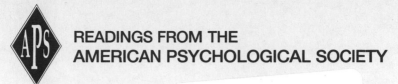

**READINGS FROM THE
AMERICAN PSYCHOLOGICAL SOCIETY**

Current
Directions
in
PERSONALITY
PSYCHOLOGY

EDITED BY

Carolyn C. Morf
University of Bern

and

Ozlem Ayduk
University of California—Berkeley

PEARSON

Prentice
Hall

Upper Saddle River, New Jersey 07458

© 2005 by PEARSON EDUCATION, INC.
Upper Saddle River, New Jersey 07458

Current Directions © American Psychological Society
1010 Vermont Avenue, NW
Suite 1100
Washington, D.C. 20005-4907

ISBN 0-13-191989-X

Printed in the United States of America

Contents

Readings from
Current Directions in Psychological Science

Personality Defined:
The Issue of Stability

Personality psychology aims to understand enduring individuating tendencies for people to experience and display particular characteristic patterns of thought, feeling, and social behavior over time and across situations. Put simply, the goals are to comprehend how people differ from each other in meaningful ways, so that we can understand and predict how each will respond and behave in a given situation. Clearly underlying this endeavor is the assumption that there is some kind of *coherence* to people's responding and that we can "decode" this coherence by examining the basic processes by which people adapt to their own particular life circumstances. As such, personality psychology is the study of the person as a whole, embedded in his or her biological and social context. To fully be able to make sense of individuals' patterns of adaptation means to understand the biological and genetic contributions to personality, the affective and cognitive mechanisms, as well as the interpersonal and social processes in which personality functions. In short, personality thus is the study of both classes and categories of dispositional tendencies, as well as the processes that underlie and define these tendencies. Articles in this volume represent current directions and most recent findings, sampling from all aspects of this contemporary definition of personality, but first we begin with a broader conceptual issue.

The notion of coherence in personality has never been in question, as personality psychology would not make sense without it. No doubt however, if personality deals with people's adaptations to their life circumstances, there will be both change and stability in personality. Thus, a particularly thorny issue that has troubled personality psychologists for a long time is what kind of consistency or stability in responding is needed for there to be coherence. The three articles in this first section illustrate this challenge and struggle to bring both variability and stability under one hat. In the end all three agree there is BOTH, but they differ in how they define stability (or variability for that matter) and its relationship to personality.

McCrae and Costa (1994) emphasize the perspective of temporal stability. They argue that there is little change in people's relative standings on broad trait categories and global tendencies across time. Despite their main emphasis on aggregating behavior across situations to show stability, they do at the same time allow, however, that traits are not completely "repetitive habits," but that they at times also interact with opportunities of the moment. In contrast, Mischel, Shoda, and Mendoza-Denton's (2002) primary focus is on consistent situationally-defined personality signatures. In their view, the most meaningful consistency is found in stable patterns of how individuals respond to

1

situations they interpret to be psychologically similar. This view depends on understanding the construal of the situation by the person who experiences it, and stability is seen in interpretable patterns of variability. In the most recent paper, Fleeson (2004) provides further evidence for the current consensus that both viewpoints are necessary for a full understanding of personality. His research shows that within-person variability around a central point of a personality trait is very high from situation to situation, but that individuals nonetheless maintain their relative position of central points compared to others from one time period to another. Thus, together these papers lead to the conclusion that personality is most usefully conceived of as a *distribution of behaviors* that can be described by both average tendencies (traits), as well as psychological processes involving characteristic responses to situations.

All papers in the remainder of this volume were chosen because they portray such a contextualized and dynamic view of personality—although they do this to a more or lesser degree. That is, enduring individual differences are the result of how person variables interact with the situational context to influence behavior. In this vein, papers were included if they make reference to psychological processes and mechanisms that result from or give rise to individual differences (or at least have the potential to). This link to individual differences is sometimes made explicitly, other times it is merely implied. Moreover, we care not only about current instantiations of these patterns, but also about how they came about and how they evolve over time. Thus, papers that address developmental processes (whether explicitly or implicitly) are included across different sections. The articles are organized into five sections, beginning with the section on stability we have already introduced.

The second section addresses individual differences in psychobiological systems, as well as genetic factors that contribute to or interact with personality characteristics. At this level, the main focus has been on specifying how the biological and genetic factors interact with the social environment in shaping who we are. The third section deals with intrapersonal processes in personality. Social processes are not universal, as they depend on the encodings of individuals. As such, this section includes papers that examine the cognitive, affective, and self-evaluatory processes that underlie social behavior. The fourth section then presents the other side of this coin, in that its focus is on the interpersonal context in which the intrapersonal processes are enacted. These papers show that personality processes vary meaningfully in relation with important longer-term social relationships. It should be noted that while we have created two separate sections, the boundaries between the intra- and interpersonal processes are fuzzy and fluid, as there is a continuous and virtually seamless interchange between the two. Thus, assignment of papers to each of these sections is somewhat arbitrary. The fifth and final section looks at the link between personality and well-being. In the end, work on personality is most exciting when it has relevance to how people live and experience their lives. Thus, understanding the adaptive and maladaptive contributions of personality is of utmost importance.

The Stability of Personality: Observations and Evaluations

Robert R. McCrae and Paul T. Costa, Jr.

"There is an optical illusion about every person we meet," Ralph Waldo Emerson wrote in his essay on "Experience":

> In truth, they are all creatures of given temperament, which will appear in a given character, whose boundaries they will never pass: but we look at them, they seem alive, and we presume there is impulse in them. In the moment it seems impulse; in the year, in the lifetime, it turns out to be a certain uniform tune which the revolving barrel of the music-box must play.[1]

In this brief passage, Emerson anticipated modern findings about the stability of personality and pointed out an illusion to which both laypersons and psychologists are prone. He was also perhaps the first to decry personality stability as the enemy of freedom, creativity, and growth, objecting that "temperament puts all divinity to rout." In this article, we summarize evidence in support of Emerson's observations but offer arguments against his evaluation of them.[2]

EVIDENCE FOR THE STABILITY OF ADULT PERSONALITY

Emerson used the term *temperament* to refer to the basic tendencies of the individual, dispositions that we call *personality traits*. It is these traits, measured by such instruments as the Minnesota Multiphasic Personality Inventory and the NEO Personality Inventory, that have been investigated in a score of longitudinal studies over the past 20 years. Despite a wide variety of samples, instruments, and designs, the results of these studies have been remarkably consistent, and they are easily summarized.

1. The mean levels of personality traits change with development, but reach final adult levels at about age 30. Between 20 and 30, both men and women become somewhat less emotional and thrill-seeking and somewhat more cooperative and self-disciplined—changes we might interpret as evidence of increased maturity. After age 30, there are few and subtle changes, of which the most consistent is a small decline in activity level with advancing age. Except among individuals with dementia, stereotypes that depict older people as being withdrawn, depressed, or rigid are unfounded.

Robert R. McCrae is Research Psychologist and **Paul T. Costa, Jr.,** is Chief, Laboratory of Personality and Cognition, both at the Gerontology Research Center, National Institute on Aging, National Institutes of Health. Address correspondence to Robert R. McCrae, Personality, Stress and Coping Section, Gerontology Research Center, 4940 Eastern Ave., Baltimore, MD 21224.

2. Individual differences in personality traits, which show at least some continuity from early childhood on, are also essentially fixed by age 30. Stability coefficients (test-retest correlations over substantial time intervals) are typically in the range of .60 to .80, even over intervals of as long as 30 years, although there is some decline in magnitude with increasing retest interval. Given that most personality scales have short-term retest reliabilities in the range from .70 to .90, it is clear that by far the greatest part of the reliable variance (i.e., variance not due to measurement error) in personality traits is stable.

3. Stability appears to characterize all five of the major domains of personality—neuroticism, extraversion, openness to experience, agreeableness, and conscientiousness. This finding suggests that an adult's personality profile as a whole will change little over time, and studies of the stability of configural measures of personality support that view.

4. Generalizations about stability apply to virtually everyone. Men and women, healthy and sick people, blacks and whites all show the same pattern. When asked, most adults will say that their personality has not changed much in adulthood, but even those who claim to have had major changes show little objective evidence of change on repeated administrations of personality questionnaires. Important exceptions to this generalization include people suffering from dementia and certain categories of psychiatric patients who respond to therapy, but no moderators of stability among healthy adults have yet been identified.[3]

When researchers first began to publish these conclusions, they were greeted with considerable skepticism—"I distrust the facts and the inferences" Emerson had written—and many studies were designed to test alternative hypotheses. For example, some researchers contended that consistent responses to personality questionnaires were due to memory of past responses, but retrospective studies showed that people could not accurately recall how they had previously responded even when instructed to do so. Other researchers argued that temporal consistency in self-reports merely meant that individuals had a fixed idea of themselves, a crystallized self-concept that failed to keep pace with real changes in personality. But studies using spouse and peer raters showed equally high levels of stability.[4]

The general conclusion that personality traits are stable is now widely accepted. Some researchers continue to look for change in special circumstances and populations; some attempt to account for stability by examining genetic and environmental influences on personality. Finally, others take the view that there is much more to personality than traits, and seek to trace the adult developmental course of personality perceptions or identity formation or life narratives.

These latter studies are worthwhile, because people undoubtedly do change across the life span. Marriages end in divorce, professional careers are started in mid-life, fashions and attitudes change with the times. Yet often the same traits can be seen in new guises: Intellectual curiosity merely shifts from one field to another, avid gardening replaces avid tennis, one abusive relationship is followed by another. Many of these changes are best regarded as variations on the "uniform tune" played by individuals' enduring dispositions.

ILLUSORY ATTRIBUTIONS IN TEMPORAL PERSPECTIVE

Social and personality psychologists have debated for some time the accuracy of attributions of the causes of behavior to persons or situations. The "optical illusion" in person perception that Emerson pointed to was somewhat different. He felt that people attribute behavior to the live and spontaneous person who freely creates responses to the situation, when in fact behavior reveals only the mechanical operation of lifeless and static temperament. We may (and we will!) take exception to this disparaging, if common, view of traits, but we must first concur with the basic observation that personality processes often appear different when viewed in longitudinal perspective: "The years teach much which the days never know."

Consider happiness. If one asks individuals why they are happy or unhappy, they are almost certain to point to environmental circumstances of the moment: a rewarding job, a difficult relationship, a threat to health, a new car. It would seem that levels of happiness ought to mirror quality of life, and that changes in circumstances would result in changes in subjective well-being. It would be easy to demonstrate this pattern in a controlled laboratory experiment: Give subjects $1,000 each and ask how they feel!

But survey researchers who have measured the objective quality of life by such indicators as wealth, education, and health find precious little association with subjective wellbeing, and longitudinal researchers have found surprising stability in individual differences in happiness, even among people whose life circumstances have changed markedly. The explanation is simple: People adapt to their circumstances rapidly, getting used to the bad and taking for granted the good. In the long run, happiness is largely a matter of enduring personality traits:[5] "Temper prevails over everything of time, place, and condition, and . . . fix[es] the measure of activity and of enjoyment."

A few years ago, William Swann and Craig Hill provided an ingenious demonstration of the errors to which too narrow a temporal perspective can lead. A number of experiments had shown that it was relatively easy to induce changes in the self-concept by providing self-discrepant feedback. Introverts told that they were really extraverts rated themselves higher in extraversion than they had before. Such studies supported the view that the self-concept is highly malleable, a mirror of the evaluation of the immediate environment.

Swann and Hill replicated this finding, but extended it by inviting subjects back a few days later. By that time, the effects of the manipulation had disappeared, and subjects had returned to their initial self-concepts. The implication is that any one-shot experiment may give a seriously misleading view of personality processes.[6]

The relations between coping and adaptation provide a final example. Cross-sectional studies show that individuals who use such coping mechanisms as self-blame, wishful thinking, and hostile reactions toward other people score lower on measures of well-being than people who do not use these mechanisms. It would be easy to infer that these coping mechanisms detract from adaptation, and in fact the very people who use them admit that they are ineffective. But the correlations vanish when the effects of prior neuroticism scores are removed; an alternative interpretation of the data is thus that individuals who score high on this personality factor use poor coping strategies and also have low well-being: The association between coping and well-being may be entirely attributable to this third variable.[7]

Psychologists have long been aware of the problems of inferring causes from correlational data, but they have not recognized the pervasiveness of the bias that Emerson warned about. People tend to understand behavior and experience as the result of the immediate context, whether intrapsychic or environmental. Only by looking over time can one see the persistent effects of personality traits.

THE EVALUATION OF STABILITY

If few findings in psychology are more robust than the stability of personality, even fewer are more unpopular. Gerontologists often see stability as an affront to their commitment to continuing adult development; psychotherapists sometimes view it as an alarming challenge to their ability to help patients;[8] humanistic psychologists and transcendental philosophers think it degrades human nature. A popular account in *The Idaho Statesman* ran under the disheartening headline "Your Personality—You're Stuck With It."

In our view, these evaluations are based on misunderstandings: At worst, stability is a mixed blessing. Those individuals who are anxious, quarrelsome, and lazy might be understandably distressed to think that they are likely to stay that way, but surely those who are imaginative, affectionate, and carefree at age 30 should be glad to hear that they will probably be imaginative, affectionate, and carefree at age 90.

Because personality is stable, life is to some extent predictable. People can make vocational and retirement choices with some confidence that their current interests and enthusiasms will not desert them. They can choose friends and mates with whom they are likely to remain compatible. They can vote on the basis of candidates' records, with some assurance that future policies will resemble past ones. They can learn which co-workers they can depend on, and which they cannot. The personal and social utility of personality stability is enormous.

But it is precisely this predictability that so offends many critics. ("I had fancied that the value of life lay in its inscrutable possibilities," Emerson complained.) These critics view traits as mechanical and static habits and believe that the stability of personality traits dooms human beings to lifeless monotony as puppets controlled by inexorable forces. This is a misunderstanding on several levels.

First, personality traits are not repetitive habits, but inherently dynamic dispositions that interact with the opportunities and challenges of the moment.[9] Antagonistic people do not yell at everyone; some people they flatter, some they scorn, some they threaten. Just as the same intelligence is applied to a lifetime of changing problems, so the same personality traits can be expressed in an infinite variety of ways, each suited to the situation.

6

Second, there are such things as spontaneity and impulse in human life, but they are stable traits. Individuals who are open to experience actively seek out new places to go, provocative ideas to ponder, and exotic sights, sounds, and tastes to experience. Extraverts show a different kind of spontaneity, making friends, seeking thrills, and jumping at every chance to have a good time, People who are introverted and closed to experience have more measured and monotonous lives, but this is the kind of life they choose.

Finally, personality traits are not inexorable forces that control our fate, nor are they, in psychodynamic language, ego alien. Our traits characterize us; they are our very selves;[10] we act most freely when we express our enduring dispositions. Individuals sometimes fight against their own tendencies, trying perhaps to overcome shyness or curb a bad temper. But most people acknowledge even these failings as their own, and it is well that they do. A person's recognition of the inevitability of his or her one and only personality is a large part of what Erik Erikson called *ego integrity*, the culminating wisdom of a lifetime.

Notes

1. All quotations are from "Experience," in *Essays: First and Second Series*, R.W. Emerson (Vintage, New York, 1990) (original work published 1844).

2. For recent and sometimes divergent treatments of this topic, see R. R. McCrae and P.T. Costa, Jr., *Personality in Adulthood* (Guilford, New York, 1990); D.C. Funder, R.D. Parke, C. Tomlinson-Keasey, and K. Widaman, Eds., *Studying Lives Through Time: Personality and Development* (American Psychological Association, Washington, DC, 1993); T. Heatherton and J. Weinberger, *Can Personality Change?* (American Psychological Association, Washington, DC, 1994).

3. I.C. Siegler, K.A. Welsh, D.V. Dawson, G.G. Fillenbaum, N.L. Earl, E.B. Kaplan, and C.M. Clark, Ratings of personality change in patients being evaluated for memory disorders, *Alzheimer Disease and Associated Disorders*, 5, 240–250 (1991); R.M.A. Hirschfeld, G.L. Klerman, P. Clayton, M.B. Keller, P. McDonald-Scott, and B. Larkin, Assessing personality: Effects of depressive state on trait measurement, *American Journal of Psychiatry*, 140, 695–699 (1983): R.R. McCrae, Moderated analyses of longitudinal personality stability, *Journal of Personality and Social Psychology*, 65, 577–585 (1993).

4. D. Woodruff, The role of memory in personality continuity: A 25 year follow-up, *Experimental Aging Research*, 9, 31–34 (1983): P.T. Costa, Jr.. and R.R. McCrae, Trait psychology comes of age, in *Nebraska Symposium on Motivation: Psychology and Aging*, T.B. Sonderegger. Ed. (University of Nebraska Press, Lincoln. 1992).

5. P.T. Costa, Jr., and R. R. McCrae, Influence of extraversion and neuroticism on subjective wellbeing: Happy and unhappy people, *Journal of Personality and Social Psychology*, 38, 668–678 (1980).

6. The study is summarized in W.B. Swann, Jr., and C.A. Hill, When our identities are mistaken: Reaffirming self-conceptions through social interactions, *Journal of Personality and Social Psychology*, 43, 59–66 (1982). Dangers of single-occasion research are also discussed in J.R. Council, Context effects in personality research, *Current Directions in Psychological Science*, 2, 31–34 (1993).

7. R.R. McCrae and P.T. Costa, Jr., Personality coping, and coping effectiveness in an adult sample. *Journal of Personality*, 54, 385–405 (1986).

8. Observations in nonpatient samples show what happens over time under typical life circumstances; they do not rule out the possibility that psychotherapeutic interventions can change personality. Whether or not such change is possible, in practice much

of psychotherapy consists of helping people learn to live with their limitations, and this may be a more realistic goal than "cure" for many patients. See P.T. Costa, Jr., and R.R. McCrae, Personality stability and its implications for clinical psychology, *Clinical Psychology Review*, 6, 407–423 (1986).

9. A. Tellegen, Personality traits: Issues of definition, evidence and assessment, in *Thinking Clearly About Psychology: Essays in Honor of Paul F. Meehl*, Vol. 2, W. Grove and D. Cicchetti, Eds. (University of Minnesota Press, Minneapolis, 1991).

10. R.R. McCrae and P.T. Costa, Jr., Age, personality, and the spontaneous self-concept, *Journals of Gerontology: Social Sciences*, 43, S177–S185 (1988).

Situation-Behavior Profiles as a Locus of Consistency in Personality

Walter Mischel,[1] Yuichi Shoda, and Rodolfo Mendoza-Denton
Psychology Department, Columbia University, New York, New York (W.M., R.M.-D.), and Psychology Department, University of Washington, Seattle, Washington (Y.S.)

Abstract

Traditional approaches have long considered situations as "noise" or "error" that obscures the consistency of personality and its invariance. Therefore, it has been customary to average the individual's behavior on any given dimension (e.g., conscientiousness) across different situations. Contradicting this assumption and practice, recent studies have demonstrated that by incorporating the situation into the search for consistency, a new locus of stability is found. Namely, people are characterized not only by stable individual differences in their overall levels of behavior, but also by distinctive and stable patterns of situation-behavior relations (e.g., she does X when A but Y when B). These *if . . . then . . . profiles* constitute behavioral "signatures" that provide potential windows into the individual's underlying dynamics. Processing models that can account for such signatures provide a new route for studying personality types in terms of their shared dynamics and characteristic defining profiles.

Keywords

personality; consistency; interactionism; *if . . . then* . . . profiles

Traditionally, personality psychology has been devoted to understanding the dispositional characteristics of the person that remain invariant across contexts and situations. Further, it has been assumed that the manifestations of invariance in personality should be seen in consistent differences between individuals in their behavior across many different situations. For example, a person who is high in conscientiousness should be more conscientious than most people in many different kinds of situations (at home, at school, with a boss, with friends). The data over the course of a century, however, made it increasingly evident that the individual's behavior on any dimension varies considerably across different types of situations, thus greatly limiting the ability to make situation-specific predictions and raising deep questions about the nature and locus of consistency in personality (Mischel, 1968; Mischel & Peake, 1982).

By the 1970s, the discrepancy between the data and the field's fundamental assumptions precipitated a paradigm crisis (Bem & Allen, 1974). The crux of this crisis was captured in the so-called personality paradox: How can our intuitions about the stability of personality be reconciled with the evidence for its variability across situations? A long-term research program was launched to try to resolve this paradox (Mischel & Peake, 1982; Mischel & Shoda, 1995). This program was motivated by the proposition that the variability of behavior across situations, at least partly, may be a meaningful expression of the enduring but dynamic personality system itself and its stable underlying organization. The findings that emerged have led to a reconceptualization of the nature and locus of personality invariance, reconciling the variability of behavior on the one hand with the stability of the personality structure on the other.

EVIDENCE FOR THE CONTEXTUALIZED *IF . . . THEN . . .* EXPRESSION OF PERSONALITY INVARIANCE

Figure 1 shows behavioral data that are typical of those found for any two individuals in a given domain of behavior across many different situations. In traditional conceptions, the variability in an individual's behavior across situations (the ups and downs along the *y*-axis) is seen as unwanted, uninformative variance reflecting either situational influences or measurement error. In dealing with this variability, the most widely accepted approach has been to aggregate the individual's behavior on a given dimension across many situations to arrive at the person's "true score." The average summary score that results allows one to ask whether individuals are different in their overall level of a disposition, and is useful for many purposes—yet it may conceal potentially valuable information about where and when individuals differ in their unique patterns of behavior. If these patterns of situation-behavior relations are indeed stable and meaningful, rather than just measurement error, they may be thought of as *if . . . then . . .* (if situation A, then the person does X, but if situation B, then the person does Y) "signatures" that contain clues about the underlying personality system that produces them.

In a study testing for the stability and meaningfulness of such situation-behavior profiles, the behavior of children was observed *in vivo* over the course of a summer within a residential camp setting (Shoda, Mischel, & Wright, 1994). The data collection yielded an extensive archival database that allowed systematic analyses of coherence in behavior as it unfolded across naturalistic situations and over many occasions, under unusually well-controlled research conditions that ensured the reliability and density of measurement.

In selecting situations for the analysis, it was important to move beyond the nominal situations specific to any given setting (such as the woodworking room, dining hall, or playground) that would necessarily be of limited generalizability and usefulness outside the specific setting. Rather, the relevant psychological features of situations—the "active ingredients" that exert a significant impact on the behavior of the person and that cut across nominal settings—were iden-

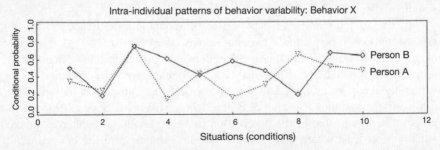

Fig. 1. Typical individual differences in the conditional probability of a type of behavior in different situations. Reprinted by permission from Mischel and Shoda (1995, Fig. 1, p. 247).

tified. Within this camp setting, five types of psychological situations that could be objectively recorded emerged: three negative situations ("teased, provoked, or threatened by peer," "warned by adult," and "punished by adult") and two positive situations ("praised by adult" and "approached socially by peer"). The children's social behavior (e.g., verbal aggression, withdrawal, friendly behavior, prosocial behavior) was unobtrusively observed and recorded as it occurred in relation to each of the selected interpersonal situations, with an average of 167 hr of observation per child over the course of the 6-week camp.

With this unusually extensive data archive, it was possible to assess the stability of the hypothesized situation-behavior relationships for each person. Figure 2 shows illustrative profiles for two children's verbally aggressive behavior across the five types of situations. The frequencies of behavior were first standardized, so that the remaining intraindividual variance in the profiles reflects behavior above and beyond what would be normally expected in the situation indicated— and is thus attributable to the individual's distinctive personal qualities. The two lines within each panel indicate the profiles based on two separate, nonoverlapping samples of situations.

As the figure shows, compared with the other children at the camp, Child 9 showed a distinctively higher level of verbal aggression when warned by adults, but a lower-than-average level when approached positively by a peer. In contrast, Child 28 displayed higher levels of verbal aggression in comparison with others when approached positively by a peer, not when warned by an adult. In contrast to the prediction that intraindividual variability in behavior across situations reflects noise and should thus have an average stability of zero, the results provided strong evidence that participants' *if . . . then . . .* profiles were both distinctive and stable.

THE PERSONALITY PARADOX RECONSIDERED

Further analyses tested the hypothesis that individuals' self-perceptions of consistency are related to the stability of their situation-behavior profiles (Mischel

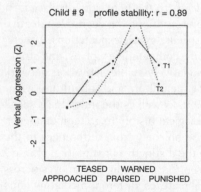 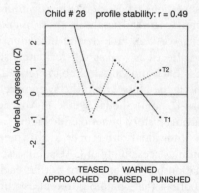

Fig. 2. Illustrative *if . . . then* signatures of verbal aggression in relation to five situations in two time samples, T1 and T2 (solid and dotted lines). Data for two children are shown in standardized scores (Z) relative to the normative levels of verbal aggression in each situation. The profile stability coefficients for the children are shown above the graphs. Reprinted by permission from Mischel and Shoda (1995, Fig. 2, p. 249).

& Shoda, 1995). These analyses utilized data from a field study in which college students were repeatedly observed on campus in various situations relevant to their conscientiousness in the college setting (Mischel & Peake, 1982). The results revealed that students who perceived themselves as consistent did not show greater overall cross-situational consistency than those who did not. However, the average correlation for situation-behavior profile stability was near .5 for individuals who perceived themselves as consistent, whereas it was trivial for those who viewed themselves as inconsistent. It is the stability in the situation-behavior profile and not the cross-situational consistency of behavior that seems to be related to the perception of consistency.

The intuition of consistency, then, seems to be neither paradoxical nor illusory. It is in fact based on a different type of behavioral consistency than has been sought for so many years. Cross-situational variability seems to be an essential expression of the enduring but dynamic personality system itself and its stable underlying organization. Given such findings, the need arose for a conception of personality that could generate—and allow one to predict and understand—not only the overall average differences between people, but also their stable and unique patterns of intraindividual variability.

TOWARD A DYNAMIC CONCEPTION OF PERSONALITY

To address this need, psychologists are beginning to reconceptualize personality not as a mere collection of attributes, but as a coherent organization of mental-emotional representations interacting within a network of relationships and constraints (e.g., Hinton, McClelland, & Rumelhart, 1986). This type of model, familiar in cognitive science, provides a framework for conceptualizing an organized personality processing system that is sensitive to different features of situations and can respond discriminatively to them in characteristic and stable ways.

Cognitive-affective personality system (CAPS) theory (Mischel & Shoda, 1995) represents one instantiation of how such a processing system might function. Within this framework, the stable units of personality consist of mental representations whose activation or inhibition leads to the behaviors displayed. At a molar level of analysis, these mental representations, or cognitive-affective units (CAUs), include the individual's construals, goals, expectations, beliefs, and affects, as well as self-regulatory standards, competencies, plans, and strategies. Each individual is characterized by a relatively stable activation network among the units within the system, reflecting the culture and subculture (Mendoza-Denton, Shoda, Ayduk, & Mischel, 1999), as well as the individual's social learning history, genetic endowment, and biological history (e.g., temperament).

Individual differences in this model arise not only from differences in the chronic accessibility of CAUs, but also from the distinctive organization of inter-relationships among them within each person. As the individual moves across situations that contain different psychological features, different mediating units and their characteristic interrelationships become activated. When the *ifs* posed by the situation change, so do the *thens* generated by the personality system, but the *if . . . then . . .* relationships remain the same, reflecting the stable organization of CAUs distinctive for that individual. Computer simulations drawing from such a conceptualization of personality have demonstrated that the CAPS model can account for both interindividual differences in mean levels of behavior and stable intraindividual variability of behavior across psychological situations (Mischel & Shoda, 1995).

FROM IDOGRAPHIC TO NOMOTHETIC ASSESSMENT OF PROCESSING DISPOSITIONS

In CAPS theory, a personality type consists of people who share a common organization of relations among mediating units in the processing of certain situational features—a common network of interrelated CAUs. The kinds of assessment tools needed to study such personality types can range from situation-specific questionnaires (e.g., Chiu, Hong, Mischel, & Shoda, 1995) to rigorously monitored daily diary studies (e.g., Ayduk, Downey, Testa, Yen, & Shoda, 1999), to experimental studies of the impact of various situational triggers on the individual's behavior (e.g., Shoda & Tiernan, in press). Such assessments can be undertaken through either a top-down or a bottom-up approach. In top-down approaches, the researcher begins with a theory of the internal processing dynamics that may characterize a type, and then hypothesizes the distinctive *if . . . then . . .* profile for that type, as well as the psychological triggers that define the profile (e.g., Downey & Feldman, 1996; Morf & Rhodewalt, 2001). Bottom-up approaches, by contrast, take advantage of recent advances in statistical techniques to extract person classes, behavior classes, and situation classes from people's responses to standardized inventories (Vansteelandt & Van Mechelen, 1998).

Such research programs are steps toward building a personality typology that takes account of both the situation and the characteristic organization of the underlying system that distinguishes each type. The CAPS model provides a framework for outlining the particular networks that distinctively characterize different individuals and personality types. From such an approach to typologies, psychologists may be able ultimately to meet a central goal in personality assessment articulated years ago (Mischel, 1968): to make specific predictions about how certain subtypes of individuals are likely to think, feel, and behave in certain kinds of situations.

Recommended Reading

Cervone, D., & Shoda, Y. (1999). *The coherence of personality: Social-cognitive bases of consistency, variability, and organization.* New York: Guilford.

Mischel, W., & Shoda, Y. (1995). (See References)

Shoda, Y., & Mischel, W. (1998). Personality as a stable cognitive-affective activation network: Characteristic patterns of behavior variation emerge from a stable personality structure. In S. Read & L.C. Miller (Eds.), *Connectionist models of social reasoning and social behavior* (pp. 175–208). Mahwah, NJ: Erlbaum.

Shoda, Y., Mischel, W., & Wright, J.C. (1994). (See References)

Acknowledgments—Preparation of this article was supported by National Institute of Mental Health Grant MH39349.

Note

1. Address correspondence to Walter Mischel, Department of Psychology, Columbia University, 406 Schermerhorn Hall, 1190 Amsterdam Ave., Mail Code 5501, New York, NY 10027; e-mail: wm@psych.columbia.edu.

References

Ayduk, O., Downey, G., Testa, A., Yen, Y., & Shoda, Y. (1999). Does rejection elicit hostility in rejection-sensitive women? *Social Cognition, 17,* 245–271.

Bem, D.J., & Allen, A. (1974). On predicting some of the people some of the time: The search for cross-situational consistencies in behavior. *Psychological Review, 81,* 506–520.

Chiu, C., Hong, Y., Mischel, W., & Shoda, Y. (1995). Discriminative facility in social competence: Conditional versus dispositional encoding and monitoring-blunting of information. *Social Cognition, 13,* 49–70.

Downey, G., & Feldman, S. (1996). Implications of rejection sensitivity for intimate relationships. *Journal of Personality and Social Psychology, 70,* 1327–1343.

Hinton, G.E., McClelland, J.I., & Rumelhart, D.E. (1986). Distributed representations. In D.E. Rumelhart & J.L. McClelland (Eds.), *Parallel distributed processing: Explorations in the microstructures of cognition, Vol. I: Foundations* (pp. 77–109). Cambridge, MA: MIT Press/ Bradford Books.

Mendoza-Denton, R., Shoda, Y., Ayduk, O., & Mischel, W. (1999). Applying cognitive-affective processing system theory to cultural differences in social behavior. In W.L. Lonner, D.L. Dinnel, D.K. Forgays, & S.A. Hayes (Eds.), *Merging past, present, and future in cross-cultural psychology: Selected proceedings from the 14th International Congress of the International Association for Cross-Cultural Psychology* (pp. 205–217). Lisse, Netherlands: Swets & Zeitlinger.

Mischel, W. (1968). *Personality and assessment.* New York: Wiley.

Mischel, W., & Peake, P.K. (1982). Beyond deja vu in the search for cross-situational consistency. *Psychological Review, 89,* 730–755.

Mischel, W., & Shoda, Y. (1995). A cognitive-affective system theory of personality: Reconceptualizing situations, dispositions, dynamics, and invariance in personality structure. *Psychological Review, 102,* 246–268.

Morf, C., & Rhodewalt, F. (2001). Unraveling the paradoxes of narcissism: A dynamic self-regulatory processing model. *Psychological Inquiry, 12,* 177–196.

Shoda, Y., Mischel, W., & Wright, J.C. (1994). Intraindividual stability in the organization and patterning of behavior: Incorporating psychological situations into the idiographic analysis of personality. *Journal of Personality and Social Psychology, 65,* 1023–1035.

Shoda, Y., & Tiernan, S. (in press). Searching for order within a person's stream of thoughts, feelings, and behaviors over time and across situations. In D. Cervone & W. Mischel (Eds.), *Advances in personality science* (Vol. 1). New York: Guilford.

Vansteelandt, K., & Van Mechelen, I. (1998). Individual differences in situation-behavior profiles: A triple typology model. *Journal of Personality and Social Psychology, 75,* 751–765.

Moving Personality Beyond the Person-Situation Debate
The Challenge and the Opportunity of Within-Person Variability

William Fleeson
Wake Forest University

Abstract

The person-situation debate is coming to an end because both sides of the debate have turned out to be right. With respect to momentary behaviors, the situation side is right: Traits do not predict, describe, or influence behavior very strongly; the typical individual's behavior is highly variable; and a process approach is needed to explain that variability. With respect to trends (e.g., a person's typical way of acting), however, the person side of the debate is right: Traits predict and describe behavior very well over long stretches of time, behavior is highly stable, and a trait approach is needed to explain differences between people. Thus, proponents of both sides are right and should continue to conduct fruitful research, and both viewpoints are necessary for a full understanding of personality. The next exciting steps in personality psychology will include integrating these two approaches in the same research paradigm.

Keywords

intraindividual variability; personality; person-situation debate; interactionism; behavior

How can we talk about the way a person typically acts if that way is always changing? The same person acts very differently on different occasions, and this simple fact has been one of the greatest challenges for personality psychologists to incorporate into the concept of personality. Indeed, initial empirical confirmations of this variability created strong reactions among psychologists, leading many to conclude that traits do not exist, people do not differ from each other, and there is no need for the study of personality. The purpose of this article is to organize and interpret the implications of such within-person variability for the study of personality. In particular, I describe my recent contributions to the growing consensus among experts that within-person variability is not a threat but an opportunity, that the stagnant person-situation debate is at an end, and that exciting new research directions lie ahead in personality psychology.

THE CHALLENGE OF WITHIN-PERSON VARIABILITY AND THE PERSON-SITUATION DEBATE

Because so much depends on this variability, it is important to establish just how differently the same person does act on different occasions. To the extent

Address correspondence to William Fleeson, Department of Psychology, Wake Forest University, Winston-Salem, NC 27109; e-mail: fleesonw@wfu.edu.

that the typical person acts similarly on different occasions, except for some normal adaptation to momentary circumstances, we need a science of traits, of individual differences in how people act. To the extent that the typical person does not act the same on different occasions (within-person variation), traits do not describe behavior, and rather than a science of traits we need a science that explains behavior variation across occasions.

The initial evidence on this question was ambiguous enough to ignite the person-situation debate. Table 1 describes the issues in the debate that have implications for (a) whether traits are useful for describing how a person acts, without referring to the situation in which he or she is acting, and (b) where personality researchers should focus their efforts. The person argument is that, because behavior is determined in large part by a person's traits, a given individual will act similarly much of the time, except for some reasonable adaptation to changing circumstances. Such stability of behavior makes it easy and useful to describe a person in terms of general traits. For example, if someone acts extraverted most of the time, it is useful and meaningful to describe him or her as extraverted. Thus, the scientific study of personality can make an important contribution by investigating the structure of individual differences—that is, by identifying which traits exist, how they correlate with each other, and how they predict important life outcomes, such as happiness, marital satisfaction, and longevity.

In contrast, the situation argument is that, because the immediate situation is the primary determinant of behavior, a given individual will act very differently on different occasions. When a person who is acting extraverted at a party subsequently goes to a seminar, for example, he or she will likely start acting introverted. Such within-person variability diminishes the usefulness of labeling a person as having a particular trait; it would be rather pointless to describe as extraverted someone who acts introverted and extraverted about equally often. Rather, the more that the same person acts differently on different occasions, the more it is incumbent upon psychologists to explain why that is the case, employing variables that vary within a person and across occasions. That is, psychologists should study the processes by which people perceive situations and react to them.

A compromise position is known as *interactionism* (Magnusson & Endler, 1977; Mischel & Peake, 1983), because interactionists agree with situationists

Table 1 The Person-Situation Debate

Issue of contention	Person position	Situation position
Central cause of behavior	Person	Situation
Similarity of multiple behaviors of one individual	Similar	Variable
Usefulness of describing an individual's way of acting	Useful	Not useful
Existence of traits	Traits exist	Traits do not exist (but personality might)
Appropriate focus of study	Structure of differences between people, correlations among differences	Process: reactions to situations, psychological functioning

that the situation is primary and that psychologists should study the processes whereby people react to changing situations, but they also hypothesize that personality does exist. They propose that personality consists of differences between individuals in how they react to situations, rather than in general ways of acting (traits). The value of interactionism—and of situationism—is enhanced to the extent that there is within-person variability in behavior to explain.

OBTAINING DISTRIBUTIONS OF BEHAVIOR

The *density-distributions* approach to determining how differently the typical person acts on different occasions (Fleeson, 2001) builds on several previous approaches (e.g., Buss & Craik, 1983; Epstein, 1979; Funder & Colvin, 1991; Shoda, Mischel, & Wright, 1994). It involves observing people as they conduct their daily lives and measuring a large number of their behaviors in a manner that allows their similarity to be assessed. For example, participants may carry personal data assistants with them for a few weeks and record their current behavior several times a day by rating, on a scale of 1 to 7, how well their behavior is described by each of five traits: extraversion, agreeableness, conscientiousness, emotional stability, and intellect. These five traits are chosen because evidence suggests that these are the best candidates for broad personality traits, if any such traits in fact exist (e.g., Goldberg, 1992). Over time, each participant's ratings will reveal a frequency distribution on each trait, showing how many times that participant acted at each level of that trait.

Figure 1 shows two possible distributions that might be obtained in such a study. Small amounts of within-person variability, as on the left, mean that the person acts similarly on different occasions and that traits would accurately describe how the person acts. For example, it would be accurate to describe the person depicted in the left panel of the figure as moderately extraverted. Higher amounts of within-person variability, as presented on the right side of the figure,

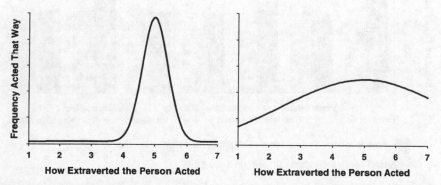

Fig. 1. Within-person variability in behavior. Each graph shows the number of times a hypothetical person acted at each level of extraversion. The distribution on the left would support a person view of personality; it would be accurate to describe the person whose behavior is graphed as moderately extraverted. In contrast, the distribution on the right would support a situation view of personality; it would not be particularly useful to label the person whose behavior is graphed on the right as extraverted.

mean that the person acts very differently from occasion to occasion. The more that actual distributions are like the right panel of the figure, the less useful is applying a trait label to a person because the label becomes a less accurate description of how the person acts. Clearly, describing the person whose behavior is depicted in the right panel as extraverted would be accurate only on occasion.

EVIDENCE FOR THE SITUATION POSITION: PEOPLE ACT VERY DIFFERENTLY ON DIFFERENT OCCASIONS

The black bars in Figure 2 show how variable the behavior of a typical person was in a typical study (the measure of variability is the within-person standard deviation of behavior across occasions). To evaluate how large these amounts of variation are, standards for comparison are needed. Emotion is one such standard that is used because emotion is commonly believed to vary so much that people primarily conceive of it as a temporary state rather than as a stable trait. Figure 2 shows that the amount of within-person variability in personality is just as large as the within-person variability in emotion (i.e., positive affect, or happiness, and negative affect, or distress).

A second standard for comparison is how much people differ from each other. The gray bars in Figure 2 represent this standard, showing the standard deviation across individuals' average ways of acting. The smaller size of the gray bars than the black bars in the figure means that the amount that one typical person varied in behavior was more than the amount that individuals differed from each other. Thus, the pattern in the right side of Figure 1 is much closer to the truth for a typical person than the pattern on the left side is: The same person changes his or her behavior quite rapidly and frequently, presumably in

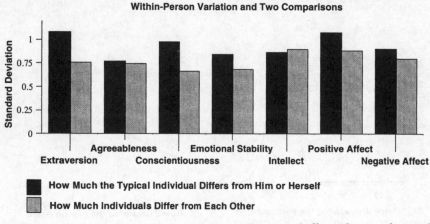

Fig. 2. Within- and between-person variability in behavior and affect. The typical person's behavior differs as much from occasion to occasion as does his or her emotion, and more than the amount people differ from each other on average. From "Towards a Structure- and Process-Integrated View of Personality: Traits as Density Distributions of States," by W. Fleeson, 2001, *Journal of Personality and Social Psychology, 80,* p. 1015. Copyright 2001 by the American Psychological Association. Adapted with permission.

response to changing situations. I have now found this pattern in several different studies using several different methodologies.

Although this within-person variance is large and presumably due to individuals adapting to situations, it is possible that individuals adapt such that they nonetheless maintain their relative position compared with others in the same situations. For example, although an extraverted person may talk less in a seminar than at a party, he or she may at least remain talkative in comparison to others in the seminar. The way researchers have tested this possibility is by correlating behavior in one situation with behavior in a different situation. Mischel (1968) reviewed several studies that did so, including the classic studies of moral character by Hartshorne and May (1928), and consistently found correlations no higher than about .3 to .4. Such correlations mean that, when adapting to circumstances, people maintain their relative positions only to a limited degree. For example, the most talkative individuals at a party are not likely to be the most talkative individuals in a seminar.

The evidence I have summarized thus far makes a powerful case for the situationist side of the person-situation debate. The variability in behavior within one person is at least as great as the variability in behavior across a group of people. Consequently, it may seem pointless to develop trait concepts or to study personality psychology. It is important, rather, to study psychological processes that might explain the large amount of within-person variability. Most likely, these processes will be found to involve reactions to specific situations.

EVIDENCE FOR THE PERSON POSITION: PEOPLE ACT VERY SIMILARLY FROM ONE WEEK TO ANOTHER

Although individuals are highly variable in their behavior, Epstein (1979) and other researchers proposed that people may differ in the central point around which they vary. Therefore, when I decided to look for behavioral similarity across occasions, or stability, I studied central points and their stability (Fleeson, 2001). The first step in testing whether individuals have different central points and whether these points are stable is to divide each person's data into equal time periods, such as Week 1 and Week 2. The average for each participant on each trait is calculated for each of the time periods and describes the central point of that person's behaviors in that time period. Figure 3 shows a typical scatter plot in which each participant's extraversion central point during one week of a study is graphed as a function of his or her extraversion central point during another week. As this example shows, different people have different central points, but two central points from the same person are not only similar to but almost identical to each other.

Scatter plots that look like the one shown in Figure 3 were found for each trait. Such scatter plots have two implications. First, they mean that one person's central points from several different time periods will be very similar to each other, forming a distribution similar to that seen in the left side of Figure 1. Second, they also mean that the position of one person's central points relative to the central points of other people will be maintained almost perfectly from one time period to another. In fact, correlations on relative position of central points at different times are typically around .9, among the highest correlations

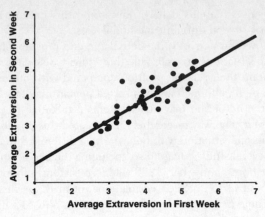

Fig. 3. Stability in behavior over time. Each point in this graph represents one person's average level of extraversion in 2 different weeks. How people act on average in one week is highly similar to how they act on average in another week.

in psychology (Fleeson, 2001). Other researchers have found similar results with various measures of behavior, and the validity of the results is not a matter of dispute (e.g., Mischel & Peake, 1983). The implication of these results is that the person side of the person-situation debate is also correct: A person's behaviors are very similar to each other when considered as averages across larger periods of time, such as weeks. Trait terms are valuable for describing how people act in everyday life, and trait psychology is needed to understand these behavioral differences between individuals.

HOW BOTH SIDES CAN BE CORRECT

Thus, the empirical evidence leads to the conclusion that both sides of the person-situation debate are correct and that an individual's personality may usefully be conceived as a distribution of behaviors rather than as one level of behavior. Generally, everyone routinely acts in a wide range of ways on a given dimension of behavior, yet different people's ranges of behaviors are centered on different portions of the dimension, and each individual's center remains very stable across large periods of time. The persuasive evidence that both the situation and the person sides of the debate are correct means that both the process and the trait approaches are needed to explain personality, and that there is no need for continued animosity. A person's momentary behaviors can indeed vary widely (as in the right side of Fig. 1), so when trying to describe and predict how a person is acting at any given moment, researchers should investigate psychological processes involving responses to situations. A person's averages over longer stretches of time are nonetheless very similar to each other (as in the left side of Fig. 1), so when trying to describe and predict how an individual acts on average, researchers should use traits. The person side has conceded that traits are not very useful for predicting momentary behavior, and the situation side has conceded that traits are very useful for predicting and describing a person's average behavior in a larger time period. There is no longer any need for debate

20

because large within-person variability and the sensitivity of behavior to situations are not a threat to the viability of traits, and the power of traits is not a threat to the need to explain the considerable amount of within-person behavioral variability. It is time for the study of personality to go forward with both approaches.

MOVING FORWARD: THE OPPORTUNITY OF WITHIN-PERSON VARIABILITY

The end of the person-situation debate creates a bright future for personality psychology. There are at least three directions in which this field is likely to generate exciting new advances. First, personality psychologists should use traits without apology. In fact, an impressive list of trait correlates is accumulating, showing that traits are among the strongest predictors of happiness, distress, career success, marital satisfaction, and even longevity, among other important life outcomes. New correlates, unfettered by doubts of the validity of traits, are likely to add further evidence that personality is critical to the length and quality of life. However, personality psychologists need to embrace a new, advanced understanding of traits, realizing that people tend to demonstrate significant flexibility in their behavior and that traits are best used for predicting trends. Second, because traits cannot explain why a person acts differently on different occasions, personality psychologists need to explain the manifestation of a trait in momentary behavior and to discover the empirical reach of interactionism. Such work would generate a rich characterization of the distinctions people make between situations and would lead to a deep integration of the process and trait viewpoints (McCrae & Costa, 2003; Shoda et al., 1994).

Finally, other parameters of behavioral distributions may turn out to be new kinds of personality variables (Larsen, 1989; Nesselroade, 1991). For example, individuals differ reliably in how variable their behavior is (Fleeson, 2001). Is being variable a sign of flexibility, a warning sign of incoherent responding to situations, or neither?

It is not possible to predict how personality psychology will proceed in the coming years. However, this is an exciting time to be a personality psychologist, unshackled by doubts about the value of one's field and encouraged by the promise of future productive integration of opposing viewpoints.

Recommended Reading

Allport, G.W. (1937). *Personality: A psychological interpretation.* New York: Henry Holt.
Fleeson, W. (2001). (See References)
Funder, D.C. (2001). Personality. *Annual Review of Psychology, 52,* 197–221.
Mischel, W., & Shoda, Y. (1998). Reconciling processing dynamics and personality dispositions. *Annual Review of Psychology, 49,* 229–258.

References

Buss, D.M., & Craik, K.H. (1983). The act frequency approach to personality. *Psychological Review, 90,* 105–126.
Epstein, S. (1979). The stability of behavior: I. On predicting most of the people much of the time. *Journal of Personality and Social Psychology, 37,* 1097–1126.

Fleeson, W. (2001). Towards a structure- and process-integrated view of personality: Traits as density distributions of states. *Journal of Personality and Social Psychology, 80,* 1011–1027.

Funder, D.C., & Colvin, C.R. (1991). Explorations in behavioral consistency: Properties of persons, situations, and behaviors. *Journal of Personality and Social Psychology, 60,* 773–794.

Goldberg, L.R. (1992). The development of markers for the Big-Five factor structure. *Psychological Assessment, 4,* 26–42.

Hartshorne, H., & May, M.A. (1928). *Studies in the nature of character, studies in deceit.* New York: Macmillan.

Larsen, R.J. (1989). A process approach to personality psychology: Utilizing time as a facet of data. In D.M. Buss & N. Cantor (Eds.), *Personality psychology: Recent trends and emerging directions* (pp. 177–193). New York: Springer-Verlag.

Magnusson, D., & Endler, N.S. (1977). *Personality at the crossroads: Current issues in interactional psychology.* Hillsdale, NJ: Erlbaum.

McCrae, R.R., & Costa, P.T., Jr. (2003). *Personality in adulthood: A five-factor theory perspective* (2nd ed.). New York: Guilford.

Mischel, W. (1968). *Personality and assessment.* New York: Wiley.

Mischel, W., & Peake, P.K. (1983). Facets of consistency: Replies to Epstein, Funder, & Bem. *Psychological Review, 90,* 394–402.

Nesselroade, J.R. (1991). The warp and the woof of the developmental fabric. In R.M. Downs & L.S. Liben (Eds.), *Visions of aesthetics, the environment & development: The legacy of Joachim F. Wohlwill* (pp. 213–240). Hillsdale, NJ: Erlbaum.

Shoda, Y., Mischel, W., & Wright, J.C. (1994). Intra-individual stability in the organization of and patterning of behavior: Incorporating psychological situations into the idiographic analysis of personality. *Journal of Personality and Social Psychology, 67,* 674–687.

Critical Thinking Questions

1. Explain what the person-situation debate was. Where does each of the articles in this section come down on this issue, and why? Be specific.

2. What are the differences between trait and process approaches to personality? If you were to do research according to the trait approach, how would it differ from research conducted in the process approach? Explain the differences between the variables you would measure and how, as well as how you would look at (analyze & interpret) the data.

3. How do McCrae & Costa differ from Mischel and colleagues in their solution to the dilemma of describing both stability and change in personality? Under what circumstances are one or the other a more useful way to approach personality? Try to give concrete examples.

4. Putting together what you have read thus far, how would you answer a friend who wants to know what are the chances of implementing a New Year's resolution to change a problematic aspect of his or her personality? That is, given what you learned from these papers about the stability/variability of personality, how easy or how difficult would it be to make such a change to some part of one's personality?

The Role of Biological Mechanisms in Personality

The contribution of biological factors to personality has always been of central interest to the field. At first it seemed like a simple question to ask how much of personality reflects nature, and how much of it nurture. The relationship between biology and personality, however, quickly proved itself to be far more complex than ever imagined. It is now clear that while many personality constructs have a biological, often genetic, component, this component interacts with the social environment to influence individuals' experiences and behaviors. Moreover, these processes operate in reciprocal directions and their interplay continues to shape the individual's personality throughout the lifespan. Thus, contemporary work no longer focuses on the "how much" question, but rather on the "how." Papers in this section address the effect of biological mechanisms on behavior, focusing on the interactions between the biological characteristics of the individual and the social environment as they jointly influence behavior and adaptation. They consider a variety of biological mechanisms, including hormones, the autonomic nervous system, neurotransmitters, and genes.

Researchers on attachment relationships commonly study the implications of unresponsive or otherwise deficient parenting on the child's development. Factors that give rise to individual differences in such parenting, however, receive relatively little attention. The first article in this section by Maestripieri (2001) brings this focus to the forefront by discussing the hormonal changes during pregnancy and postpartum that may affect motivation for caregiving. Both research on primates and humans point at higher levels of estrogen during pregnancy as a cause in increased maternal motivation and facilitation of good parenting skills. Moreover, by showing how the effect of hormones can be moderated by the prior childrearing experiences of the caregiver, this work also draws our attention to the complex interactions among biological, cognitive, and social processes in maternal motivation and caregiving behavior.

DiPietro's (2004) article that follows addresses the issue of whether and how maternal prenatal stress negatively affects fetal and child development. It turns out that the relationship between prenatal stress and a child's later development is not linear, and that optimal development may in fact require moderate levels of maternal stress. DiPietro also argues, however, that multiple factors including temperament of the child and child-rearing practices of the parents, and not only prenatal stress, are likely to affect child development. Overall, this article makes us aware that simple conceptualizations of good vs. bad is limiting, emphasizing the need to focus on the *conditions* under which stress and stress-elicited physiological processes exert their detrimental or positive effects on fetal development.

The third article in this section by Kemeny (2003) complements the preceding two by discussing how psychological stress impacts the autonomic nervous system, the hypothalamic-pituitary-adrenal axis hormones, and the immune system, as well as the interactions among these three systems in mediating the effects of stress. These effects are not uniform across individuals. Instead, the impact of stress on physical and psychological well-being crucially depends on individual differences in cognitive appraisals of stressful situations as threatening, perceptions of availability of resources for coping, and social status differences in the dominance hierarchy. This underscores the specificity and contextual nature of whether and how stress may affect physiology, and subsequent mental and physical adjustment.

Current neurological and behavioral research suggests that there are two primary affective-motivational systems that organize behavior: a *defensive system* that responds to negative, aversive stimuli (i.e., punishments, threat), disposing the individual towards defensive behaviors, and an *appetitive system* that responds to positive stimuli (i.e., rewards), motivating approach and consummatory behavior. In contrast to the first three articles that have largely focused on the mechanisms that are relevant to individual differences in the defensive system, Bevin's (2001) article turns our attention to the biological processes that mediate exploration of novelty and reward seeking, behaviors associated with the approach system. His animal model shows that novelty, in and of itself, is rewarding. Although not fully conclusive, this research suggests that a certain subtype of the neurotransmitter dopamine mediates the learning of environmental cues that predictably signal reward. The importance of understanding the mechanisms that underlie novelty-reward becomes self-evident when one considers that impulsivity of the approach system is usually involved in high-risk behaviors such as teenage exploration with sex and drugs.

The final article in this section, by Saudino (1997), addresses important methodological and conceptual issues facing behavioral genetics. Two core points are made. First, Saudino underlines the importance of including objective measures in twin research because parental ratings of similarity for identical twins are influenced by parents' expectations of greater similarity for identical compared to fraternal twins, inflating heritability coefficients for personality traits. Second, she challenges the dichotomy between the person and the situation, where causes of stability in behavior is largely attributed to the former whereas those of change and variability to the latter. The take-home message is that, to the extent that personality affects selection, construction, and perception of situations, as well as the way environment responds to the individual, we need to reconceptualize the person and the situation as incorporating one another.

Biological Bases of Maternal Attachment

Dario Maestripieri[1]
Committee on Human Development and Institute for Mind and Biology, The University of Chicago, Chicago, Illinois

Abstract

In recent years, there has been growing interest in investigating the processes affecting caregiving behavior. Recent studies of human and nonhuman primates have suggested that hormones can account, at least in part, for changes in caregiving motivation during pregnancy and the postpartum period and for variability in caregiving motivation and behavior among individuals. Although hormones may not be the primary determinants of caregiving, future research cannot afford to overlook the contribution that biological processes can make to normative and pathological attachment and parenting.

Keywords

attachment; caregiving; hormones; primates

In 1969, Bowlby published the first volume of his trilogy on *Attachment and Loss*. In it, he laid out the basic principles of a new theory aimed at explaining the nature of the social bond between infants and their caregivers, most notably their mothers. After 30 years of research focused on the processes associated with the formation, maintenance, and breaking of infants' bonds with their caregivers, psychologists are now turning their attention to attachment from the caregiver's perspective (George & Solomon, 1999).

Maternal attachment can be viewed as a set of behaviors whose function is to maintain proximity and interaction with the infant. As the early conceptualizations and empirical studies of infant attachment were informed by research with nonhuman primates (hereafter, primates), so the recent research on maternal attachment has been informed by primate studies. For example, both primate and human studies have recently investigated whether motivation for caregiving changes across pregnancy in relation to hormonal changes, whether the first few postpartum days are a sensitive period for this motivation, and whether hormonal variables predict differences in caregiving motivation and behavior among individuals. In this article, I review some recent findings in these three areas of research and discuss similarities and differences between primate and human data.

CHANGES IN CAREGIVING MOTIVATION DURING PREGNANCY

In group-living macaques, caregiving motivation during pregnancy can be measured by the frequency with which females touch, hold, groom, or carry other females' newborn infants. Interactions with young infants are by no means limited to pregnant females. Macaque females of all ages and reproductive stages show some interest in young infants and attempt to interact with them. This suggests that in primates, just as in humans and other mammals, pregnancy hormones (such as estradiol and progesterone) are not necessary for the expression of caregiving motivation. The question addressed by recent primate studies, however, is not whether hormones are necessary for caregiving motivation, but whether the hormonal changes underlying pregnancy enhance caregiving motivation.

A recent study of pigtail macaques reported that the frequency of interaction with infants increased during late pregnancy and peaked the week before birth (Maestripieri & Zehr, 1998). The increase in caregiving motivation during late pregnancy was correlated with an increase in the concentrations of estradiol in the blood and in the estradiol-to-progesterone ratio. This correlational evidence that hormones can affect caregiving motivation was corroborated by experimental manipulations. Rhesus macaque females whose ovaries had been removed increased significantly their frequency of interactions with other females' infants after receiving estradiol in doses similar to those of middle-late pregnancy (Maestripieri & Zehr, 1998). Furthermore, nonpregnant marmoset females treated with estrogen and progesterone in concentrations similar to those of late pregnancy showed a significantly higher motivation to interact with infants than nontreated females (Pryce, Döbeli, & Martin, 1993).

Human pregnancy is characterized by hormonal changes very similar to those occurring in primates and other mammals. Both longitudinal and cross-sectional studies of women in their first pregnancy have shown that, in most cases, women experience increased maternal feelings toward their own fetus at about 20 to 24 weeks of gestation (Corter & Fleming, 1995). Changes in maternal feelings during pregnancy do not appear to be correlated with changes in concentrations of hormones such as estradiol, progesterone, prolactin, or cortisol (Corter & Fleming, 1995). However, it is possible that if changes in maternal attachment during pregnancy were assessed with behavioral and psychophysiological measures (e.g., heart rate responses to infant cries) instead of women's self-reports on their feelings of attachment, an association between changes in caregiving motivation and hormones would become apparent.

IS THERE A POSTPARTUM SENSITIVE PERIOD FOR CAREGIVING MOTIVATION?

Klaus and Kennell (1976) hypothesized that there may be a sensitive period shortly after birth during which it is necessary for mothers to be in close contact with their infants for later child development to be optimal. Many subsequent studies of bonding concluded that the evidence for such a sensitive period was at best equivocal and, consequently, research on bonding was abandoned. Although the concept of mother-infant bonding was extrapolated from animal research, what most human studies attempted to demonstrate (i.e., that slight differences in time spent in contact during the postpartum period would have long-lasting consequences for the parent-child relationship) has never been demonstrated in animals either. In fact, a recent reanalysis of the primate data has provided some evidence that the postpartum period may be a sensitive period for caregiving motivation, but not necessarily for infant attachment or development (Maestripieri, 2001).

Naturalistic observations of macaques have shown that a mother whose infant dies shortly after birth may kidnap a newborn from another new mother and adopt it. Occasionally, a new mother with a live infant may adopt another newborn and raise both infants as if they were twins. Interestingly, although infant mortality is by no means limited to the early postpartum period, all cases of newborn adoption have been reported to occur within the first 2 postpartum weeks, suggesting that the potential for adoption is highest during this period.

Experimental studies in which infants have been swapped between mothers also suggest that there is a postpartum sensitive period for caregiving motivation (Maestripieri, 2001). In particular, the evidence suggests that (a) when mother and infant are separated during the sensitive period, the mother is likely to accept her own infant or an alien infant with similar characteristics if reunion occurs before the end of the sensitive period; (b) when mother and infant are separated during the sensitive period, the mother is likely to reject her own infant and any other infant if reunion occurs after the end of the sensitive period; and (c) when mother and infant are separated after the sensitive period and later reunited, the mother is likely to accept her own infant but reject any other infant. These findings are unlikely to be accounted for by learning processes related to recognition of offspring. Rather, they suggest that the physiological changes associated with childbirth and early lactation may be associated with a period of heightened responsiveness to infant stimuli and motivation for caregiving behavior.

Whether humans also have a postpartum sensitive period for caregiving motivation is not clear. Even if such a sensitive period were discovered, its implications for later parenting and child development would remain to be established. It is obvious that human adoption is the product of deliberate choice and that foster parents can provide excellent care. Nevertheless, the fact remains that if hormones and other biological variables have some effects on caregiving motivation, however small these effects might be, psychologists can no longer afford to overlook them.

INDIVIDUAL DIFFERENCES IN CAREGIVING MOTIVATION AND BEHAVIOR

Investigating whether differences in caregiving motivation or behavior among individuals are, at least in part, accounted for by hormonal or other biological variables is probably the greatest challenge for research on maternal attachment. This is because, in both primates and humans, individual differences in motivation and behavior are affected to a great extent by previous experience and the surrounding environment. Therefore, a full understanding of the causes of individual differences in caregiving would require knowledge of the complex interactions among biological, cognitive, and social processes.

Some of the most obvious individual differences in behavior are related to sex. In most mammalian species, there is a clear sex difference in caregiving motivation and behavior, with females being far more involved in caregiving than males. In only a few species of primates do males participate in caregiving, and these cases appear to reflect special reproductive and ecological circumstances.

For example, in New World monkeys such as marmosets and tamarins, females give birth to twins and fathers share the energetic costs of infant carrying with mothers. In rhesus macaques, the sex difference in interest in infants appears in the 1st year of life and persists through adulthood. A rhesus macaque female begins handling newborn infants when she is only a few months old and barely big and strong enough to lift them off the ground. In contrast, males of the same age show little or no interest in interacting with infants. A similar sex difference in interaction with infants has been reported for human children and adolescents in a number of cultures. In humans, such differences may, at least in part, be the product of socialization, and in particular the different expectations that parents in most cultures have for their sons and daughters in terms of child-care roles. In macaques, however, the sex difference in behavior toward infants is unlikely to be the product of socialization because there are no consistent differences in the way mothers, or other group members, interact with males and females during their 1st year of life (Fairbanks, 1996).

An alternative explanation has to do with prenatal hormones. In rhesus macaques, prenatal exposure to male hormones (androgens) is known to affect sex differences in play later in life, so that juvenile females prenatally exposed to excess androgens engage in the rough-and-tumble play that is typical of males (Goy & Phoenix, 1971). Unfortunately, no primate studies to date have investigated the relation between prenatal hormones and caregiving motivation. In a study with humans, however, girls affected by congenital adrenal hyperplasia (a common inherited syndrome in which the adrenal gland overproduces androgens) played less frequently with dolls than unaffected girls, suggesting that prenatal exposure to excess androgens may play a role in the development of sex differences in caregiving motivation (Geary, 1998).

Primate studies investigating differences in caregiving motivation or behavior among adult females have produced conflicting evidence. In a laboratory study of red-bellied tamarins, mothers that had poor parenting skills and whose infants did not survive had lower urinary concentrations of estradiol in the last week of pregnancy than mothers that had good parenting skills and whose infants survived (Pryce, Abbott, Hodges, & Martin, 1988). This difference, however, was found only in females without previous caregiving experience, not in experienced mothers. In macaques, not all pregnant females are more interested in infants than nonpregnant females, and individual differences in behavior toward infants are not necessarily related to differences in hormone levels. Rhesus macaque mothers who physically abuse their infants interact more frequently with other females' infants than nonabusive mothers during both pregnancy and lactation. However, the hormonal profiles of abusive and nonabusive mothers are generally similar. Moreover, individual differences in parenting styles during early lactation are largely unrelated to the levels of estradiol and progesterone circulating in the blood of both abusive and nonabusive mothers (Maestripieri & Megna, 2000).

In recent studies of humans, mothers who maintained high levels of estradiol before and after childbirth had higher feelings of attachment to their own infants in the early postpartum days than women whose levels of estradiol were lower (Fleming, Ruble, Krieger, & Wong, 1997). Interestingly, the hormone that was most closely related to maternal behavior in the early postpartum period was not estradiol but the stress hormone cortisol. Higher salivary concentrations of cortisol were associated with more intense caregiving behavior in both first-time and experienced mothers (Fleming, Steiner, & Corter, 1997). Mothers with higher salivary concentrations of cortisol on the 1st day after childbirth were also more attracted to their own infants' body odor and better able to recognize their infants' odor than mothers with lower cortisol concentrations. Mothers' attraction to infant odors was also affected by previous experience with infants, and experience, rather than cortisol, was the best predictor of individual differences in maternal responsiveness assessed with a questionnaire.

CONCLUSIONS

Taken together, these recent studies of primates and humans suggest that the study of hormonal correlates of individual differences in caregiving, and more generally of biological influences on maternal attachment, is an enterprise that is worth pursuing. Understanding the complex interaction among biological, cognitive, and social variables in the expression of caregiving behavior will not be an easy task. However, we already possess sophisticated theoretical models integrating multiple factors that may affect caregiving motivation and variability in caregiving across the life span and different individuals (e.g., Corter & Fleming, 1995; Pryce, 1995). Such models, along with comparative studies of animal parenting, can stimulate and inform future research on maternal attachment. There are still many important questions that remain to be addressed. Is there an interaction between prenatal hormonal influences and early postnatal experiences in the development of caregiving behavior? Are the influences of biological variables on caregiving mostly limited to first-time parents, or can these influences still be detected in reproductively experienced individuals? What are the specific similarities and differences between the processes affecting maternal and paternal attachment? Are there any biological correlates of neglectful or abusive parenting? Answering these questions will have important implications for understanding the normative processes underlying maternal attachment, as well as its pathologies.

Recommended Reading

Corter, C., & Fleming, A.S. (1995). (See References)
Maestripieri, D. (1999). The biology of human parenting: Insights from nonhuman primates. *Neuroscience & Biobehavioral Reviews, 23,* 411–422.

Acknowledgments—This work was supported by National Institute of Mental Health Awards R01-MH57249 and R01MH62577. I thank Martha McClintock for helpful comments on this manuscript.

Note

1. Address correspondence to Dario Maestripieri, Committee on Human Development, The University of Chicago, 5730 S. Woodlawn Ave., Chicago, IL 60637; e-mail: Dario@ccp.uchicago.edu.

References

Bowlby, J. (1969). *Attachment and loss: 1. Attachment.* New York: Basic Books.

Corter, C., & Fleming, A.S. (1995). Psychobiology of maternal behavior in human beings. In M. Bornstein (Ed.), *Handbook of parenting* (pp. 87–116). Hillsdale, NJ: Erlbaum.

Fairbanks, L.A. (1996). Individual differences in maternal styles: Causes and consequences for mothers and offspring. *Advances in the Study of Behavior, 25,* 579–611.

Fleming, A.S., Ruble, D., Krieger, H., & Wong, P.Y. (1997). Hormonal and experiential correlates of maternal responsiveness during pregnancy and the puerperium in human mothers. *Hormones and Behavior, 31,* 145–158.

Fleming, A.S., Steiner, M., & Corter, C. (1997). Cortisol, hedonics, and maternal responsiveness in human mothers. *Hormones and Behavior, 32,* 85–98.

Geary, D.C. (1998). *Male, female: The evolution of human sex differences.* Washington, DC: American Psychological Association.

George, C., & Solomon, J. (1999). Attachment and caregiving: The caregiving behavioral system. In J. Cassidy & P.R. Shaver (Eds.), *Handbook of attachment* (pp. 649–670). New York: Guilford Press.

Goy, R.W., & Phoenix, C.H. (1971). The effects of testosterone propionate administered before birth on the development of behaviour in genetic female rhesus monkeys. In C.H. Sawyer & R.A. Gorski (Eds.), *Steroid hormones and brain function* (pp. 193–201). Berkeley: University of California Press.

Klaus, M.H., & Kennell, J.H. (1976). *Maternal-infant bonding.* St. Louis, MO: Mosby.

Maestripieri, D. (2001). Is there mother-infant bonding in primates? *Developmental Review, 21,* 43–120.

Maestripieri, D., & Megna, N.L. (2000). Hormones and behavior in rhesus macaque abusive and nonabusive mothers: 2. Mother-infant interactions. *Physiology and Behavior, 71,* 43–49.

Maestripieri, D., & Zehr, J.L. (1998). Maternal responsiveness increases during pregnancy and after estrogen treatment in macaques. *Hormones and Behavior, 34,* 223–230.

Pryce, C.R. (1995). Determinants of motherhood in human and nonhuman primates: A biosocial model. In C.R. Pryce, R.D. Martin, & D. Skuse (Eds.), *Motherhood in human and nonhuman primates: Biosocial determinants* (pp. 1–15). Basel, Switzerland: Karger.

Pryce, C.R., Abbott, D.H., Hodges, J.H., & Martin, R.D. (1988). Maternal behavior is related to prepartum urinary estradiol levels in red-bellied tamarin monkeys. *Physiology and Behavior, 44,* 717–726.

Pryce, C.R., Dobeli, M., & Martin, R.D. (1993). Effects of sex steroids on maternal motivation in the common marmoset *(Callithrix jacchus)*: Development and application of an operant system with maternal reinforcement. *Journal of Comparative Psychology, 107,* 99–115.

The Role of Prenatal Maternal Stress in Child Development

Janet A. DiPietro

Johns Hopkins University

Abstract

The notion that a woman's psychological state during pregnancy affects the fetus is a persistent cultural belief in many parts of the world. Recent results indicate that prenatal maternal distress in rodents and nonhuman primates negatively influences long-term learning, motor development, and behavior in their offspring. The applicability of these findings to human pregnancy and child development is considered in this article. Potential mechanisms through which maternal psychological functioning may alter development of the fetal nervous system are being identified by current research, but it is premature to conclude that maternal prenatal stress has negative consequences for child development. Mild stress may be a necessary condition for optimal development.

Keywords

pregnancy; fetus; fetal development; stress

"Ay ay, for this I draw in many a tear,
And stop the rising of blood-sucking sighs,
Lest with my sighs or tears I blast or drown
King Edward's fruit, true heir to the English Crown"

—Queen Elizabeth's response upon learning of her husband's imprisonment in Shakespeare's *King Henry VI* (Part 3), Act IV, Scene IV

Since antiquity, people have thought that the emotions and experiences of a pregnant woman impinge on her developing fetus. Some of these notions, such as the idea that a severe fright marks a child with a prominent birthmark, no longer persist. However, the premise that maternal psychological distress has deleterious effects on the fetus is the focus of active scientific inquiry today. A resurgence of interest in the prenatal period as a staging period for later diseases, including psychiatric ones, has been fostered by the enormous attention devoted to the hypothesis of fetal programming advanced by D.J. Barker and his colleagues. Fetal programming implies that maternal and fetal factors that affect growth impart an indelible impression on adult organ function, including functioning of the brain and nervous system. That earlier circumstances, including those during the prenatal period, might affect later development is hardly newsworthy to developmentalists. In the 1930s, the Fels Research Institute initiated a longitudinal study of child development that commenced with intensive investigation of the fetal period.

Address correspondence to Janet DiPietro, Department of Population and Family Health Sciences, 624 N. Broadway, Johns Hopkins University, Baltimore, MD 21205; e-mail: jdipietr@jhsph.edu.

33

Possible effects of maternal psychological distress during pregnancy range along a continuum from the immediate and disastrous (e.g., miscarriage) to the more subtle and long term (e.g., developmental disorders). Most existing research has focused on the effects of maternal distress on pregnancy itself. For example, there are numerous comprehensive reviews of research indicating that women who express greater distress during pregnancy give birth somewhat earlier to somewhat lighter babies than do women who are less distressed. The focus of this report is on the potential for maternal stress to generate more far-reaching effects on behavioral and cognitive development in childhood.

MECHANISMS AND EVIDENCE FROM ANIMAL STUDIES

There are no direct neural connections between the mother and the fetus. To have impact on the fetus, maternal psychological functioning must be translated into physiological effects. Three mechanisms by which this might occur are considered most frequently: alteration in maternal behaviors (e.g., substance abuse), reduction in blood flow such that the fetus is deprived of oxygen and nutrients, and transport of stress-related neurohormones to the fetus through the placenta. Stress-related neurohormones, such as cortisol, are necessary for normal fetal maturation and the birth process. However, relatively slight variations in these hormones, particularly early in pregnancy, have the potential to generate a cascade of effects that may result in changes to the fetus's own stress response system.

The most compelling evidence of a link between maternal psychological functioning and later development in offspring is found in animal studies. Stress responses in rodents can be reliably induced by a variety of experimental methods. Deliberate exposure of pregnant laboratory animals to stressful events (e.g., restraint) produces effects on offspring. These include deficits in motor development, learning behavior, and the ability to cope effectively in stressful situations. There is a tendency for the effects to be greater in female than in male offspring. Changes in brain structure and function of prenatally stressed animals have also been documented (Welberg & Seckl, 2001). Yet not all documented effects of prenatal stress are negative; mild stress has been observed to benefit, not damage, later learning in rats (Fujioka et al., 2001).

In a series of studies, pregnant rhesus monkeys that were exposed to repeated periods of loud noise were shown to bear offspring with delayed motor development and reduced attention in infancy. A constellation of negative behaviors, including enhanced responsiveness to stress and dysfunctional social behavior with peers, persisted through adolescence (Schneider & Moore, 2000). In general, studies of stress in nonhuman primates find males to be more affected than females. However, although a study comparing offspring of pregnant pigtailed macaques that were repeatedly stressed with offspring of nonstressed mothers did find that the behavior of prenatally stressed males was less mature than the behavior of non-prenatally stressed males, for females the results were reversed. The females born to the stressed mothers displayed more mature behavior than non-prenatally stressed females (Novak & Sackett, 1996). Thus, although most studies have reported detrimental consequences, reports of either no effects or beneficial ones make it clear that much is left to be learned about the specific characteristics of stressors that either accelerate or retard development.

DOES MATERNAL STRESS AFFECT DEVELOPMENT IN HUMANS?

Several important factors make it difficult to generalize results based on animal studies to humans. First, there are substantial physiological differences inherent to pregnancies in different species. Second, researchers are unable to control the events that transpire after birth in humans. Women who are psychologically stressed before pregnancy are also likely to be stressed after pregnancy, so it is critical that the role of social influences after birth be carefully distinguished from pregnancy effects that are transmitted biologically. Finally, the nature of the prenatal stress studied in animals and humans is very different, and this may pose the greatest barrier to the ability to generalize. In animal research, stressors are external events that are controlled in terms of duration, frequency, and intensity. The closest parallel in human studies is found in the few studies that have taken advantage of specific events, including an earthquake and the World Trade Center disaster, to study the effects on pregnancy in women residing in physical proximity. No such study has examined children's cognitive or behavioral outcomes. However, what is measured in virtually all human studies of "stress" during pregnancy is women's affect, mood, and emotional responses to daily circumstances in their lives. Maternal anxiety and, to a lesser extent, depression are prominent foci of research. Both may reflect emotional responses to stressful circumstances, but they also represent more persistent features of personality. Thus, not only are the physiological consequences and nature of prenatal stress different between animal and human studies, but when human studies detect an association between mothers' prenatal anxiety, for example, and their children's later behavior, it may be the result of shared genes or childrearing practices related to maternal temperament.

Despite these concerns, there is a small but growing literature indicating that there is a relation between pregnant women's psychological distress and their children's behavioral outcomes. In one study, the ability of 8-month-old infants to pay attention during a developmental assessment was negatively correlated with the amount of anxiety their mothers reported about their pregnancy (Huizink, Robles de Medina, Mulder, Visser, & Buitelaar, 2002). This study is one of the few in which infants' behavior was rated by an independent observer and not a parent. Two separate studies with large numbers of participants found positive associations between maternal distress (primarily anxiety) in the first half of pregnancy and behavioral disorders or negative emotionality at preschool age (Martin, Noyes, Wisenbaker, & Huttunen, 2000; O'Connor, Heron, Golding, Beveridge, & Glover, 2002). Unfortunately, both relied on mothers' reports of their children's problems, so it is impossible to know whether the results simply indicate that anxious mothers perceive their children to be more difficult than nonanxious mothers do. However, new information about potential mechanisms whereby maternal stress might affect fetal development gives plausibility to these results. Maternal anxiety is associated with reduced blood flow to the fetus (Sjostrom, Valentin, Thelin, & Marsal, 1997), and fetal levels of stress hormones reflect those of their mothers (Gitau, Cameron, Fisk, & Glover, 1998).

Remarkably, this handful of published studies represents most of what we know about the effects of maternal distress on child development. There are several additional reports in the literature, but because of problems in methods or analysis, their results are not compelling. As the field matures, methodological, analytical, and interpretational standards will emerge over time.

THE NEXT LEVEL OF INVESTIGATION

The implicit assumption has been that prenatal stress and emotions have consequences for child development after birth because they have more immediate effects on the development of the nervous system before birth. Until recently, the fetal period of development was a black box. Although fetuses remain one of the few categories of research participants who can be neither directly viewed nor heard, opportunities to measure fetal development now exist. As pregnancy advances, the behavioral capabilities of the fetus become similar to those of a newborn infant, although the fetus is limited by the constraints of the uterus. Nonetheless, measurement of fetal motor activity, heart rate, and their relation to each other provides a fairly complete portrait of fetal development. New techniques present an opportunity to examine the manner in which the psychological state of the pregnant woman may affect development prior to birth, and perhaps permanently change the offspring's course of development.

In our first efforts to examine the link between fetal behavior and maternal stress, my colleagues and I relied on commonly used paper-and-pencil questionnaires to measure maternal psychological attributes. In a small study, we found that mothers' perception of experiencing daily hassles in everyday life was inversely related to the degree to which their fetuses' movement and heart rate were in synchrony. Such synchrony is an indicator of developing neural integration (DiPietro, Hodgson, Costigan, Hilton, & Johnson, 1996). In a second study, we found that mothers' emotional intensity, perception of their lives as stressful, and, in particular, feelings that they were more hassled than uplifted by their pregnancy were positively related to the activity level of their fetuses (DiPietro, Hilton, Hawkins, Costigan, & Pressman, 2002). We had previously reported that active fetuses tend to be active 1-year-olds, so fetal associations portend postnatal ones.

Measures of maternal stress and emotions that are based on mothers' self-reports are important only to the extent that they correspond to physiological signals that can be transmitted to the fetus; thus, they provide limited information. We turned to investigating the degree to which maternal physiological arousal, as measured by heart rate and electrical conductance of the skin, a measure of emotionality, is associated with fetal behavior. The results were unexpected in that fetal motor activity, even when it was imperceptible to women, stimulated transient increases in their heart rate and skin conductance.

It became apparent to us that the only way to truly examine the effect of stress on the fetus was to subject women to a standard, noninvasive stressor and measure the fetal response. The stressor we selected was a common cognitive challenge known as the Stroop Color-Word Test. In this test, subjects are asked to read color names that are printed in various colors and so must dissociate the color of the words from their meaning. The test is not aversive but reliably induces physiological arousal. In general, when pregnant women engaged in this task, fetal motor activity was suppressed, although individual responses varied. The degree to which individual women and fetuses responded to the Stroop test was similar from the middle to the end of pregnancy. These results lead us to propose three hypotheses. First, women respond to stress in characteristic ways that fetuses are repeatedly exposed to over the course of pregnancy. This experience serves to sensitize the developing nervous system. Second, there are both short-term and longer-term adaptive responses to stress by the fetus, depending on the intensity and repetitiveness of the stimulation. Finally, the immediacy of the fetal response to the Stroop, as well as to maternal viewing of graphic scenes from a movie on labor and delivery, suggest an additional mechanism whereby maternal stress might affect the fetus. We propose that the fetus responds to changes in the sensory environment of the uterus that occur when maternal heart rate, blood pressure, and other internal functions are abruptly altered. This proposal cannot be readily tested, but hearing is among the first perceptual systems to develop prenatally, and it is well documented that the fetus can perceive sounds that emanate from both within and outside the uterus.

Our final foray into this area of inquiry has been to follow children who participated in our studies as fetuses. Recently, we completed developmental testing on approximately one hundred 2-year-old children. The results, as is often the case in fetal research, surprised us. Higher maternal anxiety midway through pregnancy was strongly associated with better motor and mental development scores on the Bayley Scales of Infant Development, a standard developmental assessment. These associations remained even after controlling statistically for other possible contributing factors, including level of maternal education and both anxiety and stress after giving birth. This finding is in the direction opposite to that which would be predicted on the basis of most, but not all, of the animal research. Yet it is consistent with what is known about the class of neurohormones known as glucocorticoids, which are produced during the stress response and also play a role in the maturation of body organs. Our results are also consistent with findings from a series of studies on physical stress. The newborns of pregnant women who exercised regularly were somewhat smaller than the newborns of women who did not exercise much, but showed better ability to remain alert and track stimuli; the children of the regular exercisers also had higher cognitive ability at age 5 (Clapp, 1996). Exercise and psychological distress do not necessarily have the same physiological consequences to the fetus, but the parallel is intriguing.

CONCLUSIONS

At this time, there is too little scientific evidence to establish that a woman's psychological state during pregnancy affects her child's developmental outcomes. It is premature to extend findings from animal studies to women and children, particularly given the disparity in the way the animal and human studies are designed. The question of whether maternal stress and affect serve to accelerate or inhibit maturation of the fetal nervous system, and postnatal development in turn, remains open. It has been proposed that a certain degree of stress during early childhood is required for optimal organization of the brain, because stress provokes periods of disruption to existing structures (Huether, 1998), and this may be true for the prenatal period as well.

The relation between maternal stress and children's development may ultimately be found to mirror the relation between arousal and performance, which is characterized by an inverted U-shaped curve. This function, often called the Yerkes-Dodson law, posits that both low and high levels of arousal are associated with performance decrements, whereas a moderate level is associated with enhanced performance. This model has been applied to a spectrum of psychological observations, and a parallel with prenatal maternal stress may exist as well. In other words, too much or too little stress may impede development, but a moderate level may be formative or optimal. The current intensive investigation in this research area should provide better understanding of the importance of the prenatal period for postnatal life as investigators direct their efforts toward determining how maternal psychological signals are received by the fetus.

Recommended Reading

Kofman, O. (2002). The role of prenatal stress in the etiology of developmental behavioral disorders. *Neuroscience and Biobehavioral Reviews*, 26, 457–470.
Mulder, E., Robles de Medina, P., Huizink, A., Van den Bergh, B., Buitelaar, J., & Visser, G. (2002). Prenatal maternal stress: Effects on pregnancy and the (unborn) child. *Early Human Development*, 70, 3–14.
Paarlberg, K.M., Vingerhoets, A., Passchier, J., Dekker, G., & van Geijn, H. (1995). Psychosocial factors and pregnancy outcome: A review with emphasis on methodological issues. *Journal of Psychosomatic Research*, 39, 563–595.
Wadhwa, P., Sandman, C., & Garite, T. (2001). The neurobiology of stress in human pregnancy: Implications for prematurity and development of the fetal central nervous system. *Progress in Brain Research*, 133, 131–142.

Acknowledgments—This work has been supported by Grant R01 HD5792 from the National Institute of Child Health and Development.

REFERENCES

Clapp, J. (1996). Morphometric and neurodevelopmental outcome at age five years of the offspring of women who continued to exercise regularly throughout pregnancy. *Journal of Pediatrics*, 129, 856–863.
DiPietro, J., Hilton, S., Hawkins, M., Costigan, K., & Pressman, E. (2002). Maternal stress and affect influence fetal neurobehavioral development. *Developmental Psychology*, 38, 659–668.
DiPietro, J.A., Hodgson, D.M., Costigan, K.A., Hilton, S.C., & Johnson, T.R.B. (1996). Development of fetal movement-fetal heart rate coupling from 20 weeks through term. *Early Human Development*, 44, 139–151.
Fujioka, T., Fujioka, A., Tan, N., Chowdhury, G., Mouri, H., Sakata, Y., & Nakamura, S. (2001). Mild prenatal stress enhances learning performance in the non-adopted rat offspring. *Neuroscience*, 103, 301–307.

Gitau, R., Cameron, A., Fisk, N., & Glover, V. (1998). Fetal exposure to maternal cortisol. *Lancet, 352,* 707–708.

Huether, G. (1998). Stress and the adaptive self-organization of neuronal connectivity during early childhood. *International Journal of Neuroscience, 16,* 297–306.

Huizink, A., Robles de Medina, P., Mulder, E., Visser, G., & Buitelaar, J. (2002). Psychological measures of prenatal stress as predictors of infant temperament. *Journal of the American Academy of Child & Adolescent Psychiatry, 41,* 1078–1085.

Martin, R., Noyes, J., Wisenbaker, J., & Huttunen, M. (2000). Prediction of early childhood negative emotionality and inhibition from maternal distress during pregnancy. *Merrill-Palmer Quarterly, 45,* 370–391.

Novak, M., & Sackett, G. (1996). Reflexive and early neonatal development in offspring of pigtailed macaques exposed to prenatal psychosocial stress. *Developmental Psychobiology, 29,* 294.

O'Connor, T., Heron, J., Golding, J., Beveridge, M., & Glover, V. (2002). Maternal antenatal anxiety and children's behavioural/emotional problems at 4 years. *British Journal of Psychiatry, 180,* 502–508.

Schneider, M., & Moore, C. (2000). Effects of prenatal stress on development: A non-human primate model. In C. Nelson (Ed.), *Minnesota Symposium on Child Psychology: Vol. 31. The effects of early adversity on neurobehavioral development* (pp. 201–244). Mahwah, NJ: Erlbaum.

Sjostrom, K., Valentin, L., Thelin, T., & Marsal, K. (1997). Maternal anxiety in late pregnancy and fetal hemodynamics. *European Journal of Obstetrics and Gynecology, 74,* 149–155.

Welberg, L., & Seckl, J. (2001). Prenatal stress, glucocorticoids and the programming of the brain. *Journal of Neuroendocrinology, 13,* 113–128.

The Psychobiology of Stress

Margaret E. Kemeny[1]
Department of Psychiatry, University of California, San Francisco,
San Francisco, California

Abstract

Stressful life experience can have significant effects on a variety of physiological systems, including the autonomic nervous system, the hypothalamic-pituitary-adrenal axis, and the immune system. These relationships can be bidirectional; for example, immune cell products can act on the brain, altering mood and cognition, potentially contributing to depression. Although acute physiological alterations may be adaptive in the short term, chronic or repeated provocation can result in damage to health. The central dogma in the field of stress research assumes a stereotyped physiological response to all stressors (the generality model). However, increasing evidence suggests that specific stressful conditions and the specific way an organism appraises these conditions can elicit qualitatively distinct emotional and physiological responses (the integrated specificity model). For example, appraisals of threat (vs. challenge), uncontrollability, and negative social evaluation have been shown to provoke specific psychobiological responses. Emotional responses appear to have specific neural substrates, which can result in differentiated alterations in peripheral physiological systems, so that it is incorrect to presume a uniform stress response.

Keywords

stress; endocrine; autonomic; immune; physiology; emotion; cognitive

The term stress is used in the scientific literature in a vague and inconsistent way and is rarely defined. The term may refer to a stimulus, a response to a stimulus, or the physiological consequences of that response. Given this inconsistency, in this review I avoid using the term stress (except when discussing the field of stress research) and instead differentiate the various components of stress. *Stressors*, or stressful life experiences, are defined as circumstances that threaten a major goal, including the maintenance of one's physical integrity (physical stressors) or one's psychological well-being (psychological stressors; Lazarus & Folkman, 1984). *Distress* is a negative psychological response to such threats and can include a variety of affective and cognitive states, such as anxiety, sadness, frustration, the sense of being overwhelmed, or helplessness. Researchers have proposed a number of stressor taxonomies, most of which differentiate threats to basic physiological needs or physical integrity, social connectedness, sense of self, and resources. A number of properties of stressful circumstances can influence the severity of the psychological and physiological response. These properties include the stressor's controllability (whether responses can affect outcomes of the stressor), ambiguity, level of demand placed on the individual, novelty, and duration.

PHYSIOLOGICAL EFFECTS OF EXPOSURE TO STRESSFUL LIFE EXPERIENCE

Extensive research in humans and other animals has demonstrated powerful effects of exposure to stressors on a variety of physiological systems. These specific changes are believed to have evolved to support the behaviors that allow the organism to deal with the threat (e.g., to fight or flee). In order for the organism to respond efficiently, physiological systems that are needed to deal with threats are mobilized and physiological systems that are not needed are suppressed. For example, when responding to a threat, the body increases available concentrations of glucose (an energy source) to ready the organism for physical activity; at the same time, the body inhibits processes that promote growth and reproduction. Although the body is adapted to respond with little ill effect to this acute mobilization, chronic or repeated activation of systems that deal with threat can have adverse long-term physiological and health effects (McEwen, 1998; Sapolsky, 1992). A wide array of physiological systems have been shown to change in response to stressors; in this section, I summarize the effects on the three most carefully studied systems (Fig. 1).

Impact on the Autonomic Nervous System

Since Walter Cannon's work on the fight-or-flight response in the 1930s, researchers have been interested in the effects of stressful experience on the

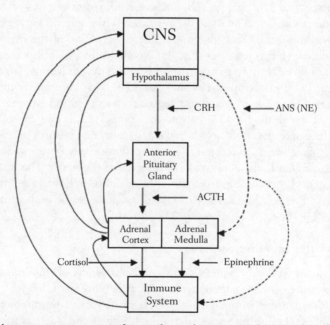

Fig. 1. Schematic representation of interrelationships among the central nervous system (CNS), the hypothalamic-pituitary-adrenal axis, the autonomic nervous system (ANS), and the immune system. Dashed lines indicate ANS neural pathways, and solid lines indicate hormonal pathways. ACTH = adrenocorticotropic hormone; CRH = corticotropin-releasing hormone; NE = norepinephrine.

sympathetic adrenomedullary system (the system is so named because the sympathetic nervous system and adrenal medulla are its key components; see Fig. 1). Cannon correctly proposed that exposure to emergency situations results in the release of the hormone epinephrine from the adrenal medulla (the core of the adrenal gland, located above the kidney). This effect was shown to be accomplished by the activity of the autonomic nervous system (ANS). The ANS has two components: the *parasympathetic nervous system*, which controls involuntary resting functions (activation of this system promotes digestion and slows heart rate, e.g.), and the *sympathetic nervous system*, which comes into play in threatening situations and results in increases in involuntary processes (e.g., heart rate and respiration) that are required to respond to physical threats. Fibers of the sympathetic nervous system release the neurotransmitter norepinephrine at various organ sites, including the adrenal medulla, causing the release of epinephrine (also known as adrenaline) into the bloodstream. Research has demonstrated that exposure to a variety of stressors can activate this system, as manifested by increased output of norepinephrine and epinephrine, as well as increases in autonomic indicators of sympathetic arousal (e.g., increased heart rate). This extremely rapid response system can be activated within seconds and results in the "adrenaline rush" that occurs after an encounter with an unexpected threat.

Impact on the Hypothalamic-Pituitary-Adrenal Axis

A large body of literature suggests that exposure to a variety of acute psychological stressors (e.g., giving a speech, doing difficult cognitive tasks), for relatively short durations, can cause an increase in the levels of the hormone cortisol in the blood, saliva, and urine. This increase is due to activation of the hypothalamic-pituitary-adrenal (HPA) axis (see Fig. 1). Neural pathways link perception of a stressful stimulus to an integrated response in the hypothalamus, which results in the release of corticotropin-releasing hormone. This hormone stimulates the anterior part of the pituitary gland to release adrenocorticotropic hormone, which then travels through the blood stream to the adrenal glands and causes the adrenal cortex (the outer layer of the adrenal gland) to release cortisol (in rodents this hormone is called corticosterone). The activation of this entire system occurs over minutes rather than seconds (as in the case of the ANS). The peak cortisol response occurs 20 to 40 min from the onset of acute stressors. Recovery, or the return to baseline levels, occurs 40 to 60 min following the end of the stressor on average (Dickerson & Kemeny, 2002).

Impact on the Immune System

Exposure to stressful experiences can diminish a variety of immune functions. For example, stressful life experiences, such as bereavement, job loss, and even taking exams, can reduce circulating levels of classes of immunological cells called lymphocytes; inhibit various lymphocyte functions, such as the ability to proliferate when exposed to a foreign substance; and slow integrated immune responses, such as wound healing (Ader, Felten, & Cohen, 2001). Individuals' autonomic reactivity to stressors correlates with the degree to which their immune system is affected by acute laboratory stressors. Extensive evidence that autonomic nerve fibers innervate (enter into) immune organs and alter the function of immune cells residing there supports the link between the ANS and the immune system. In addition, some of the immunological effects of stressors are due to the potent suppressive effects of cortisol on immunological cells. Cortisol can inhibit the production of certain cytokines (chemical mediators released by immune cells to regulate the activities of other immune cells) and suppress a variety of immune functions.

Exposure to stressors can also enhance certain immune processes, for example, those closely related to inflammation. Inflammation is an orchestrated response to exposure to a pathogen that creates local and systemic changes conducive to destroying it (e.g., increases in core body temperature). However, chronic, inappropriate inflammation is at the root of a host of diseases, including certain autoimmune diseases such as rheumatoid arthritis, and may play a role in others, such as cardiovascular disease. There is a great deal of current interest in factors that promote inappropriate inflammation outside the normal context of infection. Exposure to some psychological stressors can increase circulating levels of cytokines that promote inflammation, perhaps because stressful experience can reduce the sensitivity of immune cells to the inhibitory effects of cortisol (Miller, Cohen, & Ritchey, 2002).

Not only can the brain and peripheral neural systems (systems that extend from the brain to the body—e.g., the ANS and HPA axis) affect the immune system, but the immune system can affect the brain and one's psychological state. In rodents, certain cytokines can act on the central nervous system, resulting in behavioral changes that resemble sickness (e.g., increases in body temperature, reduction in exploratory behavior) but also appear to mimic depression (e.g., alterations in learning and memory, anorexia, inability to experience pleasure, reductions in social behavior, alterations in sleep, behavioral slowing). Emerging data indicate that these cytokines can induce negative mood and alter cognition in humans as well. These effects may explain affective and cognitive changes that have been observed to be associated with inflammatory conditions. They may also explain some depressive symptoms associated with stressful conditions (Maier & Watkins, 1998).

Health Implications

Activation of these physiological systems during exposure to a stressor is adaptive in the short run under certain circumstances but can become maladaptive if the systems are repeatedly or chronically activated or if they fail to shut down when the threat no longer exists. McEwen (1998) has coined the term *allostatic load* to refer to the cumulative toll of chronic overactivation of the physiological systems that are designed to respond to environmental perturbations. For example, evidence suggests that chronic exposure to stressors or distress (as in posttraumatic stress disorder and chronic depression) can cause atrophy in a part of the brain called the hippocampus, resulting in memory loss. Chronic exposure to stressful circumstances has also been shown to increase vulnerability to upper respiratory infections in individuals exposed to a virus. Researchers have observed effects on other health outcomes as well, but complete models of stress and health that document all the mediating mechanisms from the central nervous system to the pathophysiological processes that control disease are not yet available (Kemeny, 2003).

GENERALITY VERSUS SPECIFICITY IN THE PHYSIOLOGICAL RESPONSE TO STRESSORS

The central dogma of most stress research today is that stressors have a uniform effect on the physiological processes I have just described. Hans Selye shaped the thinking of generations of researchers when he argued that the physiological response to stressful circumstances is nonspecific, meaning that all stressors, physical and psychological, are capable of eliciting the triad of physiological changes he observed in his rodent research: shrinking of the thymus (a central immune organ), enlargement of the adrenal gland (which produces corticosterone), and ulceration of the gastrointestinal tract. Very little research has directly tested this *generality model* by determining whether or not differences in stressful conditions are associated with distinctive physiological effects in humans. Modern versions of the generality model propose that if stressors lead to the experience of distress (or perceived stress), then a stereotyped set of physiological changes will be elicited in the systems I have described. These models also emphasize the important role of a variety of psychological and environmental factors that can moderate the relationships among stressor exposure, distress, and physiological activation (see Fig. 2). However, these newer versions are essentially generality models because all of the factors are considered relevant to the extent that they buffer against or exacerbate the experience of distress, without considering that different kinds of distress (e.g., different emotional responses) might have distinctive physiological correlates. According to these models, distress has a uniform relationship to physiology.

There is, however, increasing evidence for specificity in the relationship between stressors and physiology. Weiner (1992) advocated an integrated specificity model of stressor physiology, arguing that "organisms meet . . . challenges and dangers by integrated behavioral, physiological patterns of response that are appropriate to the task" (p. 33). According to this model, both behavior and physiology are parts of an integrated response to address a specific environ-

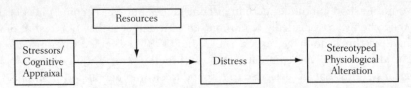

Fig. 2. The generality model of stress. This model proposes that exposure to stressors and the cognitive appraisals of those events can lead to distress. The nature of this relationship depends on the resources available to deal with the stressors (e.g., coping skills, social support, personality factors, genetics, environmental resources). Elevations in distress cause a stereotyped physiological alteration in stress-responsive systems. Bidirectional relationships between many components of the model are assumed but are not indicated here.

mental condition (see Fig. 3), and specific conditions or environmental signals elicit a patterned array of hormonal and neural changes that are designed to ready the organism to deal with the specific nature of the threat. In animals, specific neural and peripheral changes occur in concert with behaviors such as fighting, fleeing, defending, submitting, exerting dominance, and hunting prey, among others. Distinctive behaviors (fight, flight, and defeat) have also been elicited by activating specific regions of the brain with excitatory amino acids.

COGNITIVE APPRAISALS SHAPE PHYSIOLOGICAL RESPONSES

Cognitive appraisal processes can profoundly shape the specific nature of the physiological response to stressful circumstances and play a central role in the integrated specificity model. Cognitive appraisal is the process of categorizing a situation in terms of its significance for well-being (Lazarus & Folkman, 1984). Primary appraisal relates to perceptions of goal threat, whereas secondary appraisal relates to perceptions of resources available to meet the demands of the circumstance (e.g., intellectual, social, or financial resources). Three categories of cognitive appraisals have been shown to elicit distinctive affective and physiological responses.

Threat Versus Challenge

According to Blascovich and Tomaka (1996), the experience of threat results when the demands in a given situation are perceived to outweigh the resources. When resources are perceived to approximate or exceed demands, however, the individ-

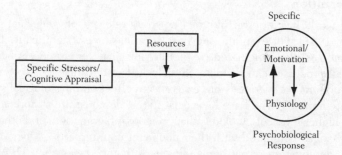

Fig. 3. The integrated specificity model of stress. This model proposes that exposure to specific stressful conditions and cognitive appraisals of those conditions shape the specific nature of an integrated psychobiological response (including emotion-motivation and physiology) to promote adaptive responses to the threat. For example, threats that are appraised as uncontrollable may lead to an integrated psychobiological response that includes disengagement from the goal that is threatened by the stressor (manifested in withdrawal, inactivity, and reduced effort), related affective states (e.g., depression), and physiological changes that support disengagement. Threats appraised as controllable may lead to an integrated response involving engagement with the threat and physiological responses supporting active coping processes. As in the generality model, resources available to deal with the stressors can moderate this relationship.

ual experiences a challenge response. These two motivational states are associated with distinctive ANS alterations. In situations that require active responses to obtain a goal, challenge is associated with increases in sympathetic arousal (increased cardiac performance) coupled with reduced or unchanged peripheral resistance (resistance to blood flow). These changes parallel those observed with metabolically demanding aerobic exercise. Threat, in contrast, although also associated with sympathetic arousal involving increased cardiac performance, is associated with *increased* peripheral resistance, leading to increased blood pressure. Thus, different cognitive appraisals can result in distinctive patterns of ANS reactivity with potentially distinguishable implications for health. The issue here is not degree of activation of the sympathetic nervous system, but rather distinctive qualities of activation depending on the specific nature of the cognitive appraisal process.

Perceived Control

Animal and human research demonstrates that uncontrollable circumstances, or those perceived as uncontrollable, are more likely to activate key stressor-relevant systems than are circumstances that the organism perceives to be controllable. For example, when rodents with and without control over exposure to identical stressors are compared, those with control show a reduced cortisol response. A meta-analysis (a statistical analysis that summarizes findings across studies) has demonstrated that humans who are exposed to stressors in an acute laboratory context are significantly more likely to experience HPA activation if the stressors are uncontrollable than if they are controllable (Dickerson & Kemeny, 2002). Threats that are appraised as controllable but in fact are uncontrollable have been shown to elicit less severe physiological alterations (e.g., in the immune system) than those appraised as uncontrollable.

Social Cognition

The social world has a powerful effect on stress-relevant physiological systems (Cacioppo, 1994). For example, social isolation has a very significant effect on health, which is likely mediated by the physiological systems described here. Other social processes can regulate physiological systems as well. For example, place in a dominance hierarchy has a significant effect on physiological systems. Subordinate animals, who have low social status, demonstrate a more activated HPA axis, higher levels of cytokines that promote inflammation, and other physiological changes compared with their dominant counterparts. A meta-analytic review has demonstrated that demanding performance tasks elicit HPA activation when one's social status or social self-esteem is threatened by performance failures, but these effects are greatly diminished when this social-status threat is not present (Dickerson & Kemeny, 2002). Cognitive appraisals of social status and social self-esteem appear to play an important role in these effects (Dickerson, Gruenewald, & Kemeny, in press).

CONCLUSIONS

The research findings on cognitive appraisal and physiological systems lead to two important conclusions. First, depending on the nature of the eliciting conditions, different patterns of physiological response can occur. Second, when cognitive appraisals of conditions are manipulated, distinctive physiological effects can be observed within the same context. Therefore, the way the individual thinks about the situation may override the impact of the specific nature of the conditions themselves.

In the integrated specificity model of stressful experience, stressful conditions and appraisals of them elicit integrated psychobiological responses (including emotion and physiology) that are tied to the nature of the threat experienced. A number of researchers have found that different neural and autonomic pathways are activated during different emotional experiences. Thus, specific emotions, in all likelihood, play a central role in the nature of the physiological response to stressful conditions. A more intensive evaluation of the role of distinct emotions would be an important contribution to future stress research. It is most likely that distinctions will be observed when researchers evaluate patterns of physiological change across systems, rather than relying on single response systems (e.g., cortisol level), and when emotional behavior is assessed in conjunction with self-report data.

Recommended Reading

Dickerson, S.S., & Kemeny, M.E. (2002). (See References)
Kemeny, M.E., & Gruenewald, T.L. (2000). Affect, cognition, the immune system and health. In E.A. Mayer & C. Saper (Eds.), *The biological basis for mind body interactions* (pp. 291–308). Amsterdam: Elsevier Science.
Lazarus, R.S., & Folkman, S. (1984). (See References)
Sapolsky, R.M. (1992). (See References)
Weiner, H. (1992). (See References)

Acknowledgments—This article is dedicated to the memory of Herbert Weiner, a pioneer in the field of stress research, who profoundly shaped the thinking of the generations of stress researchers he trained.

Note

1. Address correspondence to Margaret E. Kemeny, Health Psychology Program, Department of Psychiatry, Laurel Heights Campus, University of California, 3333 California St., Suite 465, San Francisco, CA 94143.

References

Ader, R., Felten, D.L., & Cohen, N. (2001). *Psychoneuroimmunology* (3rd ed.). New York: Academic Press.
Blascovich, J., & Tomaka, J. (1996). The biopsychosocial model of arousal regulation. *Advances in Experimental Social Psychology, 28,* 1–51.
Cacioppo, J.T. (1994). Social neuroscience: Autonomic, neuroendocrine, and immune responses to stress. *Psychophysiology, 31,* 113–128.
Dickerson, S.S., Gruenewald, T.L., & Kemeny, M.E. (in press). When the social self is threatened: Shame, physiology and health. *Journal of Personality.*
Dickerson, S.S., & Kemeny, M.E. (2002). *Acute stressors and cortisol responses: A theoretical integration and synthesis of laboratory research.* Manuscript submitted for publication.
Kemeny, M.E. (2003). An interdisciplinary research model to investigate psychosocial cofactors in disease: Application to HIV-1 pathogenesis. *Brain, Behavior & Immunity, 17,* 562–572.

Lazarus, R.S., & Folkman, S. (1984). *Stress, appraisal, and coping.* New York: Springer.

Maier, S.F., & Watkins, L.R. (1998). Cytokines for psychologists: Implications of bidirectional immune-to-brain communication for understanding behavior, mood, and cognition. *Psychological Review, 105,* 83–107.

McEwen, B.S. (1998). Protective and damaging effects of stress mediators. *New England Journal of Medicine, 338,* 171–179.

Miller, G.E., Cohen, S., & Ritchey, A.K. (2002). Chronic psychological stress and the regulation of pro-inflammatory cytokines: A glucocorticoid resistance model. *Health Psychology, 21,* 531–541.

Sapolsky, R.M. (1992). Neuroendocrinology of the stress-response. In J.B. Becker, S.M. Breedlove, & D. Crews (Eds.), *Behavioral endocrinology* (pp. 287–324). Cambridge, MA: MIT Press.

Weiner, H. (1992). *Perturbing the organism: The biology of stressful experience.* Chicago: University of Chicago Press.

Novelty Seeking and Reward: Implications for the Study of High-Risk Behaviors

Rick A. Bevins[1]

Department of Psychology, University of Nebraska-Lincoln, Lincoln, Nebraska

Abstract

Novelty seeking and sensation seeking are constructs useful in predicting human risk-taking behaviors. This predictive relation purportedly reflects some rewarding aspect of experiencing novelty. Research has confirmed this assumption. Rats display an increase in preference for an environment that has been differentially paired with novel stimuli. The physiological mechanisms mediating this rewarding effect of novelty involve the neurotransmitter dopamine, whereas those controlling novelty seeking do not. The mechanisms involved in drug seeking and reward show parallel dissociations. This concordance between novelty and drug-abuse research suggests that novelty and drug stimuli may interact in biologically and behaviorally meaningful ways. Indeed, preliminary research examining cocaine and novelty and published work with amphetamines support this suggestion. There is clear need for further systematic research on novelty reward and related processes at all levels of analysis: genetic, biological, behavioral, and social.

Keywords

cocaine; dopamine; drug abuse; sensation seeking

In 1836, Hood observed that "there are three things which the public will always clamour for, sooner or later: namely, Novelty, novelty, novelty" (cited in Darwin, 1980, p. 255). There is little doubt that human and nonhuman animals are sensitive to novelty. The startle response to a sudden loud noise provides one clear example. In contrast to this startle example, the clamor described by Hood implies some reward or positive affect from experiencing novelty. In this report, I describe recent research exploring this notion.

FRAMEWORK

In the 1950s and 1960s, researchers spent much effort elucidating concepts such as curiosity, exploration, and stimulation or novelty seeking (Fowler, 1965). Under what conditions are novel stimuli approached? Can novelty serve as a reinforcer? Is there a drive or need for novel stimulation? Is reward derived from novelty of the stimulus or novelty-elicited exploration? Only partial answers to these questions were obtained before research in this area substantially declined.

Recently, there has been a revived interest in the behavioral, cognitive, and biological processes mediating novelty seeking and reward. This interest is driven, in part, by two theoretical constructs studied in the human population: novelty seeking (Cloninger, 1987) and sensation seeking (Zuckerman, 1994). The predictive relation between these personality constructs and important health-related issues has been well documented. The popular media often depict novelty seekers as individuals engaging in extreme sports (e.g., skydiving, snowboarding). Although this portrayal is partially accurate, it is narrow and does not reflect behaviors that have a high cost for the individual and society. For example, high scores on questionnaires that assess tendency toward novelty and sensation seeking are positively correlated with early onset of drug use, frequency of multiple-drug use, and later drug abuse. Also, sensation seekers are more likely than non-sensation seekers to engage in risky sexual practices such as unprotected intercourse and multiple partners; such activities can lead to early and unwanted pregnancies and sexually transmitted diseases (see Zuckerman, 1994, for a review).

An assumption often made in the literature is that such behaviors are maintained, in part, by some rewarding quality of novel stimulation. For example, Zuckerman (1994) suggested that "an opportunity for sensation seeking often puts the person in an approach avoidance conflict where the rewards are positive sensations and experiences" (p. 124). Recently, several laboratories, including my own, have examined the assumption that novelty is rewarding. In the sections that follow, I provide an overview of basic research in this area, draw parallels with the drug-abuse literature, and discuss possible avenues for subsequent research.

DEFINITIONS AND EVIDENCE

Definitions of novelty vary in complexity and underlying assumptions. For methodological purposes, my colleagues and I defined novelty as "a change in stimulus conditions from previous experience" (Bevins, Klebaur, & Bardo, 1997, p. 114). A related but more complex definition is that novelty is "a deviation from the expected likelihood of an event on the basis of both previous information and internal estimates of conditional probabilities" (Berns, Cohen, & Mintun, 1997, p. 1272). According to these definitions, novelty is associated with events not previously experienced, as well as new combinations of familiar stimuli. For example, you may be highly familiar with your living room and automobile; however, the co-occurrence of the automobile in the living room would be very novel.

Like many physical and psychological variables, novelty should be conceptualized on a continuum. Anchoring one end of this continuum is complete familiarity (no novelty); the other end is complete novelty. Notably, this continuum varies with the stimulus, situation, and individual. Indeed, a neglected area of research is the etiology of individual differences in sensitivity to novel stimulation. Consider drug taking as an example. The alteration in physiology, behavior, and cognition induced by a drug can be considered a novel state. Drug-abuse research is replete with examples of a fixed dose of a stimulant like amphetamine producing different effects in different people. For some individuals, this novel drug state may be positive (rewarding); for other individuals, it may be aversive or neutral. There have been systematic attempts to correlate animals' sensitivity to novel stimuli and later reactivity to the behavioral and neurobiological effects of drugs. For example, Piazza, Deminière, LeMoal, and Simon (1989) first measured the activity of rats in a novel environment and then assessed their responses to amphetamine. High activity in the novel environment was correlated with sensitivity to amphetamine's stimulant effect on general activity and frequency of bar-pressing to self-administer amphetamine. This predictive relation has been replicated by several laboratories and has been extended to other drugs (e.g., alcohol, cocaine) and drug effects (Bevins et al., 1997).

Although the correlation between novelty-induced activity and drug effects suggests an overlap in the neurobiological processes involved, the relation does not indicate that novelty has a rewarding quality or that novelty and drugs have overlapping reward systems. Further, much of the early research supporting the assumption that novelty is rewarding is either nonsystematic or vulnerable to alternative explanations (see Bevins & Bardo, 1999). This situation led us to develop an animal model that would allow us to assess whether access to novel stimulation is rewarding, discount alternative nonreward explanations, examine the neural substrates of novelty seeking, and compare novelty with other rewarding stimuli.

We chose the *place-conditioning* method because it had been useful for studying the rewarding properties of such stimuli as food, copulatory opportunity, and drugs (Bardo & Bevins, 2000). In our studies, rats received access to novel objects repeatedly in one distinct environment; they spent an equal amount of time confined in a second environment without exposure to novelty (Fig. 1a). In a subsequent choice test (without novel objects), rats displayed an increase in preference for the environment that had been paired with novelty. This increase in time spent in that environment (i.e., place conditioning) indicated that access to novel stimuli has a rewarding quality. Indeed, in one study, we held every variable constant (number of pairings, duration in the environments, etc.) except intravenous cocaine replaced the novel objects. Intravenous cocaine, like novelty, produced an increase in preference for the paired environment (Bevins & Bardo, 1999). Novelty reward appears robust in that it has occurred in additional experiments using different experimental protocols and various control groups (Bevins & Bardo, 1999; Besheer, Jensen, & Bevins, 1999). It is important to note that the object that is paired with the distinct environment must be novel for place conditioning to occur. If a familiar object is repeatedly paired with the environment, rats do not show an increase in preference for that environment.

A NEURAL AND BEHAVIORAL DISSOCIATION

Given the evidence that novelty is rewarding, we turned our attention to the neural mechanisms that mediate this reward. There is a substantial literature implicating the neurotransmitter dopamine in reward-related processes (e.g., Ikemoto & Panksepp, 1999). Neurotransmitters like dopamine are naturally occurring molecules synthesized by cells. In general terms, a neurotransmitter is used by a nerve cell (i.e., neuron) to communicate information to itself or to neighboring neurons. In order for the receiving neuron to detect the presence of the neurotransmitter, it must have a receptor specific to that neurotransmitter. In the case of dopamine, pharmacological and molecular biological research has identified at least five subtypes of receptors. These subtypes may be classified into two families, the D_1-like (D_1 and D_5) and D_2-like (D_2, D_3, and D_4) families.

B

Cocaine Alone

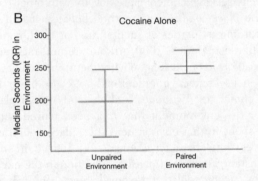

A

Cocaine + Novelty

Fig. 1. Experimental apparatus and results. One of two adjacent place-conditioning chambers (a) was black and had a rod floor and newspaper lining the litter tray; the other end compartment was white and had a wire mesh floor and pine chips lining the litter tray. The center gray area was used for placement during the choice tests. The graphs show the median time rats spent in each end compartment during choice tests after receiving cocaine alone (b) or cocaine in combination with exposure to a novel stimulus (c) in one compartment (the paired environment) and not the other (the unpaired environment). For each environment, the long horizontal line indicates the median, and the short outer lines denote the interquartile range (IQR). The asterisk indicates a significant difference ($p < .05$) between time spent in the paired and unpaired environments.

Scientists have developed drugs, termed antagonists, that prevent the action of a neurotransmitter at its receptor. Because these antagonists can be selective for different receptor subtypes, investigators are able to dissociate the function of different receptor subtypes. Rats pretreated with an antagonist for the dopamine D_1 receptor before each environment-novelty pairing did not display the increase in environmental preference shown by control rats treated with saline (placebo). In contrast, an antagonist for the dopamine D_2 receptor did not alter place conditioning (Besheer et al., 1999). Interestingly, a similar dissociation has been found with abused drugs. For example, Cervo and Samanin (1995) found that a D_1 antagonist, but not a D_2 antagonist, blocked acquisition of a cocaine-conditioned environmental preference.

There are at least two competing accounts for the role of the D_1-like dopamine receptor in reward processes. First, blocking D_1 receptors may decrease the rewarding effects of stimuli. Thus, the reason rats pretreated with D_1 antagonists do not exhibit place conditioning may be that no reward is associated with environmental cues. Second, the D_1 receptor may be a mediator that allows the reward signal to become associated with predictive environmental stimuli (Sutton & Beninger, 1999). From this perspective, the processing of novelty and its reward is not necessarily degraded. We have concluded that this latter account better fits the data (Besheer et al., 1999). If one assumes that an animal explores an object because this activity is rewarding, according to the reward-degrading account, rats pretreated with a D_1 antagonist should exhibit reduced object interaction. However, rats who received doses of a D_1 antagonist that blocked place conditioning did not show a reduction in exploration of the novel object. Thus, the data do not support the idea that D_1 antagonism directly decreases the rewarding effects of novel stimuli.

If the processing of novelty is not affected by blockade of the D_1 receptor, then performance on nonassociative tasks (i.e., tasks not requiring a learned association between environmental cues and a reward) involving novel stimuli should not be altered by a D_1 antagonist. To test this prediction, we used a task involving recognition of a novel object. Rats were exposed to an object for 10 min and an hour later were allowed to freely distribute their time interacting with the previously experienced object or a novel object for 2 min. Under these conditions, control rats interacted more with the novel object than with the experienced object. Similarly, rats pretreated with a D_1 antagonist or D_2 antagonist spent more time with the novel object (Besheer et al., 1999). This outcome provides evidence for an interesting dissociation between the physiological mechanisms underlying the rewarding effects of novelty and those involved in detecting the presence of novelty and interacting with that novelty: The dopamine D_1 receptor is involved in the former, but not the latter. Albeit preliminary, this result suggests that researchers need to conceptually separate, at least in part, the novelty-seeking behavior from the reward derived by engaging in such behavior.

McFarland and Ettenberg (1995) have found a similar dissociation between drug reward and drug seeking. In their study, rats received an intravenous infusion of heroin after traversing a straight alley maze in the presence of an odor cue. Once the rats' running speed in the maze was fast and stable as a result of the heroin reward, they were administered the dopamine receptor antagonist haloperidol before the daily session. Haloperidol did not alter running speed in the presence of the odor that signaled availability of heroin at the end of the alley. Thus, drug seeking was not affected by dopamine receptor antagonism, much as novelty seeking in our work was not affect by dopamine antagonists. Interestingly, in a subsequent session in the presence of the same odor cue, but without the antagonist, running speed was slower. This outcome suggests that haloperidol blocked the impact of heroin reward during the previous session; it was as if the rats had not received heroin for running the alley.[2] In short, the mechanisms of drug and novelty reward involve the neurotransmitter dopamine, but those of drug and novelty seeking do not.

IMPLICATIONS AND FUTURE DIRECTIONS

One interesting implication that emerges from the present discussion is that novelty may affect responses to other rewarding stimuli. Consistent with this suggestion is recent research by Badiani et al. (1998) investigating the effects of environmental novelty on reactions to amphetamine. In that research, rats were administered amphetamine in an environment that was novel for some rats and familiar for others. Behaviorally, the increase in activity induced by amphetamine was greater in the novel environment. Physiologically, the striatum (a brain region involved in motor behavior) was activated more in rats that received a combination of amphetamine and novelty than in control rats that received novelty or amphetamine alone.

Similarly, my colleagues and I have conducted a preliminary study comparing the rewarding effects of a single administration of cocaine in the presence and absence of novelty. We selected a dose of cocaine (2 mg/kg) that was not expected to produce robust place conditioning. One set of rats received a single intravenous infusion of cocaine while confined to one chamber and spent an equal amount of time, without an infusion of cocaine, confined in a second chamber (Fig. 1a). Later, when the rats were drug free, they were placed in the center compartment and given free access to both environments for 10 min (i.e., choice test). The time spent in the environment that had been paired with cocaine did not differ statistically from the time spent in the unpaired environment (Fig. 1b). Similarly, a separate set of rats that received only a single pairing of a novel object (no cocaine) with one of the environments spent equal amounts of time in the two environments during the choice test. In contrast, a separate set of rats received identical treatment except a novel stimulus co-occurred with cocaine administration. Novelty appeared to potentiate the rewarding effect of a single administration of cocaine; that is, rats in this group spent significantly more time in the paired environment than in the unpaired environment when they were later given free access to both chambers (Fig. 1c). Although this result requires replication, this initial evidence for summation between cocaine and novelty reward suggests that processes mediating the two are synergistic. Further, it remains to be determined whether this summation emerges from the same neural processes or from the convergence of separate processes.

Future research will need to refine current understanding of the dissociation between novelty seeking and reward. Proposing a neural model is beyond the scope of this review (for models, see Ikemoto & Panksepp, 1999; Zuckerman, 1994). Neuroanatomical areas that may be involved include the nucleus accumbens, hypothalamus, amygdala, hippocampus, and frontal cortex. Besides dopamine, neurotransmitters of interest include serotonin, acetylcholine, and norepinephrine. Serotonin, for example, has been implicated in drug seeking. Our laboratory has just begun to examine the interaction between novelty and cocaine reward. How will novelty reward interact with other drugs of abuse in other experimental paradigms? Do the same brain systems mediate novelty reward when novelty is and is not combined with other rewarding stimuli? Does novelty similarly affect rewarding stimuli other than drugs of abuse? The famous Coolidge effect demonstrates the role of stimulus novelty in copulatory behavior: A sexually satiated male's latency to copulate can be decreased by presenting a novel receptive female. As noted earlier, further research is needed to identify the sources of individual variation at all levels: genetic, biological, behavioral, and social. Finally, the impact of novelty on behavioral, cognitive, and biological processes should be of much interest to practitioners. That is, many high-risk behaviors that are the focus of intervention and prevention strategies occur in the presence of some novelty; this is arguably true for adolescent experimentation with sex and drugs.

Recommended Reading

Bardo, M.T., Donohew, R.L., & Harrington, N.G. (1996). Psychobiology of novelty seeking and drug seeking behavior. *Behavioural Brain Research, 77,* 23–43.
Panksepp, J. (1998). *Affective neuroscience: The foundations of human and animal emotions.* New York: Oxford University Press.
Spear, L.P. (2000). Neurobehavioral changes in adolescence. *Current Directions in Psychological Science, 9,* 111–114.
Zuckerman, M. (1994). (See References)

Acknowledgments—Research described here was supported by the National Institutes of Health (Grants DA11893 and MH57240). The place-conditioning data were collected by Heather Jensen. I thank Michael Bardo, Joyce Besheer, Gustavo Carlo, and Matthew Palmatier for their comments on this manuscript.

Notes

1. Address correspondence to Rick A. Bevins, Psychology Department, University of Nebraska-Lincoln, Lincoln, NE 68588-0308; e-mail: rbevins1@unl.edu.
2. McFarland and Ettenberg (1995) described haloperidol as a nonselective dopamine antagonist. Data indicate that haloperidol has somewhat greater selectivity for the D_2 over the D_1 receptor, suggesting a D_2 component to heroin reward. To be certain whether one receptor is more important to heroin reward than the other would require the use of more selective antagonists, such as we employed. Regardless, our main conclusion stands: Dopamine has a role in reward but not seeking.

References

Badiani, A., Oates, M.M., Day, H.E.W., Watson, S.J., Akil, H., & Robinson, T.E. (1998). Amphetamine-induced behavior, dopamine release, and c-*fos* mRNA expression: Modulation by environmental novelty. *The Journal of Neuroscience, 18,* 10579–10593.

Bardo, M.T., & Bevins, R.A. (2000). Conditioned place preference: What does it add to our preclinical understanding of drug reward? *Psychopharmacology, 153,* 31–43.

Berns, G.S., Cohen, J.D., & Mintun, M.A. (1997). Brain regions responsive to novelty in the absence of awareness. *Science, 276,* 1272–1275.

Besheer, J., Jensen, H.C., & Bevins, R.A. (1999). Dopamine antagonism in a novel-object preference and a novel-object place conditioning preparation with rats. *Behavioural Brain Research, 103,* 35–44.

Bevins, R.A., & Bardo, M.T. (1999). Conditioned increase in place preference by access to novel objects: Antagonism by MK-801. *Behavioural Brain Research, 99,* 53–60.

Bevins, R.A., Klebaur, J.E., & Bardo, M.T. (1997). Individual differences in response to novelty, amphetamine-induced activity and drug discrimination in rats. *Behavioural Pharmacology, 8,* 113–123.

Cervo, L., & Samanin, R. (1995). Effects of dopaminergic and glutamatergic receptor antagonists on the acquisition and expression of cocaine conditioning place preference. *Brain Research, 673,* 242–250.

Cloninger, C.R. (1987). A systematic method for clinical description and classification of personality variants: A proposal. *Archives of General Psychiatry, 44,* 573–588.

Darwin, B. (Ed.). (1980). *The Oxford dictionary of quotations* (3rd ed.). Oxford, England: Oxford University Press.

Fowler, H. (1965). *Curiosity and exploratory behavior.* New York: Macmillan.

Ikemoto, S., & Panksepp, J. (1999). The role of the nucleus accumbens dopamine in motivated behavior: Unifying interpretation with special reference to reward-seeking. *Brain Research Review, 31,* 6–41.

McFarland, K., & Ettenberg, A. (1995). Haloperidol differentially affects reinforcement and motivational processes in rats running an alley for intravenous heroin. *Psychopharmacology, 122,* 346–350.

Piazza, P.V., Deminière, J.-M., LeMoal, M., & Simon, H. (1989). Factors that predict individual vulnerability to amphetamine self-administration. *Science, 245,* 1511–1513.

Sutton, M.A., & Beninger, R.J. (1999). Psychopharmacology of conditioned reward: Evidence for a rewarding signal at D1-like dopamine receptors. *Psychopharmacology, 144,* 95–110.

Zuckerman, M. (1994). *Behavioral expressions and biosocial bases of sensation seeking.* New York: Cambridge University Press.

Moving Beyond the Heritability Question: New Directions in Behavioral Genetic Studies of Personality

Kimberly J. Saudino[1]
Department of Psychology, Boston University, Boston, Massachusetts

Most personality traits show some genetic influence (i.e., are to some extent inherited). Studies of personality and temperament in infancy, childhood, adolescence, adulthood, and old age consistently yield heritabilities in the range of .20 to .50, suggesting that genetic differences among individuals account for between 20 to 50%, of the variability of personality within a population. The finding of genetic influences on personality has been replicated across American, Australian, British, Finnish, Swedish, and Russian cultures. However, the conclusion that individual differences in personality are, in part, due to genetic factors is just the beginning of the story. Behavioral genetics has much more to offer to the study of personality than heritability estimates, and in this article, I describe three exciting new directions that behavioral genetic studies of personality are taking. Although basic behavioral genetic terns are defined, details of the theory and methods cannot be described in this brief article; however, they are described in textbooks on behavioral genetics (e.g., Plomin, DeFries, McClearn, & Rutter, 1997).

USING OBJECTIVE MEASURES TO ASSESS PERSONALITY

Behavioral genetic studies of personality have relied mainly on self-report questionnaires for adolescents and adults and parent reports for children. Although such measures have provided ample evidence of genetic influences on personality, they have been criticized as being subjective, reflecting raters' expectations in addition to actual behavior. A key question is whether more objective measures of personality will also show genetic influences. Thus far, this question has been examined primarily in studies of infant and child personality, or temperament, as it is referred to in the developmental literature.

The use of objective measures of temperament in behavioral genetic studies arose as a result of some puzzling outcomes that occur when parents report on their children's temperament. Identical twins typically show high correlations on ratings of temperament, whereas fraternal twins show correlations that are very low, often near zero or even slightly negative (e.g., Neale & Stevenson, 1989). Because identical twins are more similar genetically than fraternal twins, these results imply genetic influence. However, the low resemblance of fraternal twin pairs is puzzling: The simple genetic model predicts that their similarity should be half that of identical twins because fraternal twins are 50% similar genetically whereas identical twins are genetically identical. Also puzzling is the finding that adoption studies suggest little or no genetic influence on children's temperament as rated by their parents. For example, in the Colorado Adoption Project, non-adoptive siblings, who have the same biological parents and are thus 50% related genetically, were no more similar for parent-rated temperament than genetically unrelated adoptive siblings (Plomin, Coon, Carey, DeFries, & Fulker, 1991).

The problem of too-low resemblance of fraternal twin pairs and the higher heritability estimates in twin studies than adoption studies of parent-rated temperament can be explained by rating biases. Parents may either inflate the similarity of their identical twins (*assimilation effects*) or exaggerate the differences between their fraternal twins or nonadoptive siblings (*contrast effects*). Both assimilation effects and contrast effects artificially increase differences between the correlations for identical and fraternal twins and, therefore, result in overestimates of genetic influence in twin studies. Because contrast effects reduce the similarity of nonadoptive and adoptive siblings, adoption studies will underestimate heritability. Several recent articles have discussed assimilation and contrast effects (e.g., Saudino, McGuire, Reiss, Hetherington, & Plomin, 1995).

The puzzling outcomes can also be explained by the presence of *nonadditive* genetic effects, in which there is an interaction in the effects of genes. When genetic effects are nonadditive, the number of genes in common between family members does not directly translate into similarity among family members. An example of a nonadditive genetic effect is gene dominance, which occurs when one member of a gene pair is expressed and the other is not (e.g., a person with a brown-eyed gene and a blue-eyed gene will have brown eyes). Although full siblings other than identical twins have 50% of their genes in common, when nonadditive genetic influences are important to a trait, siblings will be dissimilar to the extent that one sibling has the dominant form of the gene and the other does not. Similarity of identical twins is not affected by nonadditive genetic effects because such twins are genetically identical. Nonadditive genetic effects reduce the similarity of fraternal twins and other first-degree siblings. Therefore, when nonadditive genetic effects are present, similarity of fraternal twins will be less than one half that of identical twins. Similarly, adoption designs, which are based on the difference in behavioral similarity between nonadoptive and adoptive siblings, will not uncover as much genetic influence as will twin studies.

Objective measures of temperament can help us evaluate the possible explanations of the unusual outcomes from parent-rating studies of temperament. If the outcomes are due to parental rating biases, then objective measures should show a more reasonable pattern of results. However, if the low similarity of fraternal twins and nonadoptive siblings is due to nonadditive genetic effects, then objective measures of temperament would be expected to show a similar pattern of results.

The MacArthur Longitudinal Twin Study (MALTS; Emde, in press), a collaborative longitudinal study of twins that focuses on individual differences in temperament, emotion, and cognition from infancy to early childhood, provides an opportunity to evaluate the issue of possible parental rating biases because it includes many observed behavioral measures of temperament in addition to parent ratings. In MALTS, parent ratings of emotionality, activity level, shyness, and persistence produced a pattern of moderate correlations for identical twins and near zero or negative correlations for fraternal twins (Saudino & Cherny, in press-a). This pattern for fraternal twins is significant because it implies that they are perceived as no more similar—and, in some instances, less alike—than two randomly paired children. In fact, for some dimensions, fraternal co-twins are perceived as having opposing behavioral tendencies. Observational measures of the same temperament dimensions in the MALTS sample tell a different story, however. When temperament was assessed by observer ratings, correlations for fraternal twins were positive, and the difference between correlations for identical and fraternal twins was consistent with genetic expectations (Saudino & Cherny, in press-b).

Thus, the evidence from MALTS points toward parental contrast effects, a conclusion further supported by adoption research. Correlations for nonadoptive siblings are higher when measures such as observer or teacher ratings are employed than when parent ratings are used (e.g., Schmitz, Saudino, Plomin, Fulker, & DeFries, 1996). Moreover, adoption and twin studies of objectively assessed temperament yield similar estimates of heritability (e.g., Braungart, Plomin, DeFries, & Fulker, 1992).

The finding that parent ratings and objective measures of temperament yield different results has implications more generally for personality research. The results strongly suggest that contrast biases affect parent ratings, at least for siblings. Researchers need to consider the possibility that parent ratings reflect parental expectations in addition to children's actual behavior. The lessons learned from studies of child temperament can also be applied to studies of adult personality, which have relied on self-report measures. Self-report questionnaires may be subjectively biased, and, therefore, research using more objective methods is needed to support the wealth of information that has been learned from self-report data.

EXPLORING SITUATIONAL DIFFERENCES IN PERSONALITY

In addition to signaling the need for more objective measures of personality, the findings just reviewed remind us that a single mode of assessment may not paint a complete picture of personality. That is, there may be important contextual or situational factors that are overlooked when a single measure of personality is used. By applying genetic analyses to multiple measures of the same personality dimension, researchers can capture aspects of personality that operate across multiple measures (*measure-general effects*) as well as aspects of personality that are unique to specific measures (*measure-specific effects*). When different measures assess the same dimension of personality in different situations, analysis can address cross-situational and context-specific genetic effects.

Multivariate genetic analyses differ from traditional genetic analyses in that they assess the extent to which genetic effects on one variable overlap with genetic effects on another. Such analyses allow for the examination of genetic and environmental contributions to the covariance between two measures rather than the variance of each measure considered separately. For example, in MALTS, multivariate genetic analyses have explored the extent to which genetic effects on a measure of shyness in the laboratory overlap with genetic effects on shyness in the home environment (Cherny, Fulker, Corley, Plomin, & DeFries, 1994). The same genetic influences were found to be involved in the two situations. This finding of cross-situational genetic effects for shyness in the lab and the home means that genetic factors contribute to the stability of shyness across the two situations. Indeed, the observed correlation between the two measures of shyness was almost entirely due to overlapping genetic effects. In contrast, environmental factors contributed to differences between shyness in the lab and in the home.

Although genetic factors often contribute to cross-situational stability in personality, sometimes genetic factors contribute to change as well as continuity across situations. In a recent study, Schmitz et al. (1996) examined genetic effects on teacher ratings of temperament in the classroom and tester ratings of temperament in a laboratory test situation. Schmitz et al. found that the genetic influences on teacher ratings of activity level overlapped substantially with the genetic influences on tester ratings of activity level. In fact, genetic factors were entirely responsible for the covariance between teacher and tester ratings, indicating that what teachers and testers see in common in children's activity level is due to genetics. Despite this evidence of cross-situational genetic effects, there was also genetic influence unique to tester ratings, indicating context-specific genetic effects for activity level. Context-specific genetic effects are genetic effects that are unique to a situation and, therefore, contribute to changes or differences in personality across situations. Thus, with respect to teacher and tester ratings of activity level, genetics is involved in situational change as well as stability. Similar results have emerged from a recent application of a multitrait-multimethod approach to twin data for three temperament dimensions (emotional tone, activity level, sociability), each assessed three different ways (examiner rating, playroom observation, parent rating). This study found substantial measure-specific genetic variance in addition to measure-general genetic variance (Philips & Matheny, 1997). However, the temperament measures in this study involved different methods (i.e., rating vs. observation plus rating) as well as different situations (lab vs. home vs. school), which makes it difficult to say whether the measure-specific genetic variance reflects situational change or method differences.

The fact that genes contribute to cross-situational stability for some dimensions of personality comes as no surprise because genetic factors are typically viewed as sources of stability. However, the finding of context-specific genetic effects on personality challenges the usual assumption that behavioral differences across situations are due to environmental influences. That is, situational variation in personality does not necessarily stem from environmental influences. Does this mean that there are personality genes unique to different situations or measures? Probably not. It is more likely that context-specific genetic influences arise because different measures provide different views of personality and thus detect different genetic effects specific to different contexts (Plomin & Nesselroade, 1990).

These findings offer an interesting perspective on what has been called the person-situation debate. At one time, psychologists were polarized with respect to the relative influence of the individual and situations on the individual's behavior; however, most would now agree that personality is a function of both the person (i.e., stable, enduring traits) and the specific characteristics of the situation. Multivariate genetic analyses allow us to examine the mechanisms that underlie cross-situational stability and change. Although more research is needed, initial applications of multivariate genetic analyses to personality suggest that we may have to change our conceptualization of situations to incorporate genetic influences.

PERSONALITY AND THE INTERFACE BETWEEN NATURE AND NURTURE

One of the most provocative findings to emerge from recent behavioral genetic research is that genetic factors contribute substantially to many measures that assess the environments of individuals (see Reiss, this issue). For example, genetic analyses of family environment, peer groups, social support, life events, and divorce often yield moderate heritability estimates (Plomin, 1994). Genetic influence on such environmental measures might appear paradoxical: Environments and experiences have no DNA, so how can they be affected by genetic factors? A resolution to this paradox is that the environment is not independent of the individual. Individuals play an active role in creating their own environments and experiences. Thus, to the extent that the environment reflects genetically influenced characteristics of the individual, we can expect to find genetic influence on environmental measures.

What personal characteristics might mediate genetic contributions to environmental measures? Researchers examining the mechanisms through which individuals are exposed to certain situations have found that individuals tend to choose situations or activities that reflect their personality. Therefore, personality is a good candidate for explaining genetic influences on environmental measures. That is, genetically influenced personality traits could affect how people select, construct, or perceive their environments.

Multivariate genetic analyses have been used to explore the extent to which genetic effects on environmental measures overlap with genetic effects on personality. Such studies suggest that personality traits can account for a portion of genetic effects on some environmental measures. For example, genetic effects on neuroticism and extraversion accounted for approximately 20% of the genetic variance in a measure of current family environment in a sample of Swedish adults (Chipuer, Plomin, Pedersen, McClearn, & Nesselroade, 1993). Personality has also been found to account for between 30% and 40% of the genetic influence on divorce risk (Jockin, McGue, & Lykken, 1996). Perhaps most surprising is one study's finding that for females in middle or late adulthood, genetic influences on life events were entirely mediated by neuroticism, extraversion, and openness to experience (Saudino, Pedersen, Lichtenstein, McClearn, & Plomin, 1997). That is, these three core dimensions of personality accounted for all of the genetic influences on life events. These results are not limited to adulthood. Genetic effects on a combined observational and interview measure of the home environment of 2-year-olds were mediated predominantly by genetic effects on tester ratings of task orientation, a temperament dimension reflecting attention span, persistence, and the tendency to be goal oriented (Saudino & Plomin, 1997). This finding suggests that, to some extent, parents structure infants' environments in response to genetically influenced attentional characteristics of their infants.

It should be noted, however, that personality may not explain genetic influence on all environmental measures. For example, multivariate analyses of data for adoptive and nonadoptive siblings found that genetic influences on parent-report measures of the family environment in middle childhood were largely independent of genetic influence on observed temperament in infancy and early childhood (Braungart, 1994). Similarly, a recent study of young adult twin and nontwin siblings found that there was no significant genetic covariance between personality and a self-report measure of perceptions of the classroom environment (Vernon, Jang, Harris, & McCarthy, 1997). In both of these cases, however, it is possible that measures assessing other personality traits would have produced different results. It is also possible that genetic effects on some measures of the environment may not be due to genetic effects on personality. A prudent interpretation of the research thus far suggests that genetic contributions to some measures of the environment are in part due to personality.

The finding that genetic variance in personality mediates genetic influence on environmental measures raises the question as to how the genetic effects arise. The answer depends on the extent to which the measure of the environment accurately assesses the objective environment of the individual. When the environment is measured via self-report, as was the case for the aforementioned studies of adult family environment and life events, it is possible that responses might reflect the individual's perceptions of environments or experiences, perceptions that are filtered through the individual's genetically influenced personality. Thus, personality might bias an individual's perceptions, and, consequently, the genetic covariation between personality and the environment might arise through the effects of personality on the person's perceptions, not on the environment per se. However, such perceptual processes may not tell the whole story. Genetic influences on objective, externally verifiable events such as divorce or on observations of infants' home environments provide evidence that, in some instances, environmental measures do not simply reflect genetic influences on perceptions of the environment. In these cases, the finding of significant genetic covariation between personality and environmental measures suggests a gene-environment correlation. That is, individuals are differentially exposed to environments and experiences as a function of their genetically influenced personality.

The finding that personality can explain at least some of the genetic influences on objective measures of the environment has important implications for psychologists. Traditionally, we have viewed the environment as an exogenous force that acts upon the individual. The presence of gene-environment correlations underlying the covariation between personality and environmental measures provides evidence for what many personality psychologists have long suspected: In some instances, the environment reflects rather than affects characteristics of individuals.

CONCLUSIONS

The finding of genetic influences on personality traits is only a first step in the understanding of individual differences in personality. Behavioral geneticists are taking new directions in their approach to the study of personality, and this research is yielding exciting new findings. More researchers are assessing personality through objective behavioral measures or multiple raters. This approach not only buttresses the findings from self- and parent-report questionnaires, but also can address issues of measure-specific and situational effects. Similarly, research examining the role that personality plays in the interface between nature and nurture suggests that personality mediates genetic influences on the environment. As more researchers begin to employ objective measures of the environment, the question of genetic mediation via perceptions versus gene-environment correlation will be answered. Clearly, there is much more to be discovered about personality as researchers move beyond the rudimentary heritability question.

Recommended Reading

Eaves, L.J., Eysenck, H.J., & Martin, N.G. (1989). *Genes, culture and personality.* New York: Academic Press.
Loehlin, J.C. (1992). *Genes and environment in personality development.* Newbury Park, CA: Sage.
Plomin, R., DeFries, J.C., McClearn, G.E., & Rutter, M. (1997). (See References)

Note

1. Address correspondence to Kimberly J. Saudino, Department of Psychology, Boston University, 64 Cummington St., Boston, MA 02215; e-mail: ksaudino@bu.edu.

References

Braungart. J M. (1944). Genetic influence on "environmental" measures. In J.C. DeFries, R. Plomin, & D.W. Fulker (Eds.), *Nature, nurture during middle childhood* (pp. 233–245). Cambridge, MA: Blackwell.
Braungart, J.M., Plomin, R., DeFries, J.C., & Fulker, D.W. (1.992), Genetic influence on tester-rated infant temperament as assessed by Bayley's Infant Behavior Record: Nonadoptive and adoptive siblings and twins. *Developmental Psychology, 28,* 40–47.
Cherny, S.S., Fulker, D.W., Corley, R., Plomin, R., & DeFries, J.C. (1994). Continuity and change in infant shyness from 14 to 20 months. *Behavior Genetics, 24,* 365–380.
Chipuer, H.M., Plomin, R., Pedersen, N.L., McClearn, G.E., & Nesselroade, J.R. (1993). Genetic influence on family environment: The role of personality. *Developmental Psychology, 29,* 110–118.
Emde, R. (Ed.). (in press). *The transition from infancy to early childhood: Genetic and environmental influences.* New York: Cambridge University Press.
Jockin, V., McGue, M., & Lykken, D.T. (1996). Personality and divorce: A genetic analysis. *Journal of Personality and Social Psychology, 71,* 288–299.
Neale, M.C., & Stevenson, J. (1989). Rater bias in the EASI temperament scales: A twin study. *Journal of Personality and Social Psychology, 56,* 446–455.
Philips, K., & Matheny, A.P. (1997). Evidence for genetic influence on both cross-situation and situation-specific components of behavior. *Journal of Personality and Social Psychology, 73,* 129–138.
Plomin, R. (1994). *Genetics and experience: The interplay between nature and nurture.* Newbury Park, CA: Sage.
Plomin, R., Coon, H., Carey, G., DeFries, J.C., & Fulker, D. (1991). Parent-offspring and sibling adoption analyses of parental ratings of temperament in infancy and early childhood. *Journal of Personality, 59,* 705–732.
Plomin, R., DeFries, J.C., McClearn, G.E., & Rutter, M. (1997). *Behavioral genetics* (3rd ed.). New York: W.H. Freeman.

Plomin, R., & Newsselroade, J.R. (1990). Behavioral genetics and personality change. *Journal of Personality, 58,* 191–220.

Saudino, K.J., & Cherny, S.S. (in press-a). Parent ratings of temperament in twins. In R. Emde (Ed.), *The transition from infancy to early childhood: Genetic and environmental influences.* New York: Cambridge University Press.

Saudino, K.J., & Cherny, S.S. (in press-b). Sources of continuity and change in observed temperament. In R. Emde (Ed.), *The transition from infancy to early childhood: Genetic and environmental influences.* New York: Cambridge University Press.

Saudino, K.J., McGuire, S., Reiss, D., Hetherington, E.M., & Plomin, R. (1995). Parent ratings of EAS temperaments in twins, full siblings, half siblings and step siblings. *Journal of Personality and Social Psychology, 68,* 723–733.

Saudino, K.J., Pedersen, N.L., Lichtenstein, P., McClearn, G.E., & Plomin, R. (1997). Can personality explain genetic influences on life events? *Journal of Personality and Social Psychology, 72,* 196–206.

Saudino, K.J., & Plomin, R. (1997). Cognitive and temperamental mediators of genetic contributions to the home environment during infancy. *Merrill-Palmer Quarterly, 43,* 1–23.

Schmitz, S., Saudino, K.J., Plomin, R., Fulker, D.W., & DeFries, J.C. (1996). Genetic and environmental influences on temperament in middle childhood: Analyses of teacher and tester ratings. *Child Development, 67,* 409–422.

Vernon, P.A., Jang, K.L., Harris, J.A., & McCarthy, J.M. (1997). Environmental predictors of personality differences: A twin and sibling study. *Journal of Personality and Social Psychology, 72,* 177–183.

Critical Thinking Questions

1. To what degree can people's experiences change their biology? Put another way, to what degree are people limited by their biology? Discuss with respect to findings presented in each article giving examples that argue for or against the notion that biology is destiny.

2. Saudino argues for incorporating the situation into our conceptualization of personality. How is her view similar to or different from Mischel, Shoda, and Mendoza-Denton's approach? What are the similarities and differences in what is referred to by the "situation" in these two articles? Are the solutions they propose to the so-called personality paradox compatible?

3. Discuss the maternal factors that are likely to lead to individual differences in the personality of the offspring. Discuss whether each of these factors represents nature or nurture effects or an interaction of both.

4. Discuss the positive and the negative consequences of novelty-reward. What are some of the high-risk behaviors that stem from problems in the neural and biological systems that regulate the approach system? In other words, in what ways might novelty-reward be involved in maladaptive outcomes? Draw from Bevin's discussion and give specific examples of potential behavioral problem areas.

5. Research investigating the biological underpinnings of personality often draw from animal models and research. Discuss the pros and cons of generalizing findings from animals to humans. Give specific examples from the articles.

Personality in Action:
Intrapersonal Processes

People vary a great deal in how they appraise and react to emotion-producing events. These differences are a key aspect of personality because they reveal the specific cognitive and affective mechanisms that individuals employ in their characteristic interpretations and adaptations to different types of situations. Personality here is portrayed as a distinctive system of mental-emotional mechanisms that interact with each other as well as the social environment to enable—or undermine—goal pursuit and effective emotional regulation in dealing with life stressors. The articles in this section address some basic relevant intrapersonal processes in such self-regulatory efforts as individuals adapt to the meaningful events in their lives.

Note that while each paper may focus on a different piece of such an "adaptation" process, individual differences play a role in various ways: People employ different self-regulatory strategies as a result of underlying individual differences (e.g., limitations in cognitive capacity; characteristic appraisals based on personal history; or availability of coping strategies due to prior learning conditions). But differential strategy use or styles of regulation themselves are also a reflection of personality. And finally, different styles of regulation have, in part, a direct impact on the person, as well as an indirect impact, via their impact on the social environment.

This section begins with articles addressing specific emotional and cognitive strategies people use to deal with generally difficult or upsetting situations. James Gross' (2001) process model of emotion regulation describes two commonly used strategies for down-regulation of emotions: cognitive reappraisal and suppression. Interesting for personality is that people have differential preferences for the use of these two strategies and that the use of each type has different consequences. Cognitive reappraisals, where individuals change the meaning of the event as it is occurring to decrease its emotional impact, has been shown to be much more adaptive than suppression, where individuals inhibit the emotional expression as they are experiencing the emotion. People employing appraisal strategies experience less distress, less physiological arousal, and as a result better social interactions than suppressors. The implication is that "suppressors" will experience stress more often across their lives, which is likely to have a variety of long-term consequences.

While Gross deals primarily with how people regulate negative emotion, Labouvie-Vief (2003) examines how individuals integrate positive and negative affect to moderate the effects of anxiety-producing situations. Her findings identify how the optimizing of positive emotions and experiences, and the tolerance for ambiguity and negative emotions, combine to jointly enhance adaptation and adjustment. This work also helps to clarify some of the specific cognitive mechanisms and conditions that facilitate the adaptive processing of negative emotions when individuals attempt to face them rather than to simply ignore or repress them. While not conclusive, the work suggests that individual differences in regulatory ability are likely due, at least in part, to whether individuals had the opportunity to learn regulatory strategies in relatively low stress environments that allowed for more complex cognitive integration to take place.

Both of the foregoing papers make clear that people's appraisals of events have a large impact on their emotional well-being. In the third article of this section Robinson (2004) discusses some interesting effects of habitual mental processes for categorizing various types of stimuli and their interactions with personality traits, such as agreeableness or neuroticism, as one possible contributor to such outcomes. Many factors make a difference, including the specific types of stimuli. The findings speak to the extremely complex interactions between broad personality traits and individual differences in categorization styles and tendencies in the processing of emotion-arousing stimuli.

The next three papers take these general basic cognitive and emotional mechanisms for dealing with stressful events and place them in people's life contexts more broadly. That is, they go beyond just asking about the specific operations of the mechanisms to trying to understand the more global purpose these regulatory attempts play in people's identity strivings. Cantor and Harlow (1994) investigate individual differences in the self-regulatory strategies people employ in the context of pursuing their "life tasks." According to this approach, individuals' personalities are defined by their central concerns (which are rooted in people's self-views and personal histories) and by the means and processes through which they shape situations to provide strategic "solutions" to these personal problems. In other words, situations provide different affordances for particular problems to be pursued, and individuals' personalities are characterized by the differential appraisals and subsequent responsiveness to these affordances. Interestingly, this work shows that although many of these "problem-solving" styles are successful with respect to the particular life-problem the individual is trying to solve, they simultaneously also incur costs along the way.

In a related line of research, Bill Swann (1992) examines self-verification strivings as a strategy for people to maintain their self-views—people try to get others to see them as they see themselves. He provides evidence for the counterintuitive proposition that people with negative self-views will actually seek out negative feedback about the self, if they think it is accurate, despite the fact they do not "like" it. One disconcerting consequence of the self-verification process is that people choose intimates who confirm their self-views, and that these partners then also help maintain this self-view, even when opportunity-windows for positive change arise. Thus, self-verification processes may be one vehicle through which people's personalities are maintained.

The final article in this section by Baumeister, Bushman, and Camp-bell (2000) deals with the consequences of ego-threat. This research demonstrates that for some people aggression becomes a means of defending a highly positive self-view that is being threatened at the moment. It shows that what is key is not positive self-regard per se, but rather that aggression is enacted by people motivated to protect extremely fragile self-esteem, for example, people who are narcissistic or those with unstable self-esteem. This work offers a very clear demon-stration of how personality features are not constantly active, but are brought out in personality-relevant trigger situations. Furthermore, it high-lights the interpersonal imbeddedness of intrapersonal mechanisms, as in this case it is interpersonal situations that trigger aggression, which then itself in turn has a negative impact on interpersonal relations. These interpersonal aspects are further elaborated in the next section.

Emotion Regulation in Adulthood: Timing Is Everything

James J. Gross[1]

Department of Psychology, Stanford University, Stanford, California

Abstract

Emotions seem to come and go as they please. However, we actually hold considerable sway over our emotions: We influence which emotions we have and how we experience and express these emotions. The process model of emotion regulation described here suggests that how we regulate our emotions matters. Regulatory strategies that act early in the emotion-generative process should have quite different outcomes than strategies that act later. This review focuses on two widely used strategies for down-regulating emotion. The first, reappraisal, comes early in the emotion-generative process. It consists of changing how we think about a situation in order to decrease its emotional impact. The second, suppression, comes later in the emotion-generative process. It involves inhibiting the outward signs of emotion. Theory and research suggest that reappraisal is more effective than suppression. Reappraisal decreases the experience and behavioral expression of emotion, and has no impact on memory. By contrast, suppression decreases behavioral expression, but fails to decrease the experience of emotion, and actually impairs memory. Suppression also increases physiological responding in both the suppressors and their social partners.

Keywords

emotion; mood; regulation

Some goon in a sports car careens across your lane. You brake hard. You feel like yelling, throwing something, or even ramming that idiot. Do you? Probably not. Instead, you *regulate* your emotions, and do something else that you think is more appropriate. Psychological research on emotion regulation examines the strategies we use to influence which emotions we have and how we experience and express these emotions. This research grows out of two earlier traditions, the psychoanalytic tradition and the stress and coping tradition (Gross, 1999b).[2] In this review, I describe a process model of emotion regulation that distinguishes two major kinds of emotion regulation. I illustrate each by focusing on two common forms of emotion down-regulation—reappraisal and suppression— and demonstrate how these two regulation strategies differ in their affective, cognitive, and social consequences.

A PROCESS MODEL OF EMOTION REGULATION

Emotion regulation includes all of the conscious and nonconscious strategies we use to increase, maintain, or decrease one or more components of an emotional response (Gross, 1999a). These components are the feelings, behaviors, and physiological responses that make up the emotion.

A moment's reflection suggests there are many ways to go about regulating emotions. How can we make sense of the potentially limitless number of emotion-regulation strategies? According to my process model of emotion regulation (Gross, 1998b), specific strategies can be differentiated along the timeline of the unfolding emotional response. That is, strategies differ in *when* they have their primary impact on the emotion-generative process, as shown in Figure 1.

At the broadest level, we can distinguish between *antecedent-focused* and *response-focused* emotion-regulation strategies. Antecedent-focused strategies refer to things we do before response tendencies have become fully activated and have changed our behavior and physiological responses. An example of antecedent-focused regulation is viewing an admissions interview at a school you have applied to as an opportunity to see how much you like the school, rather than a test of your worth. Response-focused strategies refer to things we do once an emotion is already under way, after response tendencies have been generated. An example of response-focused regulation is keeping a poker face while holding a great hand during an exciting card game.

As shown in Figure 1, five more specific emotion-regulation strategies can be located within this broad scheme. The first is *situation selection*, illustrated in Figure 1 by the solid arrow pointing toward Situation 1 (S1) rather than Situation 2 (S2). For example, you may decide to have dinner with a friend who always makes you laugh the night before a big exam (S1), rather than going to the last-minute study session with other nervous students (S2).

Once selected, a situation may be tailored so as to modify its emotional impact (e.g., S1x, S1y, and S1z in Fig. 1). This constitutes *situation modification*.

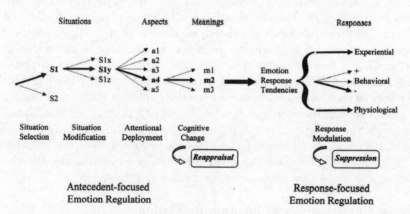

Fig. 1. A process model of emotion regulation. According to this model, emotion may be regulated at five points in the emotion-generative process: (a) selection of the situation, (b) modification of the situation, (c) deployment of attention, (d) change of cognitions, and (e) modulation of experiential, behavioral, or physiological responses. The first four of these processes are antecedent-focused, and the fifth is response-focused. The number of response options shown at each of these five points in the illustration is arbitrary, and the heavy lines indicate the particular options selected in the example given in the text. Two specific emotion-regulation strategies—reappraisal and suppression—are the primary focus of this review (Gross, 1998b).

For example, at dinner, if your friend asks whether you are ready for the exam, you can make it clear that you would rather talk about something else.

Third, situations have different aspects (e.g., a1–a5 in Fig. 1), and *attentional deployment* is used to select which aspect of the situation you focus on. An example is distracting yourself from a conversation that has taken an upsetting turn by counting ceiling tiles.

Once you have focused on a particular aspect of the situation, *cognitive change* refers to selecting which of the many possible meanings (e.g., m1–m3 in Fig. 1) you will attach to that aspect. For example, if your upcoming test is mentioned during the dinner conversation, you might remind yourself that "it's only a test," rather than seeing the exam as a measure of your value as a human being. The personal meaning you assign to the situation is crucial because it determines which experiential, behavioral, and physiological response tendencies will be generated.

Finally, *response modulation* refers to attempts to influence these response tendencies once they have been elicited, illustrated in Figure 1 by the solid arrow pointing toward decreasing expressive behavior. In our example, response modulation might take the form of hiding your embarrassment after bombing the exam. It might also take the form of altering experiential or physiological components of emotion.

CONTRASTING TWO FORMS OF EMOTION REGULATION: REAPPRAISAL AND SUPPRESSION

Antecedent-focused strategies change the emotion trajectory very early on. By contrast, response-focused strategies occur after response tendencies have already been generated. This difference in timing predicts rather different consequences for these two kinds of emotion regulation. To test this idea, my colleagues and I have focused on two specific strategies used to down-regulate emotion. One is *reappraisal*. As shown in Figure 1, this is a type of cognitive change, and thus antecedent-focused. Reappraisal means that the individual reappraises or cognitively reevaluates a potentially emotion-eliciting situation in terms that decrease its emotional impact. The second strategy we have focused on is *suppression*, a type of response modulation, and thus response-focused. Suppression means that an individual inhibits ongoing emotion-expressive behavior.[3] In the following sections, I describe our findings concerning the affective, cognitive, and social consequences of reappraisal and suppression.

Affective Consequences of Emotion Regulation

Reappraisal occurs early in the emotion-generative process and involves cognitively neutralizing a potentially emotion-eliciting situation. Thus, reappraisal should decrease experiential, behavioral, and physiological responding. By contrast, suppression occurs later and requires active inhibition of the emotion-expressive behavior that is generated as the emotion unfolds. Thus, suppression should not change emotion experience at all, but should increase physiological activation as a result of the effort expended in inhibiting ongoing emotion-expressive behavior.

72

To test these predictions, we needed to elicit emotion in the laboratory. Researchers have used a variety of methods, including music, obnoxious confederates, and films, to elicit emotion. Films have the advantage of being readily standardized, and of provoking high levels of emotion in an ethically acceptable way (Gross & Levenson, 1995). To examine the affective consequences of emotion regulation, we used a short film that showed a disgusting arm amputation (Gross, 1998a). In the reappraisal condition, participants were asked to think about the film they were seeing in such a way (e.g., as if it were a medical teaching film) that they would not respond emotionally. In the suppression condition, participants were asked to hide their emotional reactions to the film. In the natural condition, participants simply watched the film.

As expected, suppression decreased disgust-expressive behavior, but also increased physiological activation. For example, participants in the suppression condition had greater constriction of their blood vessels than participants in the natural condition. Like suppression, reappraisal decreased expressive behavior. Unlike suppression, however, reappraisal had no observable physiological consequences.[4] Another predicted difference was that reappraisal decreased the experience of disgust, whereas suppression did not.

Related studies have confirmed and extended these findings. Increases in physiological activation also have been found when participants suppress amusement and sadness (Gross & Levenson, 1993, 1997). Note that there are no such increases in physiological activation when people "suppress" during a neutral film. This shows that the physiological impact of suppression grows out of pitting attempts to inhibit expression against strong impulses to express. Absent a stimulus that produces emotional impulses, suppression has no impact on physiological responding. The finding that reappraisal decreases emotional responding has recently been replicated using a behavioral measure (the magnitude of a startle response to a loud noise burst) as an index of emotional state (Jackson, Maimstadt, Larson, & Davidson, 2000).

Cognitive Consequences of Emotion Regulation

Suppression is a form of emotion regulation that requires self-monitoring and self-corrective action throughout an emotional event. Such monitoring requires a continual outlay of cognitive resources, reducing the resources available for processing events so that they can be remembered later. Reappraisal, by contrast, is evoked early on in the emotion-generative process. Therefore, this strategy typically does not require continual self-regulatory effort during an emotional event. This would make costly self-regulation unnecessary, leaving memory intact.

We tested these predictions in several interlocking studies (Richards & Gross, 2000). In one study, participants viewed slides under one of three conditions: reappraisal, suppression, or a "just watch" control. Slides depicted injured men, and information concerning each man was provided orally as each slide was presented. Suppression led to worse performance on a memory test for information presented during slide viewing. Reappraisal did not.

To see whether our laboratory findings would generalize to everyday life, we examined memory and individual differences in emotion regulation, measured with the Emotion Regulation Questionnaire (Gross & John, 2001). Individuals with high scores on the Suppression scale of the questionnaire reported having worse memory than individuals with low Suppression scores. They also performed worse on an objective memory test in which participants were asked to recall events they had listed in a daily diary 1 week earlier. By contrast, Reappraisal scores had no relationship to either self-reported or objective memory. Together, these findings suggest that whereas suppression is cognitively costly, reappraisal is not.

Social Consequences of Emotion Regulation

Emotions serve important social functions. Thus, emotion regulation should have social consequences, and different regulation strategies should have different consequences. As postulated in my model, reappraisal selectively alters the meaning of an emotion-eliciting situation. In emotionally negative situations, reappraisal decreases negative emotion-expressive behavior, but does not decrease positive behavior. Suppression, by contrast, decreases both negative and positive emotion-expressive behavior. This decrease in positive emotion-expressive behavior should interfere with social interaction, leading to negative reactions in other individuals.

To test this prediction, we asked unacquainted pairs of women to view an upsetting film, and then discuss their reactions (Butler, Egloff, Wilhelm, Smith, & Gross, 2001). Unbeknownst to the other, one member of each dyad had been asked to either suppress her emotions, reappraise the meaning of the film, or interact naturally with her conversation partner. We expected suppression to decrease both negative and positive emotion-expressive behavior in the regulator. Positive emotion expressions are a key element of social support, and social support decreases physiological responses to stressors (Uchino, Cacioppo, & Kiecolt-Glaser, 1996). We therefore reasoned that the diminished positive emotion-expressive behavior shown by participants who suppressed their emotions would produce large physiological responses in their interaction partners. By contrast, we did not expect participants given the reappraisal instructions to show decreased positive emotion-expressive behavior. We therefore expected that their interaction partners would have physiological responses comparable to those of the partners of participants who acted naturally.

Figure 2 shows that partners of participants asked to suppress their emotions had greater increases in blood pressure than partners of participants given reappraisal instructions or asked to act naturally. Interacting with a partner who shows little positive emotion is more physiologically activating than interacting with a partner who shows greater positive emotion. This finding extends prior work by Fredrickson and Levenson (1998), who showed that positive emotions speed cardiovascular recovery from negative emotions. Emotion-regulation strategies that increase (or at least maintain) positive emotion should be calming for both the regulator and the interaction partner, whereas strategies that diminish positive emotion should increase physiological responses of both the regulator and the interaction partner.

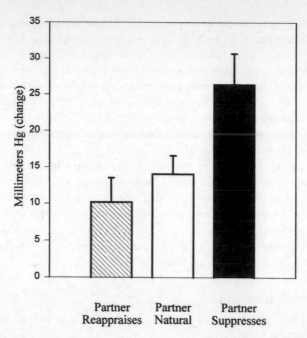

Fig. 2. Social consequences of emotion regulation. Mean change in blood pressure is shown separately for individuals whose conversation partners were asked to reappraise the situation, act naturally, or suppress their emotions (Butler, Egloff, Wilhelm, Smith, & Gross, 2001).

DIRECTIONS FOR FUTURE RESEARCH

My model suggests that adjustments made early in the emotion trajectory are more effective than adjustments made later on. The findings I have reviewed support this prediction. Reappraisal decreases expressive behavior and emotion experience, and does not adversely affect physiological responding, memory, or the regulator's interaction partner. Suppression, by contrast, has no impact on emotion experience, impairs memory, and increases physiological responding in both the regulator and the partner.

One direction for future research is to learn more about emotion regulation at each step in the emotion-generative process. This review has focused on one type of cognitive change and one type of response modulation. Do other forms of cognitive change and response modulation have similar consequences? Moreover, what are the differences among the antecedent-focused strategies of situation selection, situation modification, cognitive change, and attentional deployment? Similarly, what are the differences among the response-focused strategies?

A second important direction for future research is to explore the long-term consequences of differing emotion-regulation strategies. I have largely focused here on the immediate effects of reappraisal and suppression. However, if there are consistent individual differences in emotion and emotion regulation, such differences might have cumulative effects. For example, each time emotion is suppressed, physiological responses are magnified. Any one physiological response of increased intensity is unlikely to have deleterious consequences. But if such responses recur day after day after day, there might be adverse health consequences. A recent study illustrates how such a hypothesis might be tested. Heart attack survivors were divided into four groups, depending on their distress and their tendency to suppress emotion (Denollet et al., 1996). The subgroup scoring high on both distress and suppression had a significantly higher death rate (27%) than other patients (7%). This finding suggests that suppression indeed has important cumulative health consequences.

A third direction for future research is to explore whether people regulate emotional impulses in the same way as physical impulses such as hunger, aggression, and sexual arousal. Do strategies that help people stay emotionally cool also help them avoid eating that extra piece of cake, or steer clear of that tempting adulterous relationship? Or must each type of impulse be handled differently? Answers to such questions are of rich theoretical interest, and will also have great practical value for education and therapy.

Recommended Reading

Gross, J.J. (1998a). (See References)
Gross, J.J. (1999a). (See References)
Richards, J.M., & Gross, J.J. (2000). (See References)

Acknowledgments—Preparation of this article was supported by Grant MH53859 from the National Institute of Mental Health, I would like to thank Jo-Anne Bachorowski, Lisa Feldman Barrett, Barb Fredrickson, Oliver John, Ann Kring, Sonja Lyubomirsky, Jane Richards, Steve Sutton, and Jeanne Tsai for their helpful comments.

Notes

1. Address correspondence to James J. Gross, Department of Psychology, Stanford University, Stanford, CA 94305-2130; e-mail: james@psych.stanford.edu; http://www.psych.stanford.edu/~psyphy/.
2. This review focuses on emotion regulation in adults. For a recent review of emotion regulation in childhood, see Eisenberg, Fabes, Guthrie, and Reiser (2000).
3. The term "reappraisal" has a long history. Although some researchers find it confusing because it suggests that there is an initial appraisal that is then reworked, I use it for historical continuity. My focus here is on reappraisal that is used to cognitively transform a potentially negative-emotion-inducing situation so as to reduce its emotional impact. The term "suppression" also has a long history. It has been used to refer to inhibiting feelings, behavior, or thoughts. Here I use it to refer to inhibiting emotion-expressive behavior.
4. One puzzle is why reappraisal did not decrease physiological responding in this study. The potency and brevity of the surgical film may have made it difficult for participants to curtail their physiological responses in the time specified.

References

Butler, E.A. Egloff, B., Wilhelm, F.H., Smith, N.C., & Gross, J.J. (2001). *The social consequences of emotion regulation*. Manuscript submitted for publication.

Denollet, J., Sys, S.U., Stroobant, N., Rombouts, H., Gillebert, T.C., & Brutsaert, D.L. (1996). Personality as independent predictor of long-term mortality in patients with coronary heat disease. *The Lancet, 347,* 417–421.

Eisenberg, N., Fabes, R.A., Guthrie, I.K., & Reiser, M. (2000). Dispositional emotionality and regulation: Their role in predicting quality of social functioning. *Journal of Personality and Social Psychology, 78,* 136–157.

Fredrickson, B.L., & Levenson, R.W. (1998). Positive emotions speed recovery from the cardiovascular sequelae of negative emotions. *Cognition & Emotion, 12,* 191–220.

Gross, J.J. (1998a). Antecedent- and response-focused emotion regulation: Divergent consequences for experience, expression, and physiology. *Journal of Personality and Social Psychology, 74,* 224–237.

Gross, J.J. (1998b). The emerging field of emotion regulation: An integrative review. *Review of General Psychology, 2,* 271–299.

Gross, J.J. (1999a). Emotion and emotion regulation. In L.A. Pervin & O.P. John (Eds.), *Handbook of personality: Theory and research* (2nd ed., pp. 525–552). New York: Guilford.

Gross, J.J. (1999b). Emotion regulation: Past, present, future. *Cognition & Emotion, 13,* 551–573.

Gross, J.J., & John, O.P. (2001). *Individual differences in emotion regulation processes: Consequences affect, well-being, and relationships.* Manuscript submitted for publication.

Gross, J.J., & Levenson, R.W. (1993). Emotional suppression: Physiology, self-report, and expressive behavior. *Journal of Personality and Social Psychology, 64,* 970–986.

Gross, J.J., & Levenson, R.W. (1995). Emotion elicitation using films. *Cognition & Emotion, 9,* 87–108.

Gross, J.J., & Levenson, R.W. (1997). Hiding feelings: The acute effects of inhibiting positive and negative emotions. *Journal of Abnormal Psychology, 106,* 95–103.

Jackson, D.C., Malmstadt, J.R., Larson, C.L., & Davidson, R.J. (2000). Suppression and enhancement of emotional responses to unpleasant pictures. *Psychophysiology, 37,* 515–522.

Richards, J.M., & Gross, J.J. (2000). Emotion regulation and memory: The cognitive costs of keeping one's cool. *Journal of Personality and Social Psychology, 79,* 419–424.

Uchino, B.N., Cacioppo, J.T., & Kiecolt-Glaser, J.K. (1996). The relationship between social support and physiological processes: A review with emphasis on underlying mechanisms and implications for health. *Psychological Bulletin, 119,* 488–531.

Dynamic Integration: Affect, Cognition, and the Self in Adulthood

Gisela Labouvie-Vief[1]
Department of Psychology, Wayne State University, Detroit, Michigan

Abstract

Positive self- and emotional development is often measured by optimization of happiness, but a second aspect of positive development—the ability to tolerate tension and negativity in the interest of maintaining objective representations—needs to be integrated with this hedonic emphasis. The integration of these two aspects, optimization and differentiation, reflects a dynamic balance. Such integration is possible when emotional activation or arousal is moderate, but is impaired at very high levels of activation. From youth to middle adulthood, the capacity for integration increases, but later in life, limitations or poor regulation strategies foster compensatory processes that compromise integration.

Keywords

adulthood; affect differentiation; emotional development; integration; self-development

Research on positive self- and emotional development in adulthood and aging has revealed two seemingly contradictory patterns (Labouvie-Vief & Márquez, in press). One line of research has demonstrated that older individuals' emotion regulation improves, because the balance of positive over negative affect increases into old age. However, another research tradition has pointed to regulation problems that result from later-life decline of cognitive resources (such as planning and impulse regulation) that can affect emotion regulation. How can these two aspects of emotion regulation be reconciled? The work I report here suggests that these two bodies of research reflect different approaches to research that are based on different concepts of what is "good" regulation. One of these concepts emphasizes the *optimization* of individual well-being. The other, instead, emphasizes *differentiation and complexity* as individuals coordinate feelings in the here and now with past and future feelings and synchronize them with those of other people. Thus, at times, positive feelings must be delayed and negative affect endured, at least temporarily. In the work reported here, I suggest that, as a consequence, optimal functioning involves an integration and flexible coordination of two core emotion regulation strategies or modes—optimization and differentiation. How do individuals coordinate these dual demands?

COMPLEXITY AND DIFFERENTIATION OF EMOTIONS

Since Darwin's work on affect, researchers have developed many theories focused on primary affects, emotions hardwired by evolution to secure survival through highly automated responses. However, during development such basic emotions become embedded into more complex cognitive networks that reflect the contribution of higher-order thought processes (see Metcalfe & Mischel, 1999). My work on the relationship between feelings and thinking originally was influenced by Piaget (1981), whose writings on affect anticipated the more recent interest in complex emotions by suggesting that the individual's evolving cognitive capacities alter the very dynamics of emotional life.

As children develop complex (especially linguistic) forms of representation, emotions become less tied to the here and now and more tied to an inner world of mental states shared with other people. This gives rise to new emotions—such as embarrassment, pride, or guilt—that signal awareness that one's feelings and thoughts link one to the feelings and thoughts of other people. By adolescence, individuals experience emotions about abstract ideals and norms, and they guide their behavior through complex plans that are based on an evolving identity spanning wide segments of time and place. Even so, adolescents' representational skills remain limited (Labouvie-Vief, 1994), relying on the presence of already well-structured societal and cultural systems such as political and religious ideologies. Adults, in turn, develop more complex representations that support further development.

My colleagues and I investigated such transformations in individuals aged 10 to 80 and older (Labouvie-Vief, Chiodo, Goguen, Diehl, & Orwoll, 1995; Labouvie-Vief, DeVoe, & Bulka, 1989). We coded participants' descriptions of their emotions and their selves into qualitative levels of differing *cognitive-affective complexity*. Findings showed that from adolescence to middle adulthood, individuals acquired more conscious insight into aspects of emotions that previously were unconscious, gained clearer differentiation of self from others, and blended distinct emotions, especially ones involving positive and negative contrasts (e.g., a mixture of joy and sadness). These developments allowed many (but not all) adults to carve out a renewed sense of self that was complex, was historically situated, and entailed a more distinct sense of their individuality.

These results confirmed our expectation that significant growth in affective complexity continues through middle adulthood. However, the results also contained surprises, even disappointments: Not only did growth abate in late middle adulthood (see Fig. 1), but a significant decline occurred thereafter. These find-

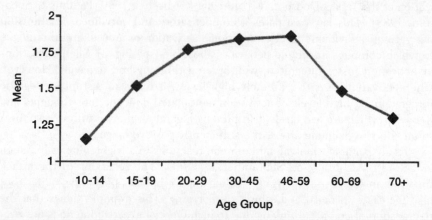

Fig. 1. Cognitive-affective complexity, based on participants' descriptions of their emotions and themselves, as a function of age.

ings highlight the role of middle-aged adults as the carriers of complex knowledge integrating mind and emotion (Labouvie-Vief, 1994) but suggest that problems with regulation of emotions occur with aging. Although the elderly reported the highest levels of positive affect, such as joy and interest, they also reported the lowest levels of negative affect, such as sadness and anger. Does this finding indicate increases in resilience among the elderly? We do not think so, because our notion of declining complexity implies reduced integration of negative affect so that as individuals age, they may find it more difficult to tolerate negative feelings. Indeed, our findings suggested such difficulty, because cognitive-affective complexity was uncorrelated with measures of hedonic tone such as wellbeing and positive affect. It was significantly positively correlated, however, with negative affect, as well as with measures of cognitive functioning. The fact that individuals of higher complexity express more negative affect goes along with our notion that affective differentiation involves coordinating positive and negative affect, but it also suggests that negative affect—but not positive affect—is related to cognitive functioning, perhaps because processing negative experience is more cognitively demanding. Is it possible, then, that individuals compensate for declines in cognitive-affective complexity with increases in optimization?

DYNAMIC INTEGRATION OF DIFFERENTIATION AND OPTIMIZATION

The notion that optimization and differentiation constitute quite different modes of regulating emotions is well embedded in the social-cognitive literature. Optimization is automatic and relatively effortless and involves experience that is personal and relatively ineffable or preconscious. Affect differentiation involves elaborative processing as individuals differentiate already existing knowledge. It requires more cognitive resources than optimization and is related to learning and knowledge that are relatively explicit and conscious.

To determine how the two modes interact, we (Labouvie-Vief & Márquez, in press) expanded Piaget's concept of an interplay between two core strategies of processing information (assimilation and accommodation) through a generalization of the Yerkes-Dodson law (Metcalfe & Mischel, 1999; Paulhus & Suedfeld, 1988). This law postulates a compensatory and curvilinear relationship between an individual's level of emotional activation or arousal and the degree to which complex, integrated behavior is possible (see Fig. 2). Slight elevations of activation foster integrated, well-ordered thinking and behavior. However, when activation rises to extremely high levels, it tends to disrupt or degrade integration. At high levels of activation, automated nonconscious thoughts and behavior, which are less easily disrupted by high arousal or activation, take over in an effort to maintain affect in a sufficiently positive range.

As an example, think about common reactions to a frightening event, such as the terrorist attack on September 11, 2001. The reactions to the attack involved an increase in patriotic feelings and emphasis on family values, but also increases in racial and ethnic stereotyping. This example shows that the degradation of complex thinking due to high emotional activation does not necessarily result in complete fragmentation, but can be relatively coherent or grace-

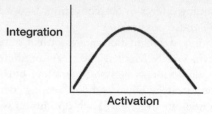

Fig. 2. Curvilinear relationship between integration (of thinking and behavior) and emotional activation. Integration is highest at moderate levels of activation and decreases at very high levels.

ful. First, behavior becomes more automatic and schematized (Metcalfe & Mischel, 1999). Second, the ability to coordinate positive and negative aspects about self and others is disrupted, leading to a positivity bias in which attention is diverted from negative information about the self. In contrast, negative affect and information often are projected onto others, resulting in increased black-and-white thinking, stereotyping, and polarization among in-groups and out-groups (e.g., Paulhus & Lim, 1994; Paulhus & Suedfeld, 1988). Finally, individuals attempt to retreat to safe havens by reducing the range of their action and seeking refuge in close social networks. Erikson (1984) has referred to these ways of simplifying psychological complexity as pseudospeciation—the exclusion of others from the circle of humanity in which one includes oneself.

In a sense, trading off differentiation and complexity in favor of optimization makes good sense in situations that pose a threat to the well-being and survival of the self. Such situations stimulate emergency responses in which resources are focused on the self-protective task of restoring equilibrium and securing survival. However, not all individuals opt for optimization; some may attempt to maintain a differentiated and fairly objective picture of reality. They may even overdifferentiate, or unsuccessfully try to reduce high levels of activation through intellectual analysis and rumination and become unable to act.

DYNAMIC INTEGRATION AND DEGRADATION OF OPTIMIZATION AND DIFFERENTIATION IN ADULT DEVELOPMENT

How does the complexity-optimization trade-off explain adult development and aging? Although the principle ideally works in a dynamic, flexible, and integrated way, two conditions can reduce flexible integration. First, normal developmental changes in cognitive resources can alter vulnerability to degradation of optimization or differentiation. As these resources grow, individuals are better able to maintain integrated behavior even when levels of activation are high. In contrast, as cognitive resources decline, individuals are more strongly affected by overactivation (Labouvie-Vief & Márquez, in press; Metcalfe & Mischel, 1999). Second, if development does not proceed in a context of relatively low and well-regulated arousal or activation, individuals are likely to develop poor strategies of affect regulation; these, in turn, should render the individuals particularly vulnerable to the degrading effects of overactivation. In our recent research, we have addressed both of these possibilities.

We began by defining two regulation modes, affect optimization and affect differentiation (Labouvie-Vief & Medler, 2002). As predicted, individuals who emphasized positive hedonic tone (high positive affect but low negative affect) displayed an optimization strategy, whereas those favoring cognitive-affective complexity adopted differentiation strategies. High optimizers were defined as individuals who minimized negative feelings; they did not engage in rich exploration of feelings and other nonrational processes (such as intuitions and dreams), and they tended to ignore unpleasant facts, but also exhibited low levels of self-doubt. High differentiators were defined as individuals who tended to analyze their emotions; they exhibited high tolerance of ambiguity and low levels of repression. Although the dimensions of optimization and differentiation were uncorrelated, they were associated with distinct patterns of additional traits. High optimizers were characterized by high ratings on self-acceptance, a sense of mastery, and purpose in life. High differentiators, in contrast, scored high on conceptual complexity, personal growth, and empathy, confirming our assumption that understanding another's perspective is a core aspect of affect complexity.

Optimizers and differentiators also reported having experienced different kinds of life events (Labouvie-Vief & Márquez, in press). Optimizers described their lives as free from major negative life events and turning points, such as emotional problems, loss of friends, experience with severe punishment or discrimination, and identity crises. In contrast, differentiators described their lives as containing major negative experiences, such as severe punishment and discrimination, and turning points, such as changes in self-concept or spiritual belief.

These results suggest that quite different pathways of development may exist in adulthood—one characterized by optimization, the other by differentiation. Do individuals develop unique styles of coordinating these modes? Through statistical analyses, we (Labouvie-Vief & Medler, 2002) identified four such styles (see Fig. 3). Following Werner (1957), we defined an *integrated* style, manifested by individuals who scored high on using both modes. These individuals displayed the most positive development: They scored high in positive but low in negative affect; reported high well-being, empathy, and health; and indicated they had a secure relationship style. In contrast, the *dysregulated* (low differentiation, low optimization) scored lowest on all of these variables, except negative affect, on which they scored highest. The *self-protective* (low differentiation, high optimization) and the *complex* (high differentiation, low optimization) displayed more mixed patterns that were nevertheless fairly coherent. Compared with the complex, the self-protective scored low in negative affect, but the two groups were similar in positive affect, relationship security, and health. The self-protective also placed less emphasis on personal growth but more on environmental mastery than the complex; they scored higher on good impression and conformance but lower on empathy. This pattern suggests that the self-protective tend to dampen negative affect, whereas the complex amplify it. The diverging affective patterns we identified appear to indicate different identity styles, each reflecting characteristic variations in how individuals integrate positive and negative affect (see Helson & Srivastava, 2001).

Integrated	Complex
High Positive Affect	Med Positive Affect
Low Negative Affect	Med Negative Affect
High Personal Growth	High Personal Growth
High Environmental Mastery	Med Environmental Mastery
High Good Impression	Med Good Impression
High Empathy	High Empathy
High Self-Related Health	Med Self-Related Health
High Relationship Security	Med Relationship Security
Self-Protective	**Dysregulated**
Med Positive Affect	Low Positive Affect
Low Negative Affect	High Negative Affect
Med Personal Growth	Low Personal Growth
High Environmental Mastery	Low Environmental Mastery
High Good Impression	Low Good Impression
Low Empathy	Low Empathy
Med Self-Related Health	Low Self-Related Health
Med Relationship Security	Low Relationship Security

Fig. 3. Four regulation styles resulting from different combinations of differentiation (high in top row, low in bottom row) and optimization (high in left column, low in right column): integrated (high differentiation, high optimization), complex (high differentiation, low optimization), self-protective (low differentiation, high optimization), and dysregulated (low differentiation, low optimization). Significant differences between the styles are indicated by different qualifiers: high, medium ("med"), and low. Environmental mastery refers to having a sense of mastery over one's environment. Good impression refers to a tendency to give socially desirable responses.

According to the principle of dynamic integration, the optimization and differentiation strategies are related in a compensatory fashion, especially among individuals, such as the elderly, who have limited resources. This is exactly what our data indicate. When we compared young, middle-aged, and old adults, our results showed that among the oldest age group, a significantly smaller than expected number of individuals fell into the complex group, whereas a disproportionately high number fell into the self-protective group: About 20% of the young and middle-aged adults (younger than 60) fell into the complex and self-protective groups, whereas only 10% of the older adults (aged 60 or older) were classified as complex, but 42% were classified as self-protective. Thus, as individuals grow older and experience declines in cognitive-affective complexity, they tend to rely more strongly on optimization strategies. This pattern was confirmed by longitudinal evidence as well: Over a 6-year interval, declines in differentiation predicted increases in optimization. On the positive side, however, our data also suggested that there were no significant declines in the number of elderly integrated individuals.

The notion of a trade-off between complexity and optimization in late life predicts not only increases in positive affect balance, but also impaired dynamic regulation of affect (i.e., degradation) in situations that require reflection to modulate emotion. Beyond our own work, much emerging experimental evidence (see Labouvie-Vief & Márquez, in press) also attests to such regulatory problems. In comparison to younger adults, older adults distort information in a positive direction, are less resistant to stereotypes, and limit their behavior to a more restricted range of tasks and goals that are directly relevant to the self (such as security); they also limit themselves to a narrower range of physical and social environments. Thus, as individuals experience reductions in cognitive-affective complexity, they can maintain a strategy of affect optimization as long as they reduce the demands made on them by their external environment.

CONCLUSIONS AND FUTURE RESEARCH

The dynamic-integration principle is able to reconcile two quite contradictory bodies of literature on adult self- and emotion regulation, one focusing on the maintenance of positive hedonic tone and the other focusing on development of cognitive-affective complexity and differentiation. Dynamic integration suggests that many elderly individuals compensate for a decrease in cognitive-affective complexity with an optimization response that involves the degradation of complex representations. The possibility of such cognitive-affective degradation means that researchers should not simply equate such concepts as well-being and positive development with positive feelings. Although the need to maintain a sufficiently positive balance of affect constrains emotional life, mature emotional development implies the ability to coordinate one's affect with that of others. This ability is widely considered a hallmark of complex emotions relating to caring, empathy, or equanimity. However, researchers still know little about the nature of those emotions. What permits some individuals to extend themselves beyond the most personal concerns with the here and now across time and to wide, perhaps unlimited, circles of others? What prevents other individuals from doing so? Researchers know little about that generation of middle-aged adults in whom these emotions come to full maturity: It is they who provide cognitive-affective scaffolding for younger generations and who, for better or for worse, regulate their development.

The concept of integration suggests that the activation of affect and the regulative function of the cognitions involved in differentiation interact in ways that can be mutually enhancing or limiting. What is the cusp that separates the two possibilities? With respect to aging, a critical threshold may be reached around the age of 60, when the capacity for conscious regulation becomes impaired. However, our data indicate that nearly half of that age group remains classified as integrated. Is it possible that many aging individuals are able to resist the degradation of complex cognitive-affective representations? If so, does a prior developmental pathway of integration differentiate them from those who embark on a less positive course?

Issues of integration extend well beyond aging, however, and raise important questions about other segments of the life span. For example, the present theory predicts that age and individual styles of regulation—with the differences in integration they imply—are important in moderating the effects of difficult and frightening events. How do individuals with different levels of cognitive-affective integration respond to a variety of emotion-activating events, both in the laboratory and in real life? Do those levels help explain why some individuals are able to grow from difficult experience, whereas others break or close down? Looking beyond behavioral data, what are the exact ways in which cognition and representation work to alter the dynamics of emotional activation? New neurobiological studies are beginning to show that this regulative function involves setting of new higher-order circuits in the brain (see Metcalfe & Mischel, 1999) that in turn are related to reduced levels of activation, as originally suggested by Freud, Luria, and Piaget. Such research brings the exciting promise of bridging the mental operations that characterize complex affects and the biological processes by which they become embodied in the brain.

Recommended Reading

Baltes, P.B., & Baltes, M.M. (1990). Psychological perspectives on successful aging: The model of selective optimization with compensation. In P.B. Baltes & M.M. Baltes (Eds.), *Successful aging: Perspectives from the behavioral sciences* (pp. 1–34). New York: Cambridge University Press.
Labouvie-Vief, G., & Márquez, M.G. (in press). (See References)
Ryan, R.M., & Deci, E.L. (2001). On happiness and human potentials: A review of research on hedonic and eudaimonic well-being. *Annual Review of Psychology, 52,* 141–166.

Acknowledgments—This research was supported by National Institute on Aging Grant AG09203.

Note

1. Address correspondence to Gisela Labouvie-Vief, Department of Psychology, Wayne State University, Detroit, MI 48202; e-mail: gvief@sun. science.wayne.edu.

References

Erikson, E.H. (1984). *The life cycle completed.* New York: Norton.
Helson, R., & Srivastava, S. (2001). Three paths of adult development: Conservers, seekers, and achievers. *Journal of Personality and Social Psychology, 80,* 995–1010.
Labouvie-Vief, G. (1994). *Psyche and Eros: Mind and gender in the life course.* New York: Cambridge University Press.
Labouvie-Vief, G., Chiodo, L.M., Goguen, L.A., Diehl, M., & Orwoll, L. (1995). Representations of self across the life span. *Psychology and Aging, 10,* 404–415.
Labouvie-Vief, G., DeVoe, M., & Bulka, D. (1989). Speaking about feelings: Conceptions of emotion across the life span. *Psychology and Aging, 4,* 425–437.
Labouvie-Vief, G., & Márquez, M.G. (in press). Dynamic integration: Affect optimization and differentiation in development. In D.Y. Dai & R.J. Sternberg (Eds.), *Motivation, emotion, and cognition.* Mahwah, NJ: Erlbaum.
Labouvie-Vief, G., & Medler, M. (2002). Affect optimization and affect complexity: Modes and styles of regulation in adulthood. *Psychology and Aging, 17,* 571–587.
Metcalfe, J., & Mischel, W. (1999). A hot/cool-system analysis of delay of gratification: Dynamics of willpower. *Psychological Review, 106,* 3–19.
Paulhus, D.L., & Lim, D.T.K. (1994). Arousal and evaluative extremity in social judgments: A dynamic complexity model. *European Journal of Social Psychology, 24,* 89–99.

Paulhus, D.L., & Suedfeld, P. (1988). A dynamic complexity model of self-deception. In J.S. Lockard & D.L. Paulhus (Eds.), *Self-deception: An adaptive mechanism* (pp. 132–145). New York: Prentice-Hall.

Piaget, J. (1981). *Intelligence and affectivity: Their relationship during child development* (T.A. Brown & C.E. Kaegi, Trans.). Palo Alto, CA: Annual Reviews.

Werner, H. (1957). *Comparative psychology of mental development*. New York: International Universities Press.

Personality as Performance Categorization Tendencies and Their Correlates

Michael D. Robinson
North Dakota State University

Abstract

As people seek to understand events within the world, they develop habitual tendencies related to categorization. Such tendencies can be measured by tasks that determine the relative ease or difficulty a person has in making a given distinction (e.g., between threatening and nonthreatening events). Researchers have sought to determine how categorization tendencies relate to personality traits on the one hand and emotional outcomes on the other. The results indicate that traits and categorization tendencies are distinct manifestations of personality. However, they often interact with each other. Three distinct interactive patterns are described. Categorization clearly does play a role in personality functioning, but its role goes beyond assimilation effects on behavior and experience.

Keywords

categorization; personality; emotion; affect; cognition

People generally recognize the role of habit in learning new skills such as square dancing, bike riding, or scientific writing. Less apparent, but probably not less important, is the role of habit in categorizing and interpreting events. Asking people why a given event is positive, threatening, or blameworthy is likely to lead to relatively inarticulate answers like "because it is." Such answers suggest that it is but a short jump from perceiving an event to interpreting it, and yet this event need not be interpreted at all or could be interpreted in a different manner.

To make the preceding points concrete, imagine two people encountering a soda machine that is empty of their preferred beverage. It is easy to imagine the two potential customers reacting very differently to this situation. One, Samantha, might react with disappointment (e.g., "I really wanted one of those") or even anger (e.g., "This soda company is completely disorganized"). In the case of disappointment, Samantha likely has categorized the event as negative; in the case of anger, she likely has categorized it as blameworthy. The second person, Tabitha, might not react with disappointment or anger, but rather might simply pick a second choice from the machine. For Tabitha, that is, the event seems to be neither negative nor blameworthy, but rather simply an occurrence.

What if Samantha and Tabitha were later asked to characterize their reactions to this incident on a self-report measure? Both women would likely claim that the incident was negative rather than neutral or positive. And yet, at the time the event actually unfolded, the two individuals made different implicit inter-

---

Address correspondence to Michael D. Robinson, Psychology Department, North Dakota State University, Fargo, ND 58105; e-mail: michael.d.robinson@ndsu.nodak.edu.

pretations. This thought experiment suggests the need for a measure of emotional appraisal that taps spontaneous categorization activity as it occurs.

PERSONALITY TRAITS AND CATEGORIZATION TENDENCIES

In recent work, my colleagues and I have found no relationships between personality traits and categorization tendencies that would seem, on the surface, to be related to those traits. For example, the personality trait of extraversion does not predict how fast a person can categorize words as positive or not (Robinson, Solberg, Vargas, & Tamir, 2003). Also, individuals more prone to experiencing distress and anxiety (i.e., those high in neuroticism) are no faster than others on a task that requires categorizing words as threatening or not (Robinson, Vargas, & Crawford, 2003). Finally, individual differences in psychological femininity, as measured by self-report, do not predict how fast a person can categorize words as feminine or not (Robinson, Vargas, & Crawford, 2003).

These experimental findings should not be surprising. Self-reports of personality fail to capture many of the cognitive processes that transpire in vivo when people are exposed to an object or event. Additionally, people do not have conscious access to how they process events in real time and therefore cannot report on such processes. Indeed, because self-reports of cognitive processes are at worst invalid and at best only uncertain indicators of how the mind transforms information, cognitive psychologists rely primarily on behavior, rather than self-report, to assess cognition (MacLeod, 1993).

Given the preceding considerations, a study investigating the relation between self-reported personality traits and categorization tendencies is likely to be a failure. Nevertheless, categorization tendencies may predict regularities in behavior and experience even when they are uncorrelated with personality traits.

CATEGORIZATION TENDENCIES AND DAILY EMOTION

My colleagues and I have undertaken a research program aimed at exploring the relations among personality traits, categorization tendencies, and everyday behavior and experience. In one investigation (Robinson, Vargas, Tamir, & Solberg, in press), we used a categorization task that required participants to classify words as neutral (e.g., *glass*, *basket*) or negative (e.g., *sweat*, *insect*). We reasoned that participants fast at the task are well practiced in making negative evaluations, and that this practice would in turn be associated with a tendency to experience negative emotional states and dissatisfaction with daily life. Three studies supported these predictions. Although the categorization measure was uncorrelated with extraversion or neuroticism, it still predicted (a) the intensity of negative affect in daily life (e.g., daily feelings of fear), (b) the frequency of self-reported symptoms suggesting a possible physical illness (e.g., nausea), and (c) the frequency with which participants classified their current situation as a negative one.

In a second investigation (Robinson, Solberg, et al., 2003), we asked people to categorize words as neutral (e.g., *jelly*, *dime*) or positive (e.g., *flower*, *smile*). In this investigation, task performance interacted with extraversion in predicting subjective well-being. Specifically, individuals who made categorizations quickly reported moderate levels of subjective well-being, regardless of whether they were introverts or extraverts. By contrast, people who were slow making these categorizations reported being particularly happy if they were extraverts, but particularly unhappy if they were introverts. The results suggested to us that participants fast at the task were capable of appreciating the distinction between neutral and positive events as they occur. Because some life events are neutral and some are positive, such a tendency should be related to moderate levels of happiness. In contrast, individuals slow at the task, lacking such discriminative information when encoding life events, would have to rely on more generalized beliefs concerning their happiness when rating their emotions within a given situation (Robinson & Clore, 2002). Because extraverts believe that they are happy, and introverts believe that they are not particularly happy, the result would be a particularly strong relation between extraversion and subjective well-being among individuals slow to distinguish neutral and positive events, exactly the pattern we found.

In a third investigation (Robinson, Vargas, & Crawford, 2003), we demonstrated the same interactive pattern for neuroticism and speed to categorize words as threatening or not. That is, neuroticism did not predict reports of daily distress among participants who were fast to distinguish threats from nonthreats in a categorization task. This result can be explained by proposing that people who make such categorizations quickly are able to determine the threat value of events as they occur and thus have no need to access their beliefs about their emotions (related to neuroticism) when determining how distressed they feel. By contrast, people who are slow at this task appear somewhat incapable of determining whether a novel event is threatening or not and therefore must rely on more dispositional sources of knowledge (related to neuroticism) in deciding how much distress they currently feel (Robinson & Clore, 2002).

In multiple investigations, we have found a second interactive pattern. People are happier when their traits are consistent, rather than inconsistent, with their categorization tendencies. For example, self-reported feminine individuals are happier if they are fast, rather than slow, to categorize words as feminine; by contrast, self-reported nonfeminine individuals are happier if they are slow, rather than fast, to categorize words as feminine (Robinson, Vargas, & Crawford, 2003). Conceptually similar results have been found in other studies (e.g., Crawford, 2001; Robinson, Vargas, & Crawford, 2003; Tamir & Robinson, 2003).

A third distinct interactive pattern was found in a recent investigation (Meier & Robinson, in press) in which participants categorized words as blame-worthy (e.g., *malpractice, addiction*) or not (e.g., *landslide, baldness*). Although speed to blame tended to predict self-reported anger and aggression in daily life, this was particularly true among individuals who scored low on a trait related to the frequency of prosocial thoughts and motives (i.e., agreeableness). In other words, anger and aggression were highest among those who were both fast to blame and low in agreeableness. We proposed that agreeable individuals have regulatory mechanisms for disconnecting activated blame from anger and aggression, whereas nonagreeable individuals do not. As a result, there is a relatively straightforward relation between blame categorizations and anger among those low, but not high, in agreeableness.

It is worth asking whether the multiple investigations I have described can be summarized in a more general way. To a certain extent this is possible. Categorization tendencies do seem to be associated with assimilation effects on experience. For example, speed at categorizing words as negative predicts negative affect (Robinson et al., in press), speed at categorizing words as blameworthy predicts anger (Meier & Robinson, in press), and speed at categorizing words as representing physical symptoms or not (e.g., *nausea, headache*) predicts the occurrence of physical symptoms (Armstrong, Wittrock, & Robinson, 2003). Beyond this general conclusion, however, further generalizations seem dubious. It appears that categorization tendencies, like traits, are content-specific. It matters whether one is assessing categorization tendencies related to blame, threat, positive evaluations, or femininity, just as it matters whether one is assessing traits related to agreeableness, neuroticism, extraversion, or femininity.

FUTURE DIRECTIONS

One considerable advantage of categorization tasks is that the experimenter specifies the category of interest to participants (e.g., blame), thus ensuring that performance reflects expertise with that category. However, a considerable disadvantage is that one does not necessarily know whether performance on the task reflects expertise with one category alternative (e.g., threat), the other category alternative (e.g., not threat), or the two alternatives in combination. This question deserves attention in future research.

A second question about categorization performance is whether it reflects familiarity with the stimuli, expertise with the category of interest, or some interactive combination of these two factors. In general, we suspect that categorization performance is most heavily dependent on the habitual use of the category rather than on the other two factors. This conclusion is buttressed by data from categorization tasks other than those used in the research I have described here (Chumbley, 1986; Fazio & Olson, 2003). However, familiarity with stimuli probably does play some role in categorization performance, therefore the issue of stimulus selection is an important one.

A third question concerns the reliability of categorization tendencies. Correlations of performance on two occasions 1 month apart (i.e., test-retest correlations) are in the neighborhood of .5 (e.g., Meier & Robinson, in press). Such coefficients compare favorably to those obtained for other performance-based personality tests (e.g., the Thematic Apperception Test: McClelland, 1987). However, they are lower than those reported for personality tests based on self-report (McCrae & Costa, 1994). It is our view that cognitive processes cannot be expected to be as stable as traits (which are measured by self-report), and therefore we are reasonably satisfied with the test-retest correlations that we have obtained (see Robinson & Neighbors, in press, for further discussion).

A fourth and final question relates to causal direction. We have been assuming that categorization tendencies lead to certain emotional outcomes rather than vice versa. And, indeed, data suggest that manipulating mood states does not alter categorization performance (e.g., Robinson et al., in press). It would be worthwhile to examine whether altering individuals' categorization tendencies changes their emotional experiences or behavior.

CONCLUSIONS

Kelly (1963) proposed a cognitive theory of personality in which categorization tendencies play an important role in determining experience and behavior. We have recently sought to validate these insights by examining correlations between categorization tendencies on the one hand and emotional outcomes on the other. The research generally supports Kelly's theorizing in that categorization tendencies are often predictive of emotional states. However, categorization tendencies frequently interact with self-reported traits, so much so that our understanding of the findings critically depended on knowing a person's traits. Overall, the findings point to the idea that traits and categorization tendencies interactively determine emotional outcomes.

Recommended Reading

Fazio, R.H., & Olson, M.A. (2003). (See References)
Kelly, G.A. (1963). (See References)
Robinson, M.D., & Neighbors, C. (in press). (See References)
Robinson, M.D., Solberg, E.C., Vargas, P.T., & Tamir, M. (2003). (See References)

Acknowledgments—The research reported here was supported by grants from the National Science Foundation (9817649) and National Institute of Mental Health (MH068241).

References

Armstrong, J., Wittrock, D., & Robinson, M.D. (2003). *Somatic categorization predicts somatic complaints.* Unpublished honor's thesis, North Dakota State University, Fargo.

Chumbley, J.I. (1986). The roles of typicality, instance dominance, and category dominance in verifying category membership. *Journal of Experimental Psychology: Learning, Memory, and Language, 12,* 257–267.

Crawford, E.G. (2001). *Can punishment sensitivity make you happy?* Unpublished master's thesis, University of Illinois, Champaign.

Fazio, R.H., & Olson, M.A. (2003). Implicit measures in social cognition research: Their meaning and uses. *Annual Review of Psychology, 54,* 297–327.

Kelly, G.A. (1963). *A theory of personality: The psychology of personal constructs.* New York: Norton.

MacLeod, C. (1993). Cognition in clinical psychology: Measures, methods, or models? *Behaviour Change, 10,* 169–195.

McClelland, D.C. (1987). *Human motivation.* New York: Cambridge University Press.

McCrae, R.R., & Costa, P.T. (1994). The stability of personality: Observations and evaluations. Current Directions in Psychological Science, 3, 173-175.

Meier, B.P., & Robinson, M.D. (in press). Does quick to blame mean quick to anger?: The role of agreeableness in dissociating blame and anger. *Personality and Social Psychology Bulletin.*

Robinson, M.D., & Clore, G.L. (2002). Belief and feeling: Evidence for an accessibility model of emotional self-report. *Psychological Bulletin, 128,* 934–960.

Robinson, M.D., & Neighbors, C. (in press). Catching the mind in action: Implicit methods in personality research and assessment. In M. Eid & E. Diener (Eds.), *Handbook of psychological assessment: A multimethod perspective.* Washington, DC: American Psychological Association.

Robinson, M.D., Solberg, E.C., Vargas, P.T., & Tamir, M. (2003). Trait as default: Extraversion, subjective well-being, and the distinction between neutral and positive events. *Journal of Personality and Social Psychology, 85,* 517–527.

Robinson, M.D., Vargas, P., & Crawford, E.G. (2003). Putting process into personality, appraisal, and emotion: Evaluative processing as a missing link. In J. Musch & C. Klauer (Eds.), *The psychology of evaluation: Affective processes in cognition and emotion* (pp. 275–306). Mahwah, NJ: Erlbaum.

Robinson, M.D., Vargas, P.T., Tamir, M., & Solberg, E.C. (in press). Using and being used by categories: The case of negative evaluations and daily well-being. *Psychological Science.*

Tamir, M., & Robinson, M.D. (2003). *Explicit and implicit components of personality interact in determining daily well-being.* Unpublished manuscript, North Dakota State University, Fargo.

Personality, Strategic Behavior, and Daily-Life Problem Solving

Nancy Cantor and Robert E. Harlow

Nonpsychologists and psychologists alike often think of personality as "having" something, such as traits. One can also think of personality as "doing" something; that is, some aspects of personality can be thought of as organizing and guiding daily behavior.[1] Individuals exhibit significant variation in the strivings, tasks, and goals that they see as important in their daily lives. These personal goals are derived in part from the tasks that cultural contexts present as important to address at points along the life course, but individuals interpret these tasks in line with their own motives and experiences. For example, establishing independence from one's family is a common task following adolescence in many Western cultures. For one person, this task might implicate handling financial matters and housekeeping independently; for another, the task might involve dealing with the loss of a valued support system; yet another individual may work on developing an identity free of the expectations of parents and siblings.[2] We refer to these personal versions of culturally mandated goals as *life tasks*. These life tasks constitute the "problems" that individuals work toward solving in daily life, and our research examines these problem-solving efforts.

STRATEGIES OF LIFE TASK PURSUIT

As with any analysis of goal-directed problem solving, examining the pursuit of life tasks includes a consideration of not only the problems being addressed but also the strategies used to work toward solutions, In our research, we have found that individuals' behavior is directed in patterned ways toward solving these important problems; that is, much of individuals' behavior is strategic. The components of a strategy include setting expectations, anticipating outcomes, monitoring behavior as events unfold, and retrospectively understanding what happened and why. Strategies for pursuing life tasks are not necessarily grandiose plans of action, nor are they strategic in the sense of being consciously drawn out blueprints for action. They are characteristic ways of responding to the challenges of a task.

Strategies for pursuing a task follow from how the individual appraises the problem at hand (e.g., as important, difficult, enjoyable). When an individual sees the demands of a specific task as being relatively straightforward and is confident in his or her ability to meet those demands, strategic efforts are straightforward as well, requiring what feels like little effort. However, task pursuit is not always straightforward, and in our work, we focus on individuals' efforts to pursue tasks that although rewarding and important are at the same

Nancy Cantor is Professor of Psychology and Department Chair at Princeton University, and **Robert E. Harlow** is a Postdoctoral Fellow at New York University. Address correspondence to Nancy Cantor, Department of Psychology, Green Hall, Princeton University, Princeton, NJ 08544-1010; e-mail: cantor@pucc.princeton.edu.

93

time difficult and daunting. These are the tasks—different ones for different people—on which people strive to make progress in the face of doubts in their abilities to master those tasks. Consider "meeting new friends," a life task that is adopted by many young adults as they move away from their families. Although some may find this task easy and enjoyable, others become anxiety-ridden at the thought of even opening a conversation with people who are unfamiliar, and this anxiety has the potential to prevent those individuals from pursuing that task. In these cases, individuals need strategies both to mobilize their task pursuit and to keep anxiety and stress at bay. In this section, we outline how these strategies direct behavior in daily life toward task pursuit and how we investigate these strategies in the context of daily life.

In explaining the nature of our approach and strategic behavior in general, we refer to three particular strategies that we have studied in detail: social constraint, defensive pessimism, and the social pursuit of academics (see Table 1). We have selected these strategies because they provide good illustrations of how strategic behavior conforms to the challenges of life tasks as individuals appraise them. These particular strategies are employed in two life domains that figure prominently in the behavior of young adults—academics and social life—to the end that much of the daily life of these individuals is relevant to these strategies. Our methods of investigation include experience sampling ("beeper") studies, in which subjects report their activities in response to a randomly programmed signal. Experience sampling is complemented by longitudinal investigations of strategic behavior and its effects over time and by laboratory investigations that allow for a microanalysis of strategy components.[3]

Strategies and the "How" of Task Pursuit

In contrast to trait analysis, strategy analysis is based on the functional significance of the behaviors a strategy comprises, not necessarily on the similarity of various acts. Consider, for example, social anxiety. A trait analysis of this dimension would focus on different acts all indicative of behavioral inhibition in social situations. The focus of a strategy analysis would be on the behaviors included in a

Table 1. Three life task strategies

Characteristic	Strategy		
	Defensive pessimism	Social pursuit of academics	Social constraint
Domain	Academic or social	Academic to social	Social
Obstacle	Anxiety	Reactivity to negative outcomes	Self-negativity
Key strategic element	Anticipatory cognition	Reassurance-seeking in social situations	Other-directedness
Side effects and sacrifices	Emotional exertion	Spillover to social satisfaction	Further self-negativity
Route to beneficial change	Savor gains as cut losses	React less to negative task outcomes	Reflect on one's active participation

coherent strategy for participating socially while keeping anxiety to a minimum, and the thoughts about the self and the task that give rise to such a strategy.

Such an extensive focus requires multiple, comprehensive assessment techniques. Our investigation of social anxiety, for example, made use of data collected from a large-scale, 5-year longitudinal analysis of 147 undergraduate students' adjustment to, and experience of, college life. Selected measures from this study included questionnaire reports of appraisals of the life task "making friends; getting along with others"; these reports were supplemented with structured interviews in which participants described how they went about pursuing social activities in daily life. From these videotaped interviews, trained judges, using a Q-sort methodology, described several different strategies of social life pursuit. The strategy of social constraint, for example, was used by individuals who "solved" their problem of feeling socially undesirable and ineffective by taking their lead from the behaviors of other people when in social situations.

Students who used this strategy appraised the task of making friends as important and desirable to pursue, but also stressful. This stress was due in part to a self-view characterized by negativity and a feeling of being less socially desirable than other people. These students exhibited a pattern of *other-directedness* in social life: Lacking confidence in their own social skills, they judged themselves according to standards set up by other people; furthermore, they considered other people's social decisions to be superior to their own, and strove to remove attention from themselves by following the lead of others in social activities.[4] This strategy afforded them active social participation by giving them a script from other people for social interaction, and thereby removed performance pressures from them, which was crucial to their participation given their self-negativity. The cognitive and behavioral elements of this strategy are separated by time and modality, but not purpose—overcoming the obstacles (in this case, a negative view of the self) to participation in social activities.

Strategies and the "When" and "Where" of Task Pursuit

Strategies also delineate conditions—times, places, partners—associated with task pursuit. For example, social constraint is associated with social situations, but not classroom behavior. One key feature of a life task strategy is that within task-relevant contexts, the behaviors included in a strategy unfold in temporally patterned ways. For example, defensive pessimism[5] is an *anticipatory* strategy used by individuals who have typically done well on important tasks, be they academic or social tasks, but who lack confidence in their own abilities to handle task-relevant challenges.

Norem and her colleagues have investigated the use of academic defensive pessimism through daily-life experience sampling as well as laboratory experiments, and these studies suggest that this lack of confidence regarding specific task-relevant challenges creates anxiety that can impair performance. Defensive pessimists prevent this performance impairment by preparing themselves cognitively before the task, setting relatively low expectations for their performance and reflecting extensively on possible outcomes, including worst-case ones. In laboratory experiments in which this anticipatory cognitive work was interfered with, either by providing encouragement to defensive pessimists before a task-relevant challenge or by preventing them from reflecting on possible outcomes, defensive pessimists performed more poorly than they did when they were able to prepare themselves before the task. By engaging in anticipatory cognitive work, they confront their anxieties before the actual challenge. In essence, they convert their anxiety into motivation so that they are able to perform as well as their counterparts whose strategies involve a consideration of more optimistic possibilities. Unlike the post hoc negative ruminations of a "true" pessimist, the critical cognitive work of a defensive pessimist occurs before the event, and this temporal patterning is absolutely critical to the success of the effort.

Post hoc efforts can be strategic as well, depending on the specific obstacles individuals need to overcome in their task pursuits. Recently, we examined another academic strategy, one that involves strategic behavior following task-relevant (in this case, academic) events. For this analysis, we used experience sampling data obtained from members of a residential college sorority whose life task pursuits we followed closely over a 15-day period. Among the 54 sorority women in our sample, there was a group of 23 women whom we labeled as outcome-focused: They were extremely focused on academic outcomes and expressed a lack of certainty about their ability to remain on top of academic challenges. When these individuals experienced negative academic outcomes—for example, had test grades—they extended their academic task pursuits into their social lives, seeking academic reassurance from friends. This concern did not extend to nonsocial situations; for example, outcome-focused women were not more likely than other women to dwell on negative academic events when alone. These individuals stepped up strategic efforts after negative academic events, when they felt especially threatened; in contrast, defensive pessimists view upcoming challenges as threatening, and therefore put their strategies into play before task-relevant events occur.[6]

Outcome-focused individuals' strategic reassurance-seeking is not only temporally and situationally patterned, but also interpersonally patterned. For example, when faced with academic difficulties, outcome-focused women in the sorority study selectively spent social time with individuals who typically encouraged them. Furthermore, these encouragers were usually non-outcome-focused women—women who felt confident of their own academic ability and therefore were probably more able than outcome-focused women to provide reassurance.

To reveal such complex strategic patterning, our methods must also be complex. In the sorority study, for example, participants reported several times daily about who they were with, what they were doing, where they were, and how they felt. In addition, we collected daily diary reports of significant task-relevant events. These daily-life data were then cross-referenced with data that study participants provided regarding who their friends were and the kinds of roles those individuals served for them, providing a full picture of their social and behavioral environments. Such cross-referencing allowed us to track contextual aspects of task pursuit, revealing, for example, the specificity of the subjects' strategic reassurance-seeking.

SIDE EFFECTS AND SACRIFICES OF STRATEGIES

Any analysis of problem solving prompts considerations regarding the effectiveness of the problem-solving strategies that individuals develop. Considerations of strategy effectiveness are not as straightforward as they might first appear, however, because although a strategy may be successful in ameliorating the problem at which it is targeted, it may create additional problems with which the person must contend. In our work with the three strategies discussed in the previous section, we have consistently uncovered unintended consequences of strategic behavior (outlined in Table 1), and these side effects cannot be ignored, especially as they accumulate with continued use. For example, in our longitudinal study of adjustment to college life, we found that the rather exhausting and unremitting preparatory work of defensive pessimists resulted in emotional wear and tear and diminished intrinsic motivation for their academic work by their 3rd year of college. Similarly, Showers demonstrated that people who are defensive pessimists in the social domain experience considerable emotional letdown after they do well in a social interaction in the laboratory.[7]

Less intuitively obvious or apparent to individuals may be those costs of strategic behavior that interfere with other life tasks. For example, in our investigation of outcome-focused individuals, we discovered that reassurance-seeking behavior converted potentially enjoyable social situations into "counseling sessions" and served to dampen enjoyment of those social situations. Reassurance-seeking was therefore strongly associated with dissatisfaction with social life. This spillover from academics to social life is especially ironic because these women initially had not appraised social life tasks as problematic for them.

Given these side effects and sacrifices, where might we draw the boundary between effective albeit costly strategies and self-defeating strategies?[8] This is a difficult question to answer, but a useful distinction may be made between strategies that at least appear to facilitate performance in the target domain and strategies that do not produce successful performance even in that domain. For example, although academic defensive pessimism is associated with emotional wear and tear, and the social pursuit of academics has a negative impact on social life, we have found that these strategies are at least associated with academic successes. In contrast, the social constraint strategy is not a particularly good way to achieve social satisfaction in the long run, even if it does help socially anxious individuals to overcome initial immobilization and participate in social activities. In our longitudinal study of college life, use of this strategy was associated with less satisfaction with social life in the junior year than would be expected based on initial social anxiety alone.[9]

Almost any strategy can become self-defeating if it is used too routinely or too loosely.[10] Habitual reliance exacerbates costs, so these strategies should not be used every time individuals face even the slightest. self-doubt. For example, outcome-focused individuals should constrain their reassurance-seeking to times when their academic control is genuinely threatened; otherwise, the gains in reassurance in the academic domain do not justify the sacrifices in social life, especially as time goes by and people in the social circle lose patience. In fact, we found in our study that people who provided encouragement to outcome-focused individuals were less available for them at the end of the semester of observation. Before they know it, outcome-focused individuals face real problems with their previously comfortable social tasks.

REVISING THE TASK

The best hope for potentially self-defeating strategies is that they will give way to ones that minimize costs. The key to such change is to promote task participation itself and thereby to encourage a change in the framing of the task (e.g., as less difficult). Such change in task appraisals can be facilitated by positive experiences, and these are possible only to the extent that individuals do not withdraw from the tasks at hand. Thus, strategies such as defensive pessimism, social constraint, and the social pursuit of academics offer some hope for individuals in that these strategies do critically facilitate task participation and prevent withdrawal. However, some of these strategies also promote experiences that actually exacerbate difficulties, as often appears to be the case for social constraint, and thereby become self-defeating.

Our future research will be focused on the possibilities for, and avenues of, beneficial change in individuals' appraisals of their life tasks. We think, for example, that if defensive pessimists can savor their successes, then gradually fewer tasks will come to arouse anticipatory anxiety, and the necessity for defensive pessimism may decline; if reassurance enables outcome-focused individuals to persist long enough in their academic pursuits, then they can achieve more self-confidence and eventually react less to every academic setback; similarly, if people who use a social constraint strategy can refrain from ruminating about their reliance on other people and instead reflect on how they have overcome a great deal just to take part in social activities, then their negative social self-images may become less threatening with time. Even apparently self-defeating strategies, if used in moderation and recognized as short-term solutions, can serve the vital function of enabling people to be active participants in the pursuit of valued life tasks, providing experiences that might just change their minds.

Acknowledgments—The research reported here was supported in part by grants from the National Science Foundation.

Notes

1. N. Cantor, From thought to behavior: "Having" and "doing" in the study of personality and cognition, *American Psychologist, 45*, 735–750 (1990); see also M. Snyder, Basic research and practical problems: The promise of a "functional" personality and social psychology, *Personality and Social Psychology Bulletin, 19*, 251–264 (1993).

2. S. Zirkel, Developing independence in a life transition: Investing the self in the concerns of the day, *Journal of Personality and Social Psychology, 62*, 506–521 (1992).

3. N. Cantor and W. Fleeson, Social intelligence and intelligent goal pursuit: A cognitive slice of motivation, in *Nebraska Symposium on Motivation: Vol. 41. Integrative views of motivation, cognition, and emotion*, W. Spaulding, Ed. (University of Nebraska Press, Lincoln, in press).

4. C. Langston and N. Cantor, Social anxiety and social constraint; When making friends is hard, *Journal of Personality and Social Psychology, 56*, 649–661 (1989); see also A. Thorne, The press of personality: A study of conversations between introverts and extraverts, *Journal of Personality and Social Psychology, 53*, 718–726 (1987).

5. For a brief review of the defensive pessimism strategy, see N. Cantor and J.K. Norem, Defensive pessimism and stress and coping, *Social Cognition, 7*, 91–112 (1989). Empirical papers include: J.K. Norem and N. Cantor, Defensive pessimism: "Harnessing" anxiety as motivation, *Journal of Personality and Social Psychology, 51*, 1208–1217 (1986); C. Showers, The motivational and emotional consequences of considering positive or negative possibilities for an upcoming event, *Journal of Personality and Social Psychology, 62*, 474–484 (1992); J. K. Norem and K S. Illingworth, Strategy-dependent effects of reflecting on self and tasks: Some implications of optimism and defensive pessimism. *Journal of Personality and Social Psychology, 65*, 822–835 (1993).

6. For details of the strategy of outcome-focused individuals, see R.E. Harlow and N. Cantor, Overcoming a lack of self-assurance in an achievement domain: Creating agency in daily life, in *Efficacy, Agency, and Self-Esteem*, M. Kernis, Ed. (Plenum, New York, in press); R.E. Harlow and N, Cantor, The social pursuit of academics: Side-effects and "spillover" of strategic reassurance-seeking, *Journal of Personality and Social Psychology, 66*, 386–397 (1994).

7. Showers, note 5; C. Showers and C. Ruben, Distinguishing defensive pessimism from depression: Negative expectations and positive coping mechanisms, *Cognitive Therapy and Research, 14*, 385–399 (1990).

8. R.F. Baumeister and S.J. Scher, Self-defeating behavior patterns among normal individuals: Review and analysis of common self-destructive tendencies, *Psychological Bulletin, 104*, 3–22 (1988).

9. Cantor and Norem, note 5; Showers, note 5; Langston and Cantor, note 4.

10. J. Bédard and M.T.H. Chi, Expertise, *Current Directions in Psychological Science, 1*, 135–139 (1992).

Recommended Reading

Buss, D.M., and Cantor, N., Eds. (1989) *Personality Psychology: Recent Trends and Emerging Directions* (Springer-Verlag, New York).

Cantor, N., and Harlow, R.E. (1994). Social intelligence and personality: Flexible life task pursuit. In *Personality and Intelligence*, R.J. Sternberg and P. Ruzgis, Eds. (Cambridge University Press, New York).

Seeking "Truth," Finding Despair: Some Unhappy Consequences of a Negative Self-Concept

William B. Swann, Jr.

"I'd never join a club that would have me as a member." Groucho Marx may have authored this quip, but I have a friend who lives it. My friend, whom I will call Kathy, is a healthy, articulate, attractive young woman who has everything going for her except for one thing—she cannot sustain satisfying relationships with men. The problem is not that she is hard to like; most men find her quite charming. The problem is that as soon as she becomes convinced that a man likes her, she leaves him. The result is that she spends most of her time in miserable relationships with men who mistreat her for a while and then leave her.

Kathy's preference for men who are unkind to her is puzzling because everyone knows that people have a deep-seated need for praise. What happened to Kathy? The research that I review here offers one answer to this question. Specifically, the findings suggest that people want to verify, and thus maintain, their self-views. To this end, they work to bring other people to see them as they see themselves—even if they think poorly of themselves. Before describing the studies that have led my students and me to this remarkable conclusion, I explain why people are motivated to seek verification of their self-views.

SELF-VERIFICATION STRIVINGS

The symbolic interactionists sowed the seeds of self-verification theory early in this century.[1] They began by assuming that the ability to predict the responses of other people is the key to successful social interaction. With this assumption in hand, they reasoned that people note how others react to them, internalize these reactions into self-conceptions, and then use these conceptions to predict the responses of others. In this way, people come to rely on stable self-concepts and prefer evaluations that are consistent with these self-concepts.[2]

Consider, for example, a man who thinks of himself as dull witted but overhears his wife characterize him as brilliant. Because her remark challenges a long-standing belief about who he is, it may induce epistemic anxiety. After all, if he lacks insight into *himself*, what does he know? Even if the man experiences no such epistemic concerns, purely pragmatic considerations might cause him to want his wife to recognize his intellectual shortcomings. That is, as long as he is convinced that she knows what to expect of him, he will remain confident that their interactions will proceed smoothly and harmoniously. Thus, pragmatic as well as epistemic considerations may cause people with negative self-views to regard unfavorable appraisals as reassuring and favorable appraisals as unsettling. Such people may accordingly prefer and seek relatively negative evaluations and relationship partners who provide such evaluations.

William B. Swann, Jr., is Professor of Psychology at the University of Texas at Austin. Address correspondence to William B. Swann, Jr., Department of Psychology, University of Texas, Austin, TX 78712.

EMPIRICAL EVIDENCE

To test the hypothesis that people seek self-verifying interaction partners, we told people who appraised themselves either positively or negatively that they had been evaluated by two persons and would soon choose the evaluator with whom they wanted to interact. We then showed them some comments that "the evaluators" (who were fictitious) had ostensibly written about them. One set of comments was favorable; the other was unfavorable. We expected that people with positive self-concepts would prefer the favorable evaluator but people with negative self-views would prefer the unfavorable one.

As can be seen in Figure 1, just such a pattern of data emerged. We and other researchers have now conducted several replications of this finding. This preference for congruent partners seems to be fueled by both global self-regard (e.g., level of depression or self-esteem) and specific self-views (e.g., "athletic," "artistic"). Moreover, people with negative self-views prefer interacting with evaluators who appraise them unfavorably over participating in an unrelated experiment. Finally, if praised about one set of characteristics, these people work to shore up globally negative self-views by seeking feedback about their limitations.[3]

Some readers of this research have wondered if the responses of people with negative self-views are akin to masochism. I think not. One difficulty with a masochist interpretation is its presumption that people with negative self-views want *only* negative evaluations. Our research suggests that such persons are ambivalent when it comes to social feedback: They want both positive and negative evaluations. For example, in one study, we had people seek feedback about several attributes, including some of their strengths and some of their limitations. Whereas

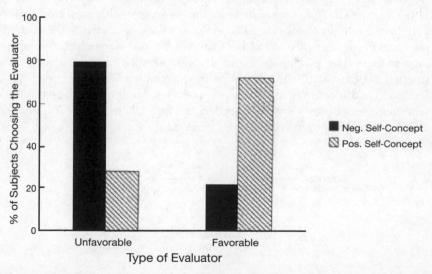

Fig. 1. Preferences for interaction partners. This graph shows that people with positive and negative self-concepts tend to prefer interacting with evaluators who verify their self-concepts. The data on which this figure is based are from KB. Swann, Jr., A. Stein-Seroussi, and R. B. Giesler.[5]

people with low self-esteem sought unfavorable information about their limitations, they sought favorable information about their strengths.[4] In another study, people thought aloud while they chose to interact with someone who appraised them favorably or unfavorably.[5] Although most participants with negative self-concepts chose the unfavorable evaluator, they expressed considerable ambivalence along the way. One participant expressed the conflict she was experiencing as follows:

> I like the (favorable) evaluation, but I am not sure that it is, ah, correct, maybe. It *sounds* good, but (the unfavorable evaluator) . . . seems to know more about me. So, I'll choose (the unfavorable evaluator).

The thought processes that go into such ambivalence seem to unfold sequentially. As shown in Figure 2, upon receiving feedback and categorizing it, people immediately experience a preference for favorable feedback. After accessing their self-concepts and comparing feedback to relevant self-concepts, however, people come to prefer feedback that confirms their self-concepts. When the self-concept is negative, the desire for self-verification will override the desire for positive evaluations.

The model implies that depriving people of cognitive resources should prevent them from engaging in the comparison process that underlies self-verification, thus prompting them to prefer favorable appraisals. To test this proposition, we had some people choose an interaction partner while they were deprived of cognitive resources (because their decision was rushed or they had to rehearse a phone number while deciding).[6] We found that people with negative self-views were less inclined to self-verify (i.e., choose a partner who appraised them unfavorably) when they were deprived of cognitive resources. Furthermore, after participants were no longer cognitively loaded, they repudiated their earlier choices in favor of self-verifying ones. The latter finding suggests that cognitively loaded participants tend to choose favorable evaluators because they lack the cognitive resources needed to self-verify, rather than because load manipulations somehow prevent them from picking up the requisite information. More generally, these findings are consistent with the notion that immediate, "affective" reactions to feedback are distinct from more reflective reactions. This may well be why people with negative self-views say that they feel unhappy when they receive unfavorable feedback but nevertheless go on to endorse its accuracy and seek it.[7]

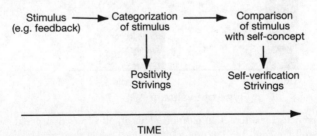

Fig. 2. The sequence by which positivity and self-verification strivings arise when people receive feedback about themselves.

But do self-verification strivings influence people's preferences for relationship partners outside the laboratory setting? To answer this question, we asked if a group of patrons of a local horse ranch and shopping mall might display self-verification strivings in the context of their marital relationships.[8] Participants completed measures of self-concept and commitment to their spouses while their spouses rated them. As expected, just as people with positive self-concepts displayed more commitment to the extent that their spouses appraised them favorably, people with negative self-concepts showed more commitment to the extent that their spouses appraised them unfavorably. Moreover, ancillary data indicated that self-verification strivings rather than several alternative processes influenced marital commitment.

CONSEQUENCES OF SELF-VERIFICATION PROCESSES

The tendency for people to gravitate toward self-verifying relationship partners may have important ramifications. Imagine, for example, the scientist with high self-esteem who learns that his grant proposal has been unequivocally and enthusiastically rejected. Devastated, he heads home to share the bad news with his intimate. If her appraisal of him is favorable, she might help dismiss the rejection notice by suggesting that the review panel was biased in some way, thus stabilizing his self-esteem. If her appraisal of him is unfavorable, however, she might reinforce the criticisms of the reviewers and further diminish his flagging self-esteem. In short, interacting with an intimate after receiving self-discrepant feedback may have a profound impact on whether that feedback influences a person's self-view.

We tested this idea by recruiting pairs of college students who were intimately involved with one another.[9] One person in each pair (the "target") had completed a measure of self-concept at the beginning of the semester. Shortly after the couple reported to the laboratory, we separated them and had the other person (the "intimate") rate the target. This procedure allowed us to categorize each relationship as relatively congruent (i.e., small discrepancy between the intimate's appraisal and the target's self-view) or incongruent (i.e., large discrepancy). Meanwhile, to set the stage for the feedback manipulation, we had targets complete a bogus psychological test. We then escorted targets to a room in which either their intimate or a stranger waited, at which point a man posing as a therapist delivered bogus feedback that contradicted their self-concepts. Targets then engaged in a brief interaction with their intimate or the stranger. They then completed a questionnaire that assessed self-concept change.

As predicted, the self-discrepant feedback caused the most self-rating change among targets who interacted with a stranger and the least amount of change among targets who interacted with a congruent intimate. Moreover, the positivity of targets' self-concepts did not moderate these effects. That is, just as congruent intimates buffered targets with positive self-views against unfavorable feedback, they also insulated targets with negative self-views against favorable feedback! This result indicates that when people with low self-esteem attempt to improve their condition by seeking therapy, their efforts may be frustrated by congruent intimates who nullify the encouraging words of the therapist.

These data suggest that the tendency for people with low self-esteem to seek self-verifying relationship partners may have disturbing consequences. Such partners may, for example, reinforce or exacerbate negative self-views by offering periodic criticism. Furthermore, self-verifying relationship partners may assault the already tenuous sense of self-worth of people with low self-esteem, thus sapping their motivation and placing them at risk for depression.

Our findings therefore suggest that although the "problem" with people with negative self-views may begin in their heads, it may later be externalized into the social environments that they construct around themselves. From this vantage point, it is easy to understand why it is sometimes useful for therapists to implement family therapy in which they treat the relationship partners of clients as well as the clients themselves.

SUMMARY AND IMPLICATIONS

This research has implications for three themes in the psychological literature: two old, one new. The first theme concerns the centuries-old debate between advocates of positive illusions and advocates of truth. In recent years, researchers have argued that positive illusions promote everything from happiness and motivation to creativity and longevity. Although there is surely merit in these contentions, our findings indicate that people do not blindly or uniformly seek positive information, but may actually prefer negative information when their self-concepts tell them that it represents the truth. Apparently, positive feedback is alluring only when it squares with people's fundamental convictions about themselves.

An implication of this conclusion is that one important task for future researchers will be to specify the boundary conditions of positivity and self-verification strivings. Our evidence that cognitive resources are often a prerequisite for self-verification processes represents one step in this direction. Nevertheless, the availability of cognitive resources means only that people will be able to access their self-views; they will actually access such views and self-verify only insofar as they are motivated to do so. At least three classes of variables influence the magnitude of this motivation. First, people are more inclined to verify firmly held, as compared with relatively uncertain, self-views. Second, self-verification is most common in social psychological contexts that foster the epistemic and pragmatic concerns underlying self-verification. For example, people are more apt to seek self-verification within enduring relationships involving high levels of commitment than within relatively casual relationships. Third, some responses are more likely to bear the mark of self-verification strivings than are others. For example, people are more apt to contemplate the epistemic and pragmatic considerations underlying self-verification strivings when they choose interaction partners than when they are asked to report how they feel about the feedback they encounter.

The second theme concerns recent suggestions that people behave so as to re-create the conceptual equivalents of relationships experienced earlier in life, First advanced by Freud in his discussions of transference, the notion that people reenact earlier relationships has gained increasing currency within developmental psychology. Indeed, a growing body of research suggests that the relationships children form with their primary caretakers will later help them—or haunt them—as they mature. Our data suggest that people's self-concepts may be an important vehicle through which childhood relationships are carried forward through life.

Finally, in recent years, there has been much talk among psychologists about the tendency for people to "construct reality." With few exceptions, these theorists have referred to a cognitive construction process through which people actively transform sensory data into beliefs and expectations about the world. Our research suggests another sense in which people may construct their social worlds. In particular, once people form and become relatively certain of their self-conceptions, they may work to maintain them by systematically recruiting friends and intimates who will verify these conceptions. In this way, people may alter the raw materials that enter into the cognitive construction process; they may create idiosyncratically skewed versions of social reality that sustain their firmly held beliefs about themselves—even if these beliefs are negative. Such is the power of people's desire to remain in touch with social reality, however harsh that reality may seem.

Acknowledgments—This research and preparation of this manuscript were supported by research funds {MH 37598) and a research scientist development award (MH 00498) from the National Institute of Mental Health. I am grateful to Kelly Brennan, Chris De La Ronde, Nancy Hazen, and Romin Tafarodi for their helpful comments on an earlier version of this manuscript.

Notes

1. C.S. Cooley, *Human nature and the social order* (G. Scribner's Sons, New York, 1902); G. H. Mead, *Mind, self and society* (University of Chicago Press, Chicago. 1934).

2. P. Lecky, *Self-consistency: A theory of personality* (Island Press, New York, 1945): E. Aronson, A theory of cognitive dissonance: A current perspective, in *Advances in Experimental Social Psychology* (Vol. 4). L. Berkowitz, Ed. (Academic Press, New York, 1968), pp. 1–34.

3. W.B. Swann, Jr., R.M. Wenzlaff, D.S. Krull, and B.W. Pelham, The allure of negative feedback: Self-verification strivings among depressed persons, *Journal of Abnormal Psychology* (in press); W.B. Swann, Jr., R.M. Wenzlaff, and R.W. Tafarodi, Depression and the search for negative evaluations: More evidence of the role of self-verification strivings, *Journal of Abnormal Psychology* (in press).

4. W.B. Swann, Jr., B.W. Pelham, and D.S. Krull, Agreeable fancy or disagreeable truth? How people reconcile their self-enhancement and self-verification needs, *Journal of Personality and Social Psychology*, 57, 782–791 (1989).

5. W.B. Swann, Jr., A. Stein-Seroussi, and R.B. Giesler, Why people self-verify, *Journal of Personality and Social Psychology* (in press).

6. W.B. Swann, Jr., J.G. Hixon, A. Stein-Seroussi, and D.T. Gilbert, The fleeting gleam of praise: Behavioral reactions to self-relevant feedback, *Journal of Personality and Social Psychology*, 59, 17–26 (1990).

7. W.B. Swann, Jr., J.J. Griffin, S. Predmore, and B. Gaines, The cognitive-affective crossfire: When self-consistency confronts self-enhancement, *Journal of Personality and Social Psychology*, 52, 881–889 (1987); Swann, Wenzlaff, Krull, and Pelham, note 3.

8. W.B. Swann, Jr., J.G. Hixon, and C. De La Ronde. Embracing the bitter "truth": Negative self-concepts and marital commitment, *Psychological Science* (in press).

9. W.B. Swann, Jr., and S.C. Predmore, Intimates as agents of social support: Sources of consolation or despair? *Journal of Personality and Social Psychology, 49,* 1609–1617 (1985).

Recommended Reading

Swann, W.B., Jr. (1983). Self-verification: Bringing social reality into harmony with the self. In *Social Psychological Perspectives on the Self* (Vol. 2), J. Suls and A.G. Greenwald, Eds. (Erlbaum, Hillsdale, NJ), pp. 33–66.

Swann, W. B., Jr. (1990). To be adored or to be known: The interplay of self-enhancement and self-verification, In *Motivation and Cognition* (Vol. 2), R.M. Sorrentino and E.T. Higgins, Eds. (Guilford. New York).

Self-Esteem, Narcissism, and Aggression: Does Violence Result From Low Self-Esteem or From Threatened Egotism?

Roy F. Baumeister,[1] Brad J. Bushman, and W. Keith Campbell

Department of Psychology, Case Western Reserve University, Cleveland, Ohio (R.F.B., W.K.C.), and Department of Psychology, Iowa State University, Ames, Iowa (B.J.B.)

Abstract

A traditional view holds that low self-esteem causes aggression, but recent work has not confirmed this. Although aggressive people typically have high self-esteem, there are also many nonaggressive people with high self-esteem, and so newer constructs such as narcissism and unstable self-esteem are most effective at predicting aggression. The link between self-regard and aggression is best captured by the theory of threatened egotism, which depicts aggression as a means of defending a highly favorable view of self against someone who seeks to undermine or discredit that view.

Keywords

aggression; violence; self-esteem; narcissism

For decades, the prevailing wisdom has held that low self-esteem causes aggression. Many authors have cited or invoked this belief or used it as an implicit assumption to explain their findings regarding other variables (e.g., Gondolf,1985; Levin & McDevitt, 1993; Staub, 1989). The origins of this idea are difficult to establish. One can search the literature without finding any original theoretical statement of that view, nor is there any seminal investigation that provided strong empirical evidence that low self-esteem causes aggression. Ironically, the theory seemed to enter into conventional wisdom without ever being empirically established.

The view of low self-esteem that has emerged from many research studies does not, however, seem easily reconciled with the theory that low self-esteem causes aggression. A composite of research findings depicts people with low self-esteem as uncertain and confused about themselves, oriented toward avoiding risk and potential loss, shy, modest, emotionally labile (and having tendencies toward depression and anxiety), submitting readily to other people's influence, and lacking confidence in themselves (see compilation by Baumeister, 1993).

None of these patterns seems likely to increase aggression, and some of them seem likely to discourage it. People with low self-esteem are oriented toward avoiding risk and loss, whereas attacking someone is eminently risky. People with low self-esteem lack confidence of success, whereas aggression is usually undertaken in the expectation of defeating the other person. Low self-esteem involves submitting to influence, whereas aggression is often engaged in to resist and reject external influence. Perhaps most relevant, people with low self-esteem are confused and uncertain about who they are, whereas aggression is likely to be an attempt to defend and assert a strongly held opinion about oneself.

PAINTING THE PICTURE OF VIOLENT MEN

An alternative to the low-self-esteem theory emerges when one examines what is known about violent individuals. Most research has focused on violent men, although it seems reasonable to assume that violent women conform to similar patterns. Violent men seem to have a strong sense of personal superiority, and their violence often seems to stem from a sense of wounded pride. When someone else questions or disputes their favorable view of self, they lash out in response.

An interdisciplinary literature review (Baumeister, Smart, & Boden, 1996) found that favorable self-regard is linked to violence in one sphere after another. Murderers, rapists, wife beaters, violent youth gangs, aggressive nations, and other categories of violent people are all marked by strongly held views of their own superiority. When large groups of people differ in self-esteem, the group with the higher self-esteem is generally the more violent one.

When self-esteem rises or falls as a by-product of other events, aggressive tendencies likewise tend to covary, but again in a pattern precisely opposite to what the low-self-esteem theory predicts. People with manic depression, for example, tend to be more aggressive and violent during their manic stage (marked by highly favorable views of self) than during the depressed phase (when self-esteem is low). Alcohol intoxication has been shown to boost self-esteem temporarily, and it also boosts aggressive tendencies. Changes in the relative self-esteem levels of African-American and white American citizens have been accompanied by changes in relative violence between the groups, and again in the direction opposite to the predictions of the low-self-esteem view. Hence, it appears that aggressive, violent people hold highly favorable opinions of themselves. Moreover, the aggression ensues when these favorable opinions are disputed or questioned by other people. It therefore seems plausible that aggression results from threatened egotism.

AGGRESSION, HOSTILITY, AND SELF-REGARD

Thus, the low-self-esteem theory is not defensible. Should behavioral scientists leap to the opposite conclusion, namely, that high self-esteem causes violence? No. Although clearly many violent individuals have high self-esteem, it is also necessary to know whether many exceptionally nonviolent individuals also have high self-esteem.

Perhaps surprisingly, direct and controlled studies linking self-esteem to aggression are almost nonexistent. Perhaps no one has ever bothered to study the question, but this seems unlikely. Instead, it seems more plausible that such investigations have been done but have remained unpublished because they failed to find any clear or direct link. Such findings would be consistent with the view that the category of people with high self-esteem contains both aggressive and non-aggressive individuals.

One of the few studies to link self-esteem to hostile tendencies found that people with high self-esteem tended to cluster at both the hostile and the non-hostile extremes (Kernis, Grannemann, & Barclay, 1989). The difference lay in stability of self-esteem, which the researchers assessed by measuring self-esteem on several occasions and computing how much variability each individual showed over time. People whose self-esteem was high as well as stable—thus, people whose favorable view of self was largely impervious to daily events— were the least prone to hostility of any group. In contrast, people with high but unstable self-esteem scored highest on hostility. These findings suggest that violent individuals are one subset of people with high self-esteem. High self-esteem may well be a mixed category, containing several different kinds of people. One of those kinds is very non-aggressive, whereas another is quite aggressive.

The view that individuals with high self-esteem form a heterogeneous category is gaining ground among researchers today. Some researchers, like Kernis and his colleagues, have begun to focus on stability of self-esteem. Others are beginning to use related constructs, such as narcissism. Narcissism is defined by grandiose views of personal superiority, an inflated sense of entitlement, low empathy toward others, fantasies of personal greatness, a belief that ordinary people cannot understand one, and the like (American Psychiatric Association, 1994). These traits seem quite plausibly linked to aggression and violence, especially when the narcissist encounters someone who questions or disputes his or her highly favorable assessment of self. Narcissism has also been linked empirically to high but unstable self-esteem, so narcissism seems a very promising candidate for aggression researchers to study.

We have recently undertaken laboratory tests of links among self-esteem, narcissism, and aggression (Bushman & Baumeister, 1998). In two studies, participants were insulted (or praised) by a confederate posing as another participant, and later they were given an opportunity to aggress against that person (or another person) by means of sounding an aversive blast of loud noise. In both studies, the highest levels of aggression were exhibited by people who had scored high on narcissism and had been insulted. Self-esteem by itself had no effect on aggression, and neither did either high or low self-esteem in combination with receiving the insult. These results confirmed the link between threatened egotism and aggression and contradicted the theory that low self-esteem causes violence.

Narcissism has thus taken center stage as the form of self-regard most closely associated with violence. It is not, however, entirely fair to depict narcissists as generally or indiscriminately aggressive. In our studies (Bushman & Baumeister, 1998), narcissists' aggression did not differ from that of other people as long as there was no insulting provocation. Narcissism is thus not directly a cause of aggression and should instead be understood as a risk factor that can contribute to increasing a violent, aggressive response to provocation. The causal role of the provocation itself (in eliciting aggression by narcissists) is clearly established by the experimental findings.

Moreover, even when the narcissists were insulted, they were no more aggressive than anyone else toward an innocent third person. These patterns show that the aggression of narcissists is a specifically targeted, socially meaningful response. Narcissists are heavily invested in their high opinion of themselves, and they want others to share and confirm this opinion. When other people question or undermine the flattering self-portrait of the narcissist, the narcissist turns aggressive in response, but only toward those specific people. The aggression is thus a means of defending and asserting the grandiose self-view.

Do laboratory studies really capture what happens out in the real world, where violence often takes much more serious and deadly forms than pushing a button to deliver a blast of aversive noise? To answer this question, we conducted another study in which we obtained self-esteem and narcissism scores from incarcerated violent felons (Bushman, Baumeister, Phillips, & Gilligan, 1999). We assumed that the prisoners' responses to some items (e.g., "I certainly feel useless at times") would be affected by being in prison as well as by the salient failure experience of having been arrested, tried, convicted, and sentenced. These factors would be expected to push all scores toward low self-esteem and low narcissism.

Despite any such tendency, however, the prisoners' scores again pointed toward high narcissism as the major cause of aggression. The self-esteem scores of this group were comparable to the scores of published samples. The narcissism scores, meanwhile, were significantly higher than the published norms from all other studies. In particular, the prisoners outscored the baselines from other (non-incarcerated) groups to the largest degree on subscales measuring entitlement and superiority. (Again, though, the fact that the participants were in prison might have artificially lowered scores on some items, such as vanity, exhibitionism, and authority.) These findings suggest that the dangerous aspects of narcissism are not so much simple vanity and self-admiration as the inflated sense of being superior to others and being entitled to special privileges. It is apparently fine to love oneself quietly—instead, the interpersonal manifestations of narcissism are the ones associated with violence.

DEEP DOWN INSIDE

A common question raised about these findings is whether the apparent egotism of aggressive, violent people is simply a superficial form of bluster that is put on to conceal deep-rooted insecurities and self-doubts. This question is actually an effort to salvage the low-self-esteem theory, because it suggests that aggressive people really do have low self-esteem but simply act as if they do not. For example, perhaps murderers and wife beaters really perceive themselves as inferior beings, and their aggressive assertion of superiority is just a cover-up.

The question can be handled on either conceptual or empirical grounds. Empirically, some investigators have sought to find this inner core of self-doubt and reported that they could not do so. For example, Olweus (1994) specifically rejected the view that playground bullies secretly have low self-esteem, and Jankowski (1991) likewise concluded that members of violent gangs do not carry around a load of inner insecurities or self-doubts. Likewise, a number of experts who study narcissism have reported that they could not support the traditional clinical view of an egotistical outer shell concealing inner self-loathing. Virtually all studies that have measured self-esteem and narcissism have found positive correlations between the two, indicating that narcissists have high self-esteem.

Even if such evidence could be found, though, the view that low self-esteem causes aggression would still be wrong. It is by now clear that overt low self-esteem does not cause aggression. How can hidden low self-esteem cause aggression if non-hidden low self-esteem has no such effect? The only possible response is that the hidden quality of that low self-esteem would be decisive. Yet focusing the theory on the hidden quality of low self-esteem requires one to consider what it is that is hiding it—which brings the analysis back to the surface veneer of egotism. Thus, again, it would be the sense of superiority that is responsible for aggression, even if one could show that that sense of superiority is only on the surface and conceals an underlying low self-esteem. And no one has shown that, anyway.

CONCLUSION

It is time to abandon the quest for direct, simple links between self-esteem and aggression. The long-standing view that low self-esteem causes violence has been shown to be wrong, and the opposite view implicating high self-esteem is too simple. High self-esteem is a characteristic of both highly aggressive individuals and exceptionally non-aggressive ones, and so attempts at direct prediction tend to be inconclusive. Moreover, it is unwarranted to conclude that self-views directly cause aggression. At best, a highly favorable self-view constitutes a risk factor for turning violent in response to perceptions that one's favorable view of self has been disputed or undermined by others.

Researchers have started trying to look more closely at the people with high self-esteem in order to find the aggressive ones. Patterns of narcissism and instability of self-esteem have proven successful in recent investigations, although more research is needed. At present, the evidence best fits the view that aggression is most likely when people with a narcissistically inflated view of their own personal superiority encounter someone who explicitly disputes that opinion. Aggression is thus a means of defending a highly favorable view of self against someone who seeks (even unwittingly) to deflate it. Threatened egotism, rather than low self-esteem, is the most explosive recipe for violence.

Further research can benefit by discarding the obsolete view that low self-esteem causes violence and building on the findings about threatened egotism. It would be helpful to know whether a highly favorable view of self contributes to violent response by increasing the perception of insult (i.e., by making people oversensitive) or instead by simply producing a more aggressive response to the same perceived provocation. Further, research on whether narcissistic individuals would aggress against people who know bad information about them (but have not specifically asserted it themselves) would shed light on whether it is the critical view itself or the expression of it that is decisive. Another question is what exactly narcissistic people hope to accomplish by responding violently to an insult: After all, violence does not really refute criticism in any meaningful way, but it may discourage other people from voicing similar criticisms. The emotion processes involved in egotistical violence also need to be illuminated: How exactly do the shameful feelings of being criticized transform into aggressive outbursts, and does aggression genuinely make the aggressor feel better?

Recommended Reading

Baumeister, R. (1997). *Evil: Inside human violence and cruelty.* New York: W.H. Freeman.
Baumeister, R., Smart, L., & Boden, J. (1996). (See References)
Bushman, B., & Baumeister, R. (1998). (See References)
Kernis, M., Grannemann, B., & Barclay, L. (1989). (See References)

Note

1. Address correspondence to R. Baumeister, Department of Psychology, Case Western Reserve University, Cleveland, OH 44106-7123; e-mail: rfb2@po.cwru.edu.

References

American Psychiatric Association. (1994). *Diagnostic and statistical manual of mental disorders* (4th ed.). Washington, DC: Author.
Baumeister, R. (1993). *Self-esteem.* New York: Plenum Press.
Baumeister, R., Smart, L., & Boden, J. (1996). Relation of threatened egotism to violence and aggression: The dark side of high self-esteem. *Psychological Review, 103,* 5-33.
Bushman, B., & Baumeister, R. (1998). Threatened egotism, narcissism, self-esteem, and direct and displaced aggression: Does self-love or self-hate lead to violence? *Journal of Personality and Social Psychology, 75,* 219-229.
Bushman, B., Baumeister, R., Phillips, C., & Gilligan, J. (1999). *Narcissism and self-esteem among violent offenders in a prison population.* Manuscript submitted for publication.
Gondolf, E. (1985). *Men who batter.* Holmes Beach, FL: Learning Publications.
Jankowski, M.S. (1991). *Islands in the street: Gangs and American urban society.* Berkeley: University of California Press.
Kernis, M., Grannemann, B., & Barclay, L. (1989). Stability and level of self-esteem as predictors of anger arousal and hostility. *Journal of Personality and Social Psychology, 56,* 1013-1022.
Levin, J. & McDevitt, J. (1993). *Hate crimes.* New York: Plenum Press.
Olweus, D. (1994). Bullying at school: Long-term outcomes for the victims and an effective school-based intervention program. In R. Huesmann (Ed.), *Aggressive behavior: Current perspectives* (pp. 97-130). New York: Plenum Press.
Staub, E. (1989). *The roots of evil.* New York: Cambridge University Press.

Critical Thinking Questions

1. In each of the papers in this section cognitive and affective processes interact in some way to affect behavior and well-being. Discuss the similarities and differences in how this interaction is seen across papers. Do cognitive processes always precede affective ones, or vice versa?

2. For each article in this section, identify what role individual differences play in people's efforts to adapt to their life circumstances.

3. Think about and explain to what degree there is a one-to-one correspondence between trait and behavior in each paper. Presumably, you will find that correspondence is more direct in some papers than in others. Can you explain why this is? (Hint: it may help to look at differences in how "trait" is being defined.)

4. The self-regulatory strategies described across the papers all appear to be "strategic," i.e., they serve a purpose. Does that mean people are always fully aware of and have control over them? Although virtually none of the papers discuss this explicitly, think about what may be the role of "automaticity" in the processes people employ.

5. Cantor and Harlow state: "Almost any strategy can become self-defeating if it is used too routinely or too loosely." Evaluate this statement by extrapolating from the articles in this section. Support your answer with specific examples.

Personality in Relational Contexts

Personality is inherently relational in nature. As we have already seen, personality develops and evolves not in isolation, but rather through continuous reciprocal interactions between the dynamics of the intrapersonal system and the demands and affordances of the particular situation and contexts. Of these contexts, the most meaningful involve social and interpersonal relationships. From the very beginning, personality is shaped through its caregiving relationships. These early experiences are then carried forward because they serve in part as guides through which subsequent relationship experiences may be selected, filtered, and interpreted. Individuals, thus, shape their own social contexts through processes such as their expectations about others, their relationship goals, and their construals of and reactions to interpersonal situations. These social contexts in turn affect the individual by reacting and providing social feedback to which the person then must continuously adapt anew. Thus, social and interpersonal relationships serve as contexts through with personality is both maintained and altered. The articles in this section focus on these relational aspects of personality.

This section opens with an article by Goldsmith and Harman (1994) that situates the contrasting views between attachment and temperament research in the broader context of the nature vs. nurture debate. The authors argue that both constructs are relevant to explaining individual differences in emotionality but they differ in where they see the locus of causality. Temperament research assigns it to biologically-based personality traits whereas attachment assigns it to the quality of the parent-child relationship. The article makes recommendations for both conceptual and methodological changes that may help resolve this conflict, with the recognition that the impact of each on personality development needs to be considered in the context of the other.

A common premise of psychodynamic, neo-Freudian, and attachment theories is that patterns of relating to others are laid down early in childhood through our relationship with primary caregivers and that these patterns tend to recur over and over throughout the life-span. But how does this recurrence happen? What psychological mechanism can account for why and how past relationships are relived in the present ones? Anderson and Berk (1998) present a social-cognitive model of Freud's notion of transference to explain this process. It draws heavily from the social cognitive principle of knowledge activation and seeks to examine the process of transference as it applies to everyday interpersonal interactions. Although Anderson and Berk do not discuss explicitly the implications for personality, it is should be apparent that everyday transference is likely one of the fundamental mechanisms through which individual differences in affect, relationship behavior, and self-conceptions arise.

In the next article, Leary's (1999) sociometer model focuses on the social origins and functions of self-esteem. The model states that self-esteem has evolved to serve as a sociometer that monitors and signals relational devaluation, and motivates change in behaviors to minimize social rejection. It is thus not low self-esteem that is conceptualized as a cause of psychological problems, but rather a history of low relational evaluations, of which low self-esteem is simply an expression. In this view, self-esteem is no longer an attribute of the person that is *independent* of the context in which he/she operates; rather it is an evaluation of how well the person functions *within* particular relationships, underscoring the relational and contextual nature of personality.

Existing research on personality and relationships concentrates predominantly on how personality affects and is affected by interactions with parents, peers, and romantic partners. The role of siblings in the development of personality within the family is an often-neglected domain of inquiry. The article by Brody (2004) presents the recent literature on this issue, outlining the ways in which siblings may form the context of development for each other. Siblings affect each other's development directly through their encounters and interactions with one another, as well as indirectly, as when one sibling impacts the way parents treat and take care of other brothers and sisters. Parental differential treatment of siblings may also have an impact on the well-being of children. This work represents a first step in what will likely be a long-term emphasis in research in child development.

Marital conflict presents huge costs not only to the individuals involved but also to the society at large. It is not surprising, therefore, that a large corpus of literature has sprung up on understanding the correlates, structure, and context of marital conflicts. Fincham's (2002) work shows that the frequency of marital conflict, as well as how each spouse behaves during conflicts, are mediated by the way people construe and explain their partner's behavior, as well as by their level of commitment to the relationship and their willingness and capacity to forgive their partner's transgressions. These mechanisms are related to spouses' backgrounds and characteristics, most notably to individual differences in their attachment styles. However, the effect of marital conflict on satisfaction and other marital outcomes are also moderated by the level of support-giving and affectional expression present in the relationship, as well as by broader contextual factors (such as the presence of external stressors). These latter findings again provide clear evidence for the utility of adopting a contextual and interactionist approach to personality.

The final article in this section by McCullough (2001) follows up on a theme raised by the preceding article on forgiveness. Given that people's willingness to forgive their partners have positive influences on marital harmony, the question of interest becomes who does it and how do they do it. McCullough conceptualizes forgiveness as a complex set of motivational transformations whereby one's desire to harm and revenge a transgressor is replaced by benevolent and constructive motives aimed at maintaining and repairing the relationship. The work finds that some personality traits (e.g., high agreeableness, emotional stability) as well as some social-cognitive mechanisms (e.g., empathy with the transgressor's perspective, benign attributions to the transgressor) are associated with forgiveness. More systematic empirical work on the combined and/or interactional effects between these psychological mechanisms and their associations to agreeableness and emotional stability will further facilitate advances in personality trait theory by linking it to process level variables such as expectations, goals, appraisals, and attributions.

Temperament and Attachment;
Individuals and Relationships

H.H. Goldsmith and Catherine Harman

For the past 15 years, the most researched topics in the field of early socioe-motional development have been temperament and attachment. Our review summarizes the associations and distinctions between temperament and attachment and places them in broader context. Proponents of each construct have made strong claims about the relative influence of infant temperament and parenting behavior on the formation of attachment relationships. They have also considered the relative power of temperament and attachment to predict personality and later adaptive functioning. Why have these issues been so hotly debated? One reason is that the definitions of temperament and attachment cover common ground. Temperament refers primarily to emotional individuality. Attachment refers to the fundamental emotional bond between caregiver and infant, mediated in part by the infant's internal working model of the caregiver. Thus, one reason for conflict is that both concepts concern emotions and emotional development. Of course, this is also a reason for collaboration among temperament and attachment researchers.

These turf wars in the study of emotion involve, in part, definitional uncertainties. The term temperament is a rubric for several noncognitive, dispositional constructs, despite some laypersons' tendencies to equate temperament with the notion of irritability. Temperamental constructs include activity level, fearfulness, irritability, joyfulness, and a variety of other behavioral tendencies.[1] The constructs included in any one researcher's list of temperamental characteristics vary, but most definitions share four features: The constructs are largely, but not exclusively, emotional in nature; they appear in infancy; they are relatively stable for significant periods of development; and they have biological substrates. Temperament research has diverse roots, dating back to the ancient Greeks and deriving impetus from neo-Pavlovians, psychophysiologists, clinicians, educators, and developmentalists. Currently, questions about the categorical versus dimensional nature of temperament and the structure of temperament (e.g., can early temperament be conceptualized in terms of the "Big 5" factors of adult personality?) are being subjected to empirical test. Current theory also recognizes the developmental plasticity and regulatory functions of temperament; these latter features invite integration with attachment theory.

There is more theoretical consensus concerning the construct of attachment, due chiefly to attachment researchers' adherence to the theorizing of Bowlby.[2] Attachment quality refers principally to one aspect of the infant—

H.H. Goldsmith is Professor of Psychology at the University of Wisconsin-Madison, and **Catherine Harman** is a Ph.D. candidate in developmental psychology at the University of Oregon. Address correspondence to H.H. Goldsmith, Department of Psychology, 1202 West Johnson St., University of Wisconsin, Madison, WI 53706-1611; e-mail: hhg@macc.wisc.edu.

mother relationship—its security. Security is surely an overarching quality of the relationship, involving as it does trust and love. A definition of attachment follows:

> Attachment refers to an affective tie (or bond) between infant and caregiver, and to a behavioral system that operates in the service of the goal of providing a sense of security for the infant. Attachment is mediated by feeling states, and it interacts with other behavioral systems such as fear and exploration. Attachment is not a trait or a set of behaviors that are constantly operative. Although it is not reducible to infant-caregiver interaction, attachment is a product of that interaction.[3]

THE TEMPERAMENT-ATTACHMENT ISSUE IN BROADER CONTEXT

Their common grounding in emotionality is not the only reason for conflict between temperament and attachment perspectives. Another fundamental reason for the conflict is that the field has not developed enough paradigms for understanding characteristics of individuals independent of the context of their relationships or for understanding relationships independent of the characteristics that individuals bring to them. We also suggest that the issue of temperament versus attachment is a surrogate for several other issues that psychologists like to debate. These issues are outlined in Table 1.

As Table 1 shows, the omnipresent nature-nurture debate arises in discussions of temperament and attachment, and the fading controversy over the importance of traits in personality development is also involved. These differing theoretical perspectives have led to very different literatures. For example, there are several behavioral genetic studies of temperament,[4] but only recent, very tentative, evidence about genetic contributions to individual differences in attachment.

Methodological approaches need to be diversified in both fields. Attachment research with infants depends crucially on the "strange situation" (described in the next section), and temperament research depends on eco-

Table 1. Conceptual contrasts between temperament and attachment

Issue	Classical posture		Likely grounds for resolution
	Temperament field	Attachment field	
Origin	Nature oriented	Nurture oriented	Developmental genetic approaches
Theoretical perspective	Trait theory	Psychoanalytic psychology, ethology	Systems approaches, emotion theory
Measurement paradigm	Questionnaire	Strange situation	Methodological diversity
Level of analysis	Individual	Relationship	Recognition that goals of explanation are different at different levels

nomical parental report questionnaires. Both of these assessment techniques have been subjected to extensive criticism. Temperament methodology has recently become more pluralistic, including, for example, our own construction of laboratory-based assessment techniques.[5] Attachment methodology has also become more pluralistic as researchers have expanded assessment to ages at which the strange situation is inappropriate. Still, the strange situation remains the criterion measure for many researchers.

However important the other contrasts in Table 1 might be, we believe that the fundamental issue concerns the interplay between characteristics of the individual and of the relationship. A comparable issue is the interplay between personality or attitudes of individual marriage partners and the dyadic quality of their marital adjustment. The perspectives of the individual and of the relationship are just two of the levels at which behavior may be understood (e.g., two other levels are neurophysiology and culture). Some apparent controversy is simply the result of analysis at different levels. The last column of Table 1 suggests likely grounds for resolution of issues in which temperament and attachment are both likely to play a role. Some of these integrative possibilities are inherent in the empirical work reviewed in this article.

How should one view the relation between temperament and attachment? Two of the more extreme possibilities are that an infant's temperament plays a critical role in determining the attachment bond between mother and infant or that the attachment relationship crucially shapes the development of temperamental characteristics. Another position is that the parent's cognitive representation of the child—existing even before birth and conditioned by the parent's own attachment history—is fine-tuned by the infant's temperament during the 1st year of life. Although such an explanation is not parsimonious or simple, it seems probable that attachment and temperament exert reciprocal influences on one another or that each provides an important context for development of the other. Another possibility is that aspects of temperament bias assessment of attachment in the strange situation, or that attachment quality biases the assessment of temperament when social assessment contexts are employed.

It is no wonder that disentangling the effects of temperament and attachment has been so difficult, especially given that both constructs are most commonly inferred from infant behavior on one occasion. Both systems of behavior are undoubtedly multidetermined, both develop concurrently, and sensitive measures of both systems should probably change over the course of infancy in concert with the infant's motoric, perceptual, and cognitive growth.

ATTACHMENT ASSESSMENT AND RESEARCH

It is difficult to discuss attachment without describing its assessment in the strange situation.[6] After a 20-min laboratory session involving two separations and reunions with the caregiver (usually the mother), researchers classify an infant as A (anxious-avoidant), B (secure), or C (anxious-resistant), based mainly on the infant's behavior toward the mother during reunions. Key behaviors include seeking or avoiding proximity with the mother and maintaining or resisting contact. To a lesser extent, stability across episodes, the level of the infant's distress during separation, and ease of comforting and soothing are also considered. A infants avoid their mothers. They could also be described as emotionally controlled and restrained in the presence of their mothers. C infants resist contact with their mothers but do not avoid proximity; they often cry upon separation and continue to cry upon reunion. Thus, their behavior conveys a sense of ambivalence toward the mother. C infants can be described also as angry and unsoothable. Research has explored antecedents and consequences of these behavioral patterns.

According to attachment theory, the key antecedent is interaction in the home between infant and mother during the 1st year. Sensitive, responsive parenting is a predictor of secure attachment, but the effect may be substantially less than commonly assumed. Contrary to lore based on isolated studies, meta-analyses showed associations between strange-situation classifications conducted with mothers versus fathers[7] and cross-national differences in attachment types.[8] Although intracultural variation exceeded cross-cultural variation and secure attachment was the norm in all cultures, infants from some Western European cultures tended toward avoidant behavior, and infants from Asian cultures and Israel tended toward resistant behaviors, with U.S. infants being intermediate. The most common interpretation of this finding is that the strange situation is sensitive to differences in culture-based parenting differences.

Attachment security is important because of its consequences. Differences between infants classified as securely and insecurely attached have been explored primarily during the toddler and early childhood years. For instance, securely attached children approach problem-solving tasks with greater persistence and positive affect than insecurely attached children. In social situations, securely attached children are more likely to be generally competent—empathetic, compliant, and unconflicted in their relationships with both peers and adults. Insecure, resistant children show greater dependency on parents and teachers, although they continue to show elevated levels of anger directed toward these same people. Additionally, they are less compliant, enthusiastic, and persistent than their securely attached peers. In interactions with strange adults, they may be less sociable. There is suggestive evidence that avoidant children are hostile and distant in social relationships. In contrast to secure and resistant children, they are less likely to seek help from adults when injured or disappointed. Securely attached infants tend to grow into ego-resilient toddlers and children who are high in self-esteem and positive affect, and low in negative affect. However, as is the case for much research on complex social processes (including the effects of temperament on later behavior), differences between outcomes of securely versus insecurely attached infants are often only modest in strength, difficult to replicate, and resistant to unambiguous causal interpretation.

SUMMARY OF EMPIRICAL STUDIES

With hundreds of studies on temperament or attachment and a few dozen on temperament *and* attachment in the literature, our review must be very selective. A 1987 meta-analysis[9] found little evidence for an association between temperament and later attachment security. Early negative emotionality was associated with resistant behavior in the strange situation, but the mean effect size was only .16.

Since this meta-analysis, studies of negative emotionality and strange-situation behavior have enriched the common understanding that negative emotionality per se does not distinguish securely from insecurely attached infants. Evidence from the strange situation itself shows that separation distress predicts resistant behavior in the reunion episodes. Other careful research has examined patterns of affect regulation not typically scored during the strange situation (gaze aversion, self-comforting, object orientation, etc.) and shown different patterns of regulation depending on both attachment security and distress. Several studies with temperament questionnaires as well as laboratory-based measures of temperament show that negative emotionality predicts separation distress in the strange situation. Some, but not all, of these results are accommodated by a proposal that insecure A infants and subsets of the secure B infants who show minor avoidance and minimal distress can be differentiated on temperamental grounds (primarily distress proneness, or negative emotionality) from the insecure C infants and the remainder of the B's.[10] However, these studies do not suggest that an infant's negative emotionality affects attachment security directly. Recent data reopen the possibility that extreme temperament has direct effects on attachment, In two Dutch samples, highly irritable neonates were likely to be insecurely attached at 12 months, and their mothers showed some caregiving strategies that were less than optimal for dealing with irritability during the 1st year of life.[11]

Six studies have included both a temperament questionnaire and Waters and Deane's Attachment Behavior Q-set, the only established alternative to the strange situation in infant attachment research.[12] Across the studies, negative affectivity scores derived from temperament questionnaires tend to be moderately correlated with attachment insecurity. Both individual characteristics and relationships can modulate reactions to affective stimuli. Also, these correlations tend to increase with age, thus highlighting the difficulty of distinguishing the constructs in later development.

ASSOCIATIONS BETWEEN ATTACHMENT CLASSIFICATIONS AND PHYSIOLOGICAL VARIABLES

Improved physiological methods might help clarify the relation between attachment and temperament. A simpleminded view is that physiological variables reflect biological bases of temperament in early infancy and that studying physiology obviates the difficulty of distinguishing individual and relational constructs on a solely behavioral level. However, we doubt that physiological methods provide clairvoyance in understanding of temperament. Like behavioral methods, each physiological technique carries interpretive ambiguities well documented in the literature.[13] At the least, however, recent studies[11] are contributing to a descriptive corpus that must be accommodated by process-oriented theories.

One study indicated that high vagal tone, indicative of parasympathetic nervous system function, is characteristic of the insecure infant. Other intriguing research in progress examines the relations among the pattern of behaviors known as temperamental inhibition, left versus right frontal electroencephalographic asymmetry (which differentiates infants who express more positive vs. negative affect, respectively), and attachment classification in the strange situation. The relationship between neuroendocrine response, specifically, adrenocortical activity, and attachment classification has also been explored. Although infants who were temperamentally more negative showed greater increases in adrenocortical activity during testing, no relationship was found between adrenocortical response and quality of attachment.

THE FUTURE

Behavioral scientists who wish to monitor this field can anticipate several developments over the next few years. These developments might include expansion of intergenerational studies of parenting to include studying attachment in infants of young parents who themselves were once assessed in the strange situation; more research on infant physiological predictors of later attachment, including studies of the effects of relationships on physiological differences; studies of how attachment is related to the extremes of temperament (e.g., highly inhibited children) and how temperament is related to the extremes of attachment (e.g., relationships involving abuse and neglect); consideration of aspects of early relationships other than security, such as expressiveness, exclusiveness, and stability; consideration of parental personality as well as infant temperament in studies of relationships; and studies of the associations between adult personality and adult resolutions of early attachment relationships.

Acknowledgments—The National Institute of Mental Health (NIMH) supported some of the research reviewed (MH41200, awarded to Goldsmith). NIMH also supported Harman with a predoctoral traineeship in emotion research (MH18935). We appreciate comments and suggestions by Sarah Mangelsdorf and two reviewers.

Notes

1. H.H. Goldsmith, A.H. Buss, R. Plomin, M.K. Rothbart, A. Thomas, S. Chess, R.A. Hinde, and R.B. McCall, Roundtable: What is temperament? Four approaches, *Child Development, 58*, 505–529 (1987).

2. J. Bowlby, *Attachment and Loss: Vol. 1. Attachment*, 2nd ed. (Basic Books, New York, 1982).

3. Paraphrased from L.A. Sroufe and E. Waters, Attachment as an organizational construct, *Child Development, 48*, 1184–1199 (1977).

4. H.H. Goldsmith, Behavior-genetic approaches to temperament, in *Temperament in Childhood*, D.A. Kohnstamm, J.E. Bates, and M.K. Rothbart, Eds. (Wiley, Chichester, England, 1989).

5. H.H Goldsmith and M.K. Rothbart, Contemporary instruments for assessing early temperament by questionnaire and in the laboratory, in *Explorations in Temperament: Contemporary Conceptualizations, Measurement and Methodological Issues*, A. Angleitner and J. Strelau, Eds. (Plenum Press, New York, 1991). The laboratory procedures reported in this chapter—and developed more recently—allow assessment of fearfulness, anger proneness, activity level, joy-pleasure, and interest-persistence in both prelocomotor infants and locomotor infants and toddlers. Ongoing research is expanding this tem-

perament assessment battery to the period after children begin to use language fluently. (Information is available from the first author.)

6. M.D.S. Ainsworth, M.C. Blehar, E. Waters, and S. Wall, *Patterns of Attachment: A Psychological Study of the Strange Situation* (Erlbaum, Hillsdale, NJ. 1978).

7. N.A. Fox, N.L. Kimmerly, and W.D. Schafer, Attachment to mother/attachment to father: A meta-analysis, *Child Development*, 62, 210–225 (1991).

8. M.H. van Ijzendoorn and P.M. Kroonenberg, Cross-cultural patterns of attachment: A meta-analysis of the strange situation, *Child Development*, 59, 147–156 (1988),

9. H.H. Goldsmith and J.A. Alansky, Maternal and infant temperamental predictors of attachment: A meta-analytic review, *Journal of Consulting and Clinical Psychology*, 55, 805–816 (1987).

10. J. Belsky and M. Rovine, Temperament and attachment security in the Strange Situation: An empirical rapprochement, *Child Development*, 58, 787–795 (1987); A. Frodi and R. Thompson, Infants' affective reactions in the Strange Situation: Effects of prematurity and of quality of attachment. *Child Development*, 56, 1280–1291 (1985).

11. A reference list of these studies and others included in this review, but not cited because of space limitations, is available from the first author.

12. R.E. Vaughn, J. Stevenson-Hinde, E. Waters, A. Kotsaftis, G.B. Levfever, A. Shouldice, M. Trodel, and I. Belsky, Attachment security and temperament in infancy and early childhood: Some conceptual clarifications, *Developmental Psychology*, 28, 463–473 (1992).

13. J.T. Cacioppo and L.G. Tassinary, Eds., *Principles of Psychophysiology* (Cambridge University Press, Cambridge, England, 1990).

The Social-Cognitive Model of Transference: Experiencing Past Relationships in the Present

Susan M. Andersen and Michele S. Berk[1]

Department of Psychology, New York University, New York, New York

Personal experience, as well as psychological theory and research, suggests that relationships with significant individuals from one's past may have a profound impact on present-day relationships. The notion that aspects of past relationships may reemerge in later social relations also forms the basis of the clinical concept of transference (Freud, 1912/1958; Sullivan, 1953), which involves old issues in past relationships emerging in new relations, especially in analysis. Transference in everyday life is the focus of our research, even though historically, transference has been examined mainly theoretically and as it pertains to psychotherapy (e.g., Ehrenreich, 1989). Despite its potential importance to social relations in daily life, until recently, little empirical work of any kind has examined transference (although see Luborsky & CritsChristoph, 1990).

In our work, we have developed a social-cognitive model of transference in everyday social relations (Andersen & Glassman, 1996; Andersen, Reznik, & Chen, 1997; Chen & Andersen, in press; for related models, see Singer, 1988; Wachtel, 1981; Westen, 1988). We have shown that mental representations of significant others are stored in memory, and that the fundamental processes underlying transference are the activation and application of these representations to new people. Such activation and application occur particularly when the new person resembles the significant other. This research provides the first experimental demonstrations of the transference concept and is relevant to a variety of related literatures, ranging from those dealing with relational schemas (Baldwin, 1992; Bugental, 1992) and attachment theory (e.g., Bowlby, 1969; Collins & Read, 1990; Hazan & Shaver, 1987), to those concerned with the self (e.g., Aron, Aron, Tudor, & Nelson,1991), close relationships (Berscheid, 1994; Murray & Holmes, 1993), and basic processes in social cognition (Higgins, 1996; Higgins & King, 1981).

In this article, we provide an overview of this research. To begin, we describe the basic tenets of the model, highlighting its social-cognitive and clinical origins, and also outline our experimental paradigm. We then summarize the experimental research supporting the model, which has demonstrated transference as measured by inference and memory derived from significant-other representations, as well as by representation-derived evaluation. We also review research that shows the pervasive impact of transference on interpersonal relations, summarizing findings involving affect, motivation, expectancies, interpersonal roles, and self-definition.

THE SOCIAL-COGNITIVE MODEL OF TRANSFERENCE

Basic Assumptions

Research suggests that the activation and use of significant-other representations in relation to new people are the basic processes by which transference occurs in everyday social relations (Andersen & Glassman, 1996; Chen & Andersen, in press). Basic principles of social cognition, and social-construct theory in particular (e.g., Higgins, 1996; Higgins & King, 1981; Kelly, 1955), suggest that people should "go beyond the information given" about a new person using an existing social construct (Bruner, 1957). Thus, when a significant-other representation, as a construct, is used to interpret a new individual, representation-derived inferences should be made about him or her, by attributing qualities to him or her that are in fact part of the significant-other representation. This is exactly what the findings on transference have shown. Perceivers appear to believe that they learned about a new person what they simply inferred on the basis of a significant-other representation, remembering the new person "as if" he or she were more like the significant other than is actually the case.

The theory of schema-triggered affect says that the "summary" evaluation of a social category or stereotype is transferred to a new person classified in terms of that category (S.T. Fiske & Pavelchak, 1986). In accordance with this theory, a central assumption of our social-cognitive model is that triggering a significant-other representation should lead representation-derived evaluation to be activated and used with a new person. The overall evaluative tone of the significant-other representation should be transferred to the new person in transference, and this is exactly what occurs. Participants like a new person more when he or she triggers a positively toned rather than a negatively toned significant-other representation from their own lives (Andersen & Baum, 1994; Andersen, Reznik, & Manzella, 1996; see also Baum & Andersen, in press). Both representation-derived memory and representation-derived evaluation are basic indices of transference.

Clinical Origins

The concept of transference originates in the work of Freud (1912/1958). In his view, a person in analysis experiences transference with his or her analyst, and this transference involves unconscious psychosexual conflicts with a past significant other (typically a parent). Although he acknowledged that transference occurs in daily life as well, in his drive-structure model (i.e., the id, ego, and superego, driven by libido; see Greenberg & Mitchell, 1983), psychosexual conflict and defense underlie transference, an assumption with which we do not agree. We concur, however, with the basic premise that aspects of past relationships resurface in the present (Chen & Andersen, in press).

Our view of transference is similar to Sullivan's (1953). In Sullivan's model, "personifications" of the self and significant others are formed on the basis of early relations with significant others, as are "dynamisms" (or dynamics) representing typical relational patterns between self and other. When "parataxic distortion" (transference) occurs, the new person is experienced in terms of the significant other, and the interpersonal patterns learned with the significant other are experienced in the new relationship. Although Sullivan did not conceive of personifications and dynamisms in social-cognitive terms, they can easily be conceptualized accordingly, without altering his model. Hence, Sullivan's model corresponds nicely with our social-cognitive view, in which we assume that significant other representations are highly emotionally laden and that relational linkages between the self and other exist and are activated with new people, producing transference and its various effects (Andersen et al., 1997).

Fundamental to our model is the assumption that transference occurs in daily life, as well as in psychotherapy. We assume that the process of transference occurs uniformly across individuals, but that the content of transference—that is, the content of significant-other representations—differs across individuals (Andersen & Berk, 1998). We also assume that this content may change over time (i.e., it is not entirely fixed or static; Horney, 1939; Wachtel, 1981). In addition, we contend that transference occurs for all types of significant others, and not primarily or only for parents, as assumed in many psychodynamic models. Our work has demonstrated transference based on a wide variety of significant other representations (i.e., sibling, best friend, spouse). Of course, numerous clinical models of transference exist, as well as empirical work tracking repetitive interpersonal patterns that are reported by patients in psychotherapy and thought to be transference-based (e.g., Luborsky & Crits-Christoph, 1990). Our social-cognitive model and research are relevant to these lines of thinking, even though we focus on everyday life, and then consider the clinical implications of our findings (see Andersen & Berk, 1998).

Social-Construct Theory and Transference

Research in social cognition now includes a growing literature on significant other representations, their links to the self in memory, and their role in transference (Andersen et al., 1996; Andersen, Glassman, & Gold, 1998; Hinkley & Andersen, 1996). Research on social constructs, in particular, has typically examined constructs designating groups of people (i.e., the stereotype and trait-based notions people use to categorize and interpret others; e.g., Andersen & Klatzky, 1987; Higgins & King, 1981; Wyer & Martin, 1986). Relatively less work has been done on "n-of-one" constructs, or individual-person exemplars (e.g., Smith & Zarate, 1992; see also Higgins & King, 1981), which denote a single individual and are also used to interpret new individuals when activated. We argue that this process is especially likely to occur when the exemplar is a significant other, as shown in our research (e.g., Andersen, Glassman, Chen, & Cole, 1995).

Research on social-construct theory has identified both chronic and transient sources of construct activation (e.g., Bargh, Bond, Lombardi, & Tota, 1986; Higgins, 1996). A construct can be activated by virtue of its chronic accessibility, that is, its chronically high readiness to be activated, which arises from the frequency of its past activation (e.g., Higgins & King, 1981). Indeed, chronic activation is associated with the same effects as is transient activation, which occurs on the basis of either advanced priming or applicability cues in the stimulus person (2). There is also an additive relationship between chronicity and transient activation in transference (i.e., for significant other representations;

Andersen et al., 1995), just as there is for other social constructs (Bargh et al., 1986; Higgins & Brendl, 1985).

Specifically, significant-other representations have been shown to be chronically accessible in that they are used to interpret a new person in the absence of any transient activation. Hence, these representations have a general readiness to be used, suggesting that transference may be ubiquitous in social relations. At the same time, significant-other representations are still more likely to be activated and used in responding to new others when transient activation also occurs. In particular, we suggest that when a new person resembles the significant other, applicability-based transient activation of the significant-other representation occurs. Indeed, we speculate that the phenomenon may be particularly likely to occur in face-to-face encounters with others, and thus emphasize cues emanating from a new person in triggering transference. Overall, then, we assume that both chronic and applicability-based activation typically contribute to the activation and use of significant-other representations in interpreting new people, and much research on transference supports this view (see Chen & Andersen, in press).

THE BASIC TRANSFERENCE PARADIGM

One distinguishing feature of our transference paradigm is that we use idiographic research methods, often considered crucial in personality measurement (Allport, 1937; Kelly, 1955), in combination with a nomothetic (standard across all participants) experimental design (Andersen & Glassman, 1996). Given that experiences with significant others are highly personal and unique, it is essential that each participant describe his or her own significant other. These idiographic (or idiosyncratic) descriptions are then used in a standard, nomothetic paradigm in which the basic process of transference is examined across participants. The use of this combined idiographic-nomothetic methodology allows measurement of the uniform process of transference while at the same time accounting for the idiosyncratic nature of the content of significant-other representations.

In our research, we hold a pretest session in which each participant generates a series of sentences to describe a significant other (in a sentence-completion procedure), and sometimes various control representations (e.g., a stereotype) as well. In the experimental session, held at least 2 weeks later and allegedly unrelated to the pretest, the participant is presented with a series of sentences describing one or several new target persons. In the experimental condition, one of these targets is portrayed so as to resemble the significant other, by being characterized in terms of some of the sentences provided in the pretest session, in combination with irrelevant filler items. We regard these stimuli as an analogue for the types of cues perceivers would encounter in a new person in a real social encounter. In the control condition, no resemblance to the significant other exists in the target person or persons. In some studies, each participant in the control condition is yoked with a participant in the experimental condition, so that the control participant is presented with the experimental participant's significant-other descriptors (e.g., Andersen et al., 1996). Participants are yoked in this way on a one-to-one basis, to ensure that all participants in the experimental and control conditions are exposed to the same set of target descriptors, so that stimulus content is controlled entirely. Alternatively, other types of representations, such as nonsignificant others, stereotypes, and traits, have also been used as controls (e.g., Andersen et al., 1995).

After learning about the new person, all participants in the experiment complete a series of dependent measures, including the basic transference indices of representation-derived inference and memory, as well as evaluation. Measures of affect, motivation, expectancies, and self-definition are also examined selectively.

OVERVIEW OF EXPERIMENTAL EFFECTS ASSOCIATED WITH TRANSFERENCE

Representation-Derived Inference and Memory in Transference

Using this experimental paradigm, we have demonstrated the occurrence of representation-derived inference and memory based on an activated significant-other representation. Participants complete a standard recognition-memory test consisting of representation-derived descriptive sentences (as well as filler items), some of which were presented earlier to describe the new target person and some of which were not. Participants rate their confidence that they remember seeing each descriptor about the target. Of interest are those descriptors that were not presented about the target, but that are representation-derived (i.e., from the original significant-other descriptors listed in the pretest). These not-presented descriptors index the tendency to "go beyond the information given" about the target (Bruner, 1957) in representation-derived ways. Across several studies, participants exhibited reliably greater memory confidence for representation-derived target descriptors not actually presented about the target when he or she resembled the participant's own significant other rather than a yoked participant's significant other or another type of control representation (Andersen & Baum, 1994; Andersen & Cole, 1990; Andersen et al., 1995, 1996; Baum & Andersen, in press; Hinkley & Andersen, 1996). This basic transference effect occurs for both positively toned and negatively toned significant others, and the robustness of the effect is shown in the fact that it appears to persist and to be exacerbated over time (as measured in weeks; Glassman & Andersen, in press).

Representation-Derived Evaluation in Transference

Evaluative responses toward a new person derived from an activated significant-other representation also serve as a basic index of transference. To examine such representation-derived evaluation in transference, we ask participants in the pretest to identify a significant other whom they evaluative positively or negatively, so that evaluative responses deriving from the significant-other representation can be assessed. The evidence shows that participants evaluate a target person resembling their own positively toned significant other more favorably than a target resembling their own negatively toned significant other (Andersen & Baum, 1994; Andersen et al., 1996; Baum & Andersen, in press). These findings do not occur in a control condition in which the target resembles a yoked participant's significant other; thus, these evaluations are based on significant other resemblance in the new person and transference, in accord with the theory of schema-triggered affect (S.T. Fiske & Pavelchak, 1986), extended to n-of-one representations.

Although the model of schema-triggered affect focuses primarily on evaluative responses, we argue that affect, motivation, and expectancies should emerge in transference via a similar schema-triggering process, because significant-other representations are highly emotionally laden (Andersen et al., 1997, 1998). Indeed, because significant-other representations should be linked to the self via relational linkages (see also Baldwin, 1992), affect, motivation, expectancies, roles, and aspects of self experienced in the relationship with the significant other should be activated and experienced when a significant-other representation is activated with a new person and should be used in relation to this new person in transference. The following research tested these assumptions in depth.

Facial Affect in Transference

Because emotional responses may be fleeting, we examined participants' facial expressions of affect—as an immediate, nonverbal index of affect in transference (Andersen et al., 1996). Participants' facial expressions were covertly videotaped while the participants read each descriptor to learn about the target person and were later rated by trained, independent judges. As predicted, participants' facial expressions were judged to be more pleasant when participants were learning about a target who resembled their own positively toned significant other rather than their own negatively toned significant other (Andersen et al., 1996). This pattern in facial expressions did not occur in the control condition, in which the target resembled a yoked participant's significant other. Hence, representation-derived affect, as indexed by instantaneous facial affect, occurs in transference. Because this same study did not find self-reported mood effects—as assessed by participants' reports of their current mood states after learning about the target—it suggests that this affect may be fleeting. Prior work found some evidence of representation-derived mood states in transference, based on the overall tone of the activated significant other representation (Andersen & Baum, 1994). However, these effects were weak, and hence, mood derived from significant-other representations (from the overall tone of the representations) in transference appears to be inconsistent at best.

Interpersonal Roles and Mood in Transference

Of potential relevance to how mood states emerge in transference are the normative interpersonal roles held by the self in relation to the significant other, which should be stored in linkages between the self and the significant other in memory, and hence activated in transference. When the significant-other representation and relationship are positive, the interpersonal role with this significant other is associated with positive feeling. Hence, if this role is activated in transference and it appears feasible to pursue it with the new person, a positive mood should result. By contrast, if this role does not appear feasible, negative mood and disappointment should result. This is exactly what findings have shown (Baum & Andersen, in press). When the participant's positively toned significant-other representation was activated in transference with a new person and this new person's role was incongruent, rather than congruent, with the significant other's role, the participant came to be in a more negative mood. Perhaps this occurred because the incongruent role signaled a potential disruption in the positively regarded interaction goals and interaction patterns typically pursued in that particular role with that particular significant other. These findings occurred only in the transference condition—that is, when the new person resembled the participant's own significant other and not a yoked participant's significant other—and thus provide evidence that the activation of a significant-other representation in transference also activates role structures in transference, with consequences for current mood states. This work is relevant to the literature on interpersonal roles in relationships (e.g., A.P. Fiske, Haslam, & Fiske, 1991; Mills & Clark, 1993), as well as to the general notion that aspects of past relationships with significant others are activated when the relevant significant-other representations are activated.

Motivational Responses in Transference

Our model of transference assumes that motivational information regarding the significant other is stored in the linkages between the significant-other representation and the self (as roles are) and thus should be activated and applied to a new person when the significant-other representation is activated and applied (Andersen et al., 1996). In particular, our focus has been on motivation for interpersonal closeness—that is, the desire to be close and emotionally connected to, and liked or loved by, the significant other, a motivation of central importance in close relationships (Andersen et al., 1996). It is also a basic human motivation (see Andersen et al., 1997, Bakan, 1966; Baumeister & Leary, 1995; Bowlby, 1969). As expected, participants indicated greater motivation to emotionally approach (and not increase distance from) a target if the target resembled their own positively toned significant other than if the target resembled their own negatively toned significant other; positive versus negative tone of the significant other did not have an effect in the control condition with yoked participants (Andersen et al., 1996). Hence, motivations pursued in relationships with significant others also emerge in transference.

Expectancies in Transference

Expectancies about the significant other's likely responses toward the self should also be stored in the linkages between the significant-other representation and the self, and should be used in transference. As anticipated, participants indicated expecting targets who resembled their own positively toned significant other to like and accept them more than targets resembling their own negatively toned significant other, and tone of the significant other did not have an effect with yoked participants in the control condition (Andersen et al.,

1996). Expectancies derived from the significant-other representation thus appear to be activated in transference. This finding is of relevance to social relations because expectancies directly influence interpersonal behavior (e.g., Olson, Roese, & Zanna, 1996). Recent work has in fact found evidence that representation-derived behavior occurs in transference (Berk & Andersen, 1996), an important extension.

The Self in Transference: The Working Self-Concept and Self-Evaluation

Research described thus far supports the contention that linkages between the self and significant other exist in memory and are traversed in transference, a premise central to our model. In another study, these linkages were assessed directly—in the shifts that occur in the working self-concept (e.g., Linville & Carlston, 1994; Markus & Wurf, 1987) when a significant-other representation is activated. If linkages between the self and significant other exist, then the activation of significant-other representations should activate aspects of the self-concept linked with the significant other, producing changes in the working self-concept that reflect the self-when-with-the-significant-other (Hinkley & Andersen, 1996; see also Ogilvie & Ashmore, 1991).

As expected, the research showed that significant-other resemblance in the target person did in fact produce changes in the working self-concept reflecting the self-when-with-the-significant-other. We assessed these changes by examining the participant's working self-concept in the experiment. That is, after learning about the new person in the experiment, each participant provided self-generated descriptors of himself or herself, and we then computed the overlap of these descriptors with the self-with-significant-other descriptors the participant provided at pretest, before learning about the new person. To tap change in the working self-concept in the experiment, we examined this overlap score while covarying out the same overlap at pretest (i.e., the overlap between the participant's pretest working self-concept and self-with-significant-other descriptors). The findings revealed that in the transference condition, a reliably greater increase emerged in the self's overlap with the self-with-significant-other, showing changes in the working self-concept in the predicted direction. Coupled with independent evidence demonstrating that transference occurred in the condition in which the new person resembled the participant's own significant other, these data suggest that self-concept changes occurred as predicted in the context of transference (Hinkley & Andersen, 1996). In short, in relation to the new person, one becomes the version of self one is with the significant other.

Furthermore, relevant self-evaluation changes also occurred in transference, driven by the overall tone of the significant-other representation. That is, those aspects of the self-concept that changed in the direction of the self-with-the-significant-other became more positive in the positive transference than in the negative transference. The effect did not occur in the no-resemblance control condition, showing that the effect was limited to the transference condition.

These findings clearly demonstrate that the self is activated in conjunction with transference, revealing that the self is indeed interpersonal and defined in part by the self-with-each-significant-other (Andersen et al., 1997; see also Aron et al., 1991; Baldwin, 1992; Ogilvie & Ashmore, 1991).

CONCLUDING COMMENTS

We have provided an overview of the social-cognitive model of transference and presented experimental research demonstrating that transference occurs in everyday social relations. The experimental findings stemming from the model show that activation of mental representations of significant others and the use of these representations in relation to new individuals underlie transference, and thus that transference occurs as a result of basic principles that govern the activation and use of social constructs. Significant-other representations are chronically accessible—that is, they have a chronic readiness to be used in social perception, even when the new person does not resemble the significant other—suggesting that transference is rather ubiquitous in interpersonal relations (Andersen et al., 1995). However, the research also demonstrates the importance of the new person's resemblance to the significant other (applicability cues in the new person) in triggering transference. The new person's resemblance to the significant other leads to the activation and use of significant-other representations by the perceiver, which is reflected in inference and memory, evaluation, affect, motivation, and expectancy effects, as well as effects associated with the activation of interpersonal roles and with changes in self-definition in relation to the new person (relative to the no-significant-other-resemblance baseline). In short, transference has wide-ranging, multifaceted effects that demonstrate the pervasive role of past interpersonal relationships in present ones (Chen & Andersen, in press).

This work contributes to the literature on close relationships, especially the literature on attachment. It also shares common ground with work on relational schemas and on linkages between self and others in memory. Clearly, the research also contributes to long-standing theories of personality dealing with transference. Personality models and measures focused on the idiographic are also relevant to the present work. Finally, these findings contribute to the social-cognitive literature on how social constructs and exemplars constrain interpersonal perception, while highlighting the specific role of significant-other representations in such basic processes. (For detailed discussion of the model's convergence with other literatures, see Andersen & Berk, 1998; Andersen et al., 1997; Chen & Andersen, in press.) In sum, past experiences with significant others appear to have a broad and profound impact on present relationships, and transference is critical in this process as it occurs in everyday social relations.

Acknowledgements—We would like to thank Serena Chen, Noah Glassman, and Ira Reznik for their comments on a draft of this article.

Notes

1. Address correspondence to Susan M. Andersen, Department of Psychology, New York University, 6 Washington Pl., 4th Floor, New York, NY 10003. 2.

2. Priming involves presentation of a stimulus related to a particular mental representation (or construct) before information about the new person is encountered, with the result that the representation is activated and used to interpret this new person. Transient activation based on cues in the stimulus person—applicability—occurs when information presented about the new person is in itself related to a representation (or construct), again with the result that the representation is activated and used to interpret the new person.

References

Allport, G. (1937). *Personality: A psychology interpretation*. New York: Holt, Rinehart, & Winston.

Andersen, S.M., & Baum, A.B. (1994). Transference in interpersonal relations: Inferences and affect based on significant-other representations. *Journal of Personality, 62,* 460–497.

Andersen, S.M., & Berk, M.S. (1998). Transference in everyday experience: Implications of experimental research for relevant clinical phenomena. *Review of General Psychology, 2,* 81–120.

Andersen, S.M., & Cole, S.W. (1990). "Do I know you?" The role of significant others in general social perception. *Journal of Personality and Social Psychology, 59,* 384–399.

Andersen, S.M., & Glassman, N.S. (1996). Responding to significant others when they are not there: Effects on interpersonal inference, motivation, and affect. In R.M. Sorrentino & E.T. Higgins (Eds.), *Handbook of motivation and cognition* (Vol. 3, pp. 262–321). New York: Guilford Press.

Andersen, S.M., Glassman, N.S., Chen, S., & Cole, S.W. (1995). Transference in social perception: The role of chronic accessibility in significant-other representations. *Journal of Personality and Social Psychology, 69,* 41–57.

Andersen, S.M., Glassman, N.S., & Gold, D. (1998). Mental representations of the self, significant-others, and nonsignificant others: Structure and processing of private and public aspects. *Journal of Personality and Social Psychology, 75,* 845–861.

Andersen, S.M., & Klatzky, R.L. (1987). Traits and social stereotypes: Levels of categorization in person perception. *Journal of Personality and Social Psychology, 53,* 235–246.

Andersen, S.M., Reznik, I., & Chen, S. (1997). The self and others: Cognitive and motivational underpinnings. In J.G. Snodgrass & R.L. Thompson (Eds.), *The self across psychology: Self-recognition, self-awareness, and the self-concept* (pp. 233–275). New York: New York Academy of Science.

Andersen, S.M., Reznik, I., & Manzella, L.M. (1996). Eliciting facial affect, motivation, and expectancies in transference: Significant-other representations in social relations. *Journal of Personality and Social Psychology, 71,* 1108–1129.

Aron, A., Aron, E.N., Tudor, M., & Nelson, G. (1991). Close relationships and including other in the self. *Journal of Personality and Social Psychology, 60,* 241–253.

Bakan, D. (1966). *The duality of human existence*. Chicago: Rand-McNally.

Baldwin, M.W. (1992). Relational schemas and the processing of information. *Psychological Bulletin, 112,* 461–484.

Bargh, J.A., Bond, R.N., Lombardi, W.L., & Tota, M.E. (1986). The addictive nature of chronic and temporary sources of construct accessibility. *Journal of Personality and Social Psychology, 50,* 869–878.

Baum, A., & Andersen, S.M. (in press). Interpersonal roles in transference: Transient mood effects under the condition of significant-other resemblance. *Social Cognition*.

Baumeister, R.F., & Leary, M.R. (1995). The need to belong: Desire for interpersonal attachments as a fundamental human motivation. *Psychological Bulletin, 117,* 497–529.

Berk, M.S., & Andersen, S.M. (1996, July). *Eliciting behavioral confirmation by activating significant-other representations*. Poster presented at the annual meeting of the American Psychological Society, San Francisco.

Berscheid, E. (1994). Interpersonal relationships. *Annual Review of Psychology, 45,* 79–129.

Bowlby, J. (1969). Attachment and loss: Vol. 1. *Attachment.* New York: Basic Books.

Bruner, J.S. (1957). Going beyond the information given. In H.E. Gruber, K.R. Hammond, & R. Jessor (Eds.), *Contemporary approaches to cognition* (pp. 41–60). Cambridge, MA: Harvard University Press.

Bugental, D. (1992). Affective and cognitive processes within threat-oriented family systems. In I.E. Sigel, A. McGillicuddy-de Lissi, & J. Goodnow (Eds.), *Parental belief systems: The psychological consequences for children* (pp. 219–248). Hillsdale, NJ: Erlbaum.

Chen, S., & Andersen, S.M. (in press). Relationships from the past in the present: Significant-other representations and transference in interpersonal life. In M.P. Zanna (Ed.), *Advances in experimental social psychology* (Vol. 31). San Diego: Academic Press.

Collins, N.L., & Read, S.J. (1990). Adult attachment, working models, and relationship quality in dating couples. *Journal of Personality and Social Psychology, 58,* 644–663.

Ehrenreich, J.H. (1989). Transference: One concept or many? *The Psychoanalytic Review, 76,* 37–65.

Fiske, A.P., Haslam, N., & Fiske, S.T. (1991). Confusing one person with another: What errors reveal about the elementary forms of social relations. *Journal of Personality and Social Psychology, 60,* 656–674.

Fiske, S.T., & Pavelchak, M. (1986). Category-based versus piecemeal-based affective responses: Developments in schema-triggered affect. In R.M. Sorrentino & E.T. Higgins (Eds.), *Handbook of motivation and cognition* (Vol. 1, pp. 167–203). New York: Guilford Press.

Freud, S. (1958). The dynamics of transference. In J. Strachey (Ed. and Trans.), *The standard edition of the complete psychological works of Sigmund Freud* (Vol. 12, pp. 99–108). London: Hogarth Press. (Original work published 1912)

Glassman, N.S., & Andersen, S.M. (in press). Transference in social cognition: Persistence and exacerbation of significant-other based inferences over time. *Cognitive Therapy and Research.*

Greenberg, J.R., & Mitchell, S.A. (1983). *Object relations in psychoanalytic theory.* Cambridge, MA: Harvard University Press.

Hazan, C., & Shaver, P. (1987). Romantic love conceptualized as an attachment process. *Journal of Personality and Social Psychology, 52,* 511–524.

Higgins, E.T. (1996). Knowledge activation: Accessibility, applicability, and salience. In E.T. Higgins & A.W. Kruglansh (Eds.), *Social psychology: Handbook of basic principles* (pp. 133–168). New York: Guilford Press.

Higgins, E.T., & Brendl, C.M. (1995). Accessibility and applicability: Some "activation rules" influencing judgment. *Journal of Experimental Social Psychology, 31,* 218–243.

Higgins, E.T., & King, G.A. (1981). Accessibility of social constructs: Information processing consequences of individual and contextual variability. In N. Canto & J.F. Kihlstrom (Eds.), *Personality, cognition and social interaction* (pp. 69–121). Hillsdale, NJ: Erlbaum.

Himkley, K., & Andersen, S.M. (1996). The working self-concept in transference: Significant-other activation and self-change. *Journal of Personality and Social Psychology, 71,* 1279–1295.

Horney, K. (1939). *New ways in psychoanalysis.* New York: Norton.

Kelly, G. (1955). *The psychology of personal constructs.* New York: Norton.

Linville, P.W., & Carlston, D.E. (1994). Social cognition of the self. In P.G. Devine, D.C. Hamilton, & T.M. Ostrom (Eds.), *Social cognition: Impact on social psychology* (pp. 143–193). New York: Academic Press.

Luborsky, L., & Crits-Cristoph, P. (1990). *Understanding transference: The CCRT method.* New York: Basic Books.

Markus, H., & Wurf, E. (1987). The dynamic self-concept: A social psychological perspective. *Annual Review of Psychology, 38,* 299–337.

Mills, J., & Clark, M.S. (1993). Communal and exchange relationships: New research and old controversies. In R.G. Gilmour & R. Erber (Eds.), *Theoretical approaches to new relationships* (pp. 29–42). Hillsdale, NJ: Erlbaum.

Murray, S.L., & Holmes, J.G. (1993). Seeing virtues in faults: Negativity and the transformation of interpersonal narratives in close relationships. *Journal of Personality and Social Psychology, 65,* 707–722.

Ogilvie, D.M., & Ashmore, R.D. (1991). Self-with-other representation as a unit of analysis in self-concept research. In R.C. Curtis (Ed.), *The relational self Theoretical convergences in psychoanalysis and social psychology* (pp. 282–314). New York: Guilford Press.

Olson, J.M., Roese, N.J., & Zanna, M.P. (1996). Expectancies. In E.T. Higgms & A.W. Kruglanski (Eds.), *Social psychology: Handbook of basic principles* (pp. 211–238). New York: Guilford Press.

Singer, J.L. (1988). Reinterpreting the transference. In D.C. Turk & P. Salovey (Eds.), *Reasoning, inference, and judgment in clinical psychology* (pp. 182–205). New York: Free Press.

Smith, E.R., & Zarate, M.A. (1992). Exemplar-based model of social judgment. *Psychological Review, 99,* 3–21.

Sullivan, H.S. (1953). *The interpersonal theory of psychiatry.* New York: Norton.

Wachtel, P.L. (1981). Transference, schema, and assimilation: The relevance of Piaget to the psychoanalytic theory of transference. *The Annual of Psychoanalysis, 8,* 59–76.

Westen, D. (1988). Transference and information processing. *Clinical Psychology Review, 8,* 161–179.

Wyer, R.S., Jr., & Martin, L.L. (1986). Person memory: The role of traits, group stereotypes, and specific behaviors in the cognitive representation of persons. *Journal of Personality and Social Psychology, 50,* 661–675.

Making Sense of Self-Esteem

Mark R. Leary[1]
Department of Psychology, Wake Forest University, Winston-Salem, North Carolina

Abstract

Sociometer theory proposes that the self-esteem system evolved as a monitor of social acceptance, and that the so-called self-esteem motive functions not to maintain self-esteem per se but rather to avoid social devaluation and rejection. Cues indicating that the individual is not adequately valued and accepted by other people lower self-esteem and motivate behaviors that enhance relational evaluation. Empirical evidence regarding the self-esteem motive, the antecedents of self-esteem, the relation between low self-esteem and psychological problems, and the consequences of enhancing self-esteem is consistent with the theory.

Keywords

self-esteem; self; self-regard; rejection

Self-esteem has been regarded as an important construct since the earliest days of psychology. In the first psychology textbook, William James (1890) suggested that the tendency to strive to feel good about oneself is a fundamental aspect of human nature, thereby fueling a fascination—some observers would say obsession—with self-esteem that has spanned more than a century. During that time, developmental psychologists have studied the antecedents of self-esteem and its role in human development, social psychologists have devoted attention to behaviors that appear intended to maintain self-esteem, personality psychologists have examined individual differences in the trait of self-esteem, and theorists of a variety of orientations have discussed the importance of self-regard to psychological adjustment. In the past couple of decades, practicing psychologists and social engineers have suggested that high self-esteem is a remedy for many psychological and social problems.

Yet, despite more than 100 years of attention and thousands of published studies, fundamental issues regarding self-esteem remain poorly understood. Why is self-esteem important? Do people really have a need for self-esteem? Why is self-esteem so strongly determined by how people believe they are evaluated by others? Is low self-esteem associated with psychological difficulties and, if so, why? Do efforts to enhance self-esteem reduce personal and social problems as proponents of the self-esteem movement claim?

PERSPECTIVES ON THE FUNCTION OF SELF-ESTEEM

Many writers have assumed that people seek to maintain their self-esteem because they possess an inherent "need" to feel good about themselves. However, given the apparent importance of self-esteem to psychological functioning, we must ask why self-esteem is so important and what function it might serve.

Humanistic psychologists have traced high self-esteem to a congruency between a person's real and ideal selves and suggested that self-esteem signals people as to when they are behaving in self-determined, autonomous ways. Other writers have proposed that people seek high self-esteem because it facilitates goal achievement. For example, Bednar, Wells, and Peterson (1989) proposed that self-esteem is subjective feedback about the adequacy of the self. This feedback—self-esteem—is positive when the individual copes well with circumstances but negative when he or she avoids threats. In turn, self-esteem affects subsequent goal achievement; high self-esteem increases coping, and low self-esteem leads to further avoidance.

The ethological perspective (Barkow, 1980) suggests that self-esteem is an adaptation that evolved in the service of maintaining dominance in social relationships. According to this theory, human beings evolved mechanisms for monitoring dominance because dominance facilitated the acquisition of mates and other reproduction-enhancing resources. Because attention and favorable reactions from others were associated with being dominant, feelings of self-esteem became tied to social approval and deference. From this perspective, the motive to evaluate oneself positively reduces, in evolutionary terms, to the motive to enhance one's relative dominance.

One of the more controversial explanations of self-esteem is provided by terror management theory, which suggests that the function of self-esteem is to buffer people against the existential terror they experience at the prospect of their own death and annihilation (Solomon, Greenberg, & Pyszczynski, 1991). Several experiments have supported aspects of the theory, but not the strong argument that the function of the self-esteem system is to provide an emotional buffer specifically against death-related anxiety.

All of these perspectives offer insights into the nature of self-esteem, but each has conceptual and empirical difficulties (for critiques, see Leary, 1999; Leary & Baumeister, in press). In the past few years, a novel perspective—sociometer theory—has cast self-esteem in a somewhat different light as it attempts to address lingering questions about the nature of self-esteem.

SOCIOMETER THEORY

According to sociometer theory, self-esteem is essentially a psychological meter, or gauge, that monitors the quality of people's relationships with others (Leary, 1999; Leary & Baumeister, in press; Leary & Downs, 1995). The theory is based on the assumption that human beings possess a pervasive drive to maintain significant interpersonal relationships, a drive that evolved because early human beings who belonged to social groups were more likely to survive and reproduce than those who did not (Baumeister & Leary, 1995). Given the disastrous implications of being ostracized in the ancestral environment in which human evolution occurred, early human beings may have developed a mechanism for monitoring the degree to which other people valued and accepted them. This psychological mechanism—the *sociometer*—continuously monitors the social environment for cues regarding the degree to which the individual is being accepted versus rejected by other people.

The sociometer appears to be particularly sensitive to changes in relational evaluation—the degree to which others regard their relationship with the individual as valuable, important, or close. When evidence of low relational evaluation (particularly, a decrement in relational evaluation) is detected, the sociometer attracts the person's conscious attention to the potential threat to social acceptance and motivates him or her to deal with it. The affectively laden self-appraisals that constitute the "output" of the sociometer are what we typically call self-esteem.

Self-esteem researchers distinguish between *state self-esteem*—momentary fluctuations in a person's feelings about him- or herself—and *trait self-esteem*—the person's general appraisal of his or her value; both are aspects of the sociometer. Feelings of state self-esteem fluctuate as a function of the degree to which the person perceives others currently value their relationships with him or her. Cues that connote high relational evaluation raise state self-esteem, whereas cues that connote low relational evaluation lower state self-esteem. Trait self-esteem, in contrast, reflects the person's general sense that he or she is the sort of person who is valued and accepted by other people. Trait self-esteem may be regarded as the resting state of the sociometer in the absence of incoming information relevant to relational evaluation.

SELF-ESTEEM AND ITS RELATIONSHIP TO BEHAVIOR

Sociometer theory provides a parsimonious explanation for much of what we know about self-esteem. Here I examine how sociometer theory answers four fundamental questions about self-esteem raised earlier.

The Self-Esteem Motive

As noted, many psychologists have assumed that people possess a motive or need to maintain self-esteem. According to sociometer theory, the so-called self-esteem motive does not function to maintain self-esteem but rather to minimize the likelihood of rejection (or, more precisely, relational devaluation). When people behave in ways that protect or enhance their self-esteem, they are typically acting in ways that they believe will increase their relational value in others' eyes and, thus, improve their chances of social acceptance.

The sociometer perspective explains why events that are known (or potentially known) by other people have much greater effects on self-esteem than events that are known only by the individual him- or herself. If self-esteem involved only private self-judgments, as many psychologists have assumed, public events should have no greater impact on self-esteem than private ones.

Antecedents of Self-Esteem

Previous writers have puzzled over the fact that self-esteem is so strongly tied to people's beliefs about how they are evaluated by others. If self-esteem is a *self*-evaluation, why do people judge themselves by *other* people's standards? Sociometer theory easily explains why the primary determinants of self-esteem involve the perceived reactions of other people, as well as self-judgments on dimensions that the person thinks are important to significant others. As a monitor of relational evaluation, the self-esteem system is inherently sensitive to real and potential reactions of other people.

Evidence shows that state self-esteem is strongly affected by events that have implications for the degree to which one is valued and accepted by other people (Leary, Haupt, Strausser, & Chokel, 1998; Leary, Tambor, Terdal, & Downs, 1995). The events that affect self-esteem are precisely the kinds of things that, if known by other people, would affect their evaluation and acceptance of the person (Leary, Tambor, et al., 1995). Most often, self-esteem is lowered by failure, criticism, rejection, and other events that have negative implications for relational evaluation; self-esteem rises when a person succeeds, is praised, or experiences another's love—events that are associated with relational appreciation. Even the mere possibility of rejection can lower self-esteem, a finding that makes sense if the function of the self-esteem system is to warn the person of possible relational devaluation in time to take corrective action.

The attributes on which people's self-esteem is based are precisely the characteristics that determine the degree to which people are valued and accepted by others (Baumeister & Leary, 1995). Specifically, high trait self-esteem is associated with believing that one possesses socially desirable attributes such as competence, personal likability, and physical attractiveness. Furthermore, self-esteem is related most strongly to one's standing on attributes that one believes are valued by significant others, a finding that is also consistent with sociometer theory.

In linking self-esteem to social acceptance, sociometer theory runs counter to the humanistic assumption that self-esteem based on approval from others is false or unhealthy. On the contrary, if the function of self-esteem is to avoid social devaluation and rejection, then the system must be responsive to others' reactions. This system may lead people to do things that are not always beneficial, but it does so to protect their interpersonal relationships rather than their inner integrity.

Low Self-Esteem and Psychological Problems

Research has shown that low self-esteem is related to a variety of psychological difficulties and personal problems, including depression, loneliness, substance abuse, teenage pregnancy, academic failure, and criminal behavior. The evidence in support of the link between low self-esteem and psychological problems has often been overstated; the relationships are weaker and more scattered than typically assumed (Mecca, Smelser, & Vasconcellos, 1989). Moreover, high self-esteem also has notable drawbacks. Even so, low self-esteem tends to be more strongly associated with psychological difficulties than high self-esteem.

From the standpoint of sociometer theory, these problems are caused not by low self-esteem but rather by a history of low relational evaluation, if not outright rejection. As a subjective gauge of relational evaluation, self-esteem may parallel these problems, but it is a coeffect rather than a cause. (In fact, contrary to the popular view that low self-esteem causes these problems, no direct evidence exists to document that self-esteem has any causal role in thought, emotion, or behavior.) Much research shows that interpersonal rejection results in emotional problems, difficulties relating with others, and maladaptive efforts to be accepted (e.g., excessive dependency, membership in deviant groups), precisely the concomitants of low self-esteem (Leary, Schreindorfer, & Haupt, 1995). In addition, many personal problems lower self-esteem because they lead other people to devalue or reject the individual.

Consequences of Enhancing Self-Esteem

The claim that self-esteem does not cause psychological outcomes may appear to fly in the face of evidence showing that interventions that enhance self-esteem do, in fact, lead to positive psychological changes. The explanation for the beneficial effects of programs that enhance self-esteem is that these interventions change people's perceptions of the degree to which they are socially valued individuals. Self-esteem programs always include features that would be expected to increase real or perceived social acceptance; for example, these programs include components aimed at enhancing social skills and interpersonal problem solving, improving physical appearance, and increasing self-control (Leary, 1999).

CONCLUSIONS

Sociometer theory suggests that the emphasis psychologists and the lay public have placed on self-esteem has been somewhat misplaced. Self-esteem is certainly involved in many psychological phenomena, but its role is different than has been supposed. Subjective feelings of self-esteem provide ongoing feedback regarding one's relational value vis-à-vis other people. By focusing on the monitor rather than on what the monitor measures, we have been distracted from the underlying interpersonal processes and the importance of social acceptance to human well-being.

Recommended Reading

Baumeister, R.F. (Ed.). (1993). *Self-esteem: The puzzle of low self-regard.* New York: Plenum Press.
Colvin, C.R., & Block, J. (1994). Do positive illusions foster mental health? An examination of the Taylor and Brown formulation. *Psychological Bulletin, 116,* 3–20.
Leary, M.R. (1999). (See References)
Leary, M.R., & Downs, D.L. (1995). (See References)
Mecca, A.M., Smelser, N.J., & Vasconcellos, J. (Eds.). (1989). (See References)

Note

1. Address correspondence to Mark Leary, Department of Psychology, Wake Forest University, Winston-Salem, NC 27109; e-mail: leary@wfu.edu.

References

Barkow, J. (1980). Prestige and self-esteem: A biosocial interpretation. In D.R. Omark, F.F. Strayer, & D.G. Freedman (Eds.), *Dominance relations: An ethological view of human conflict and social interaction* (pp. 319–332). New York: Garland STPM Press.
Baumeister, R.F., & Leary, M.R. (1995). The need to belong: Desire for interpersonal attachments as a fundamental human motivation. *Psychological Bulletin, 117,* 497–529.

Bednar, R.L., Wells, M.G., & Peterson, S.R. (1989). *Self-esteem: Paradoxes and innovations in clinical theory and practice*. Washington, DC: American Psychological Association.

James, W. (1890). *The principles of psychology* (Vol. 1). New York: Henry Holt.

Leary, M.R. (1999). The social and psychological importance of self-esteem. In R.M. Kowalski & M.R. Leary (Eds.), *The social psychology of emotional and behavioral problems: Interfaces of social and clinical psychology* (pp. 197–221). Washington, DC: American Psychological Association.

Leary, M.R., & Baumeister, R.F. (in press). The nature and function of self-esteem: Sociometer theory. *Advances in Experimental Social Psychology.*

Leary, M.R., & Downs, D.L. (1995). Interpersonal functions of the self-esteem motive: The self-esteem system as a sociometer. In M.H. Kernis (Ed.), *Efficacy, agency, and self-esteem* (pp. 123–144). New York: Plenum Press.

Leary, M.R., Haupt, A.L., Strausser, K.S., & Chokel, J.L. (1998). Calibrating the sociometer: The relationship between interpersonal appraisals and state self-esteem. *Journal of Personality and Social Psychology, 74,* 1290–1299.

Leary, M.R., Schreindorfer, L.S., & Haupt, A.L. (1995). The role of self-esteem in emotional and behavioral problems: Why is low self-esteem dysfunctional? *Journal of Social and Clinical Psychology, 14,* 297–314.

Leary, M.R., Tambor, E.S., Terdal, S.J., & Downs, D.L. (1995). Self-esteem as an interpersonal monitor: The sociometer hypothesis. *Journal of Personality and Social Psychology, 68,* 518–530.

Mecca, A.M., Smelser, N.J., & Vasconcellos, J. (Eds.). (1989). *The social importance of self-esteem.* Berkeley: University of California Press.

Solomon, S., Greenberg, J., & Pyszczynski, T. (1991). A terror management theory of social behavior: The psychological functions of self-esteem and cultural worldviews. *Advances in Experimental Social Psychology, 24,* 93–159.

Siblings' Direct and Indirect Contributions to Child Development

Gene H. Brody

Department of Child and Family Development and Center for Family Research, University of Georgia

Abstract

Since the early 1980s, a growing body of research has described the contributions of sibling relationships to child and adolescent development. Interactions with older siblings promote young children's language and cognitive development, their understanding of other people's emotions and perspectives, and, conversely, their development of antisocial behavior. Studies address the ways in which parents' experiences with older children contribute to their rearing of younger children, which in turn contributes to the younger children's development. Finally, by virtue of having a sibling, children may receive differential treatment from their parents. Under some conditions, differential treatment is associated with emotional and behavioral problems in children.

Keywords

siblings; interaction; development; differential treatment

The first studies of the contributions that older siblings make to their younger brothers' and sisters' development were conducted in Britain around the turn of the 20th century by Sir Francis Galton, a cousin of Charles Darwin. Sibling research, however, only recently has begun to address many of the issues that concern families. Parents, clinicians, and now researchers in developmental psychology recognize the significance of the sibling relationship as a contributor to family harmony or discord and to individual children's development. Since the early 1980s, a growing interest in the family has prompted research on those aspects of sibling relationships that contribute to children's cognitive, social, and emotional adjustment. These contributions can be direct, occurring as a result of siblings' encounters with one another, or indirect, occurring through a child's impact on parents that influences the care that other brothers and sisters receive. Differential treatment by parents is a third way in which having a sibling may contribute to child development. Children may be treated differently by their parents than their siblings are, or at least believe that they are treated differently. The development of this belief has implications for children's and adolescents' mental health. In this article, I present an overview of the ways in which siblings' direct and indirect influences and parental differential treatment contribute to child development.

Address correspondence to Gene H. Brody, University of Georgia, Center for Family Research, 1095 College Station Rd., Athens, GA 30602-4527.

SIBLINGS' DIRECT CONTRIBUTIONS TO DEVELOPMENT

Currently, research suggests that naturally occurring teaching and caregiving experiences benefit cognitive, language, and psychosocial development in both older and younger siblings. Studies conducted in children's homes and in laboratories show that older siblings in middle childhood can teach new cognitive concepts and language skills to their younger siblings in early childhood. Across the middle childhood years, older siblings become better teachers as they learn how to simplify tasks for their younger siblings. The ability to adjust their teaching behaviors to their younger siblings' capacities increases as older siblings develop the ability to take other people's perspectives (Maynard, 2002). Older siblings who assume teaching and caregiving roles earn higher reading and language achievement scores, gain a greater sense of competence in the caregiving role, and learn more quickly to balance their self-concerns with others' needs than do older siblings who do not assume these roles with their younger siblings (Zukow-Goldring, 1995). When caregiving demands on the older sibling become excessive, however, they may interfere with the older child's time spent on homework or involvement in school activities. Caregiving responsibilities during middle childhood and adolescence can compromise older siblings' school performance and behavioral adjustment (Marshall et al., 1997).

Children who are nurtured by their older siblings become sensitive to other people's feelings and beliefs (Dunn, 1988). As in all relationships, though, nurturance does not occur in isolation from conflict. Sibling relationships that are characterized by a balance of nurturance and conflict can provide a unique opportunity for children to develop the ability to understand other people's emotions and viewpoints, to learn to manage anger and resolve conflict, and to provide nurturance themselves. Indeed, younger siblings who experience a balance of nurturance and conflict in their sibling relationships have been found to be more socially skilled and have more positive peer relationships compared with children who lack this experience (Hetherington, 1988).

Sibling relationships also have the potential to affect children's development negatively. Younger siblings growing up with aggressive older siblings are at considerable risk for developing conduct problems, performing poorly in school, and having few positive experiences in their relationships with their peers (Bank, Patterson, & Reid, 1996). The links between older siblings' antisocial behavior and younger siblings' conduct problems are stronger for children living in disadvantaged neighborhoods characterized by high unemployment rates and pervasive poverty than for children living in more advantaged neighborhoods (Brody, Ge, et al., 2003). Younger siblings who live in disadvantaged neighborhoods have more opportunities than do children living in more affluent areas to practice the problematic conduct that they learn during sibling interactions as they interact with peers who encourage antisocial behavior.

The importance of the sibling relationship is probably best demonstrated by older siblings' ability to buffer younger siblings from the negative effects of family turmoil. Younger siblings whose older siblings provide them with emotional support (caring, acceptance, and bolstering of self-esteem) during bouts of intense, angry interparental conflict show fewer signs of behavioral or emotional problems than do children whose older siblings are less supportive (Jenkins, 1992).

SIBLINGS' INDIRECT CONTRIBUTIONS

Conventional wisdom suggests that parents' experiences with older children influence their expectations of subsequent children and the child-rearing strategies that parents consider effective. Similarly, the experiences that other adults, particularly teachers, have with older siblings may influence their expectations and treatment of younger siblings. Research has confirmed the operation of these indirect effects on younger siblings' development. Whiteman and Buchanan (2002) found that experiences with earlier-born children contributed to parents' expectations about their younger children's likelihood of experiencing conduct problems, using drugs, displaying rebellious behavior, or being helpful and showing concern for others. Teachers are not immune from the predisposing effects of experiences with older siblings. As a result of having an older sibling in class or hearing about his or her accomplishments or escapades, teachers develop expectations regarding the younger sibling's academic ability and conduct even before the younger child becomes their student (Bronfenbrenner, 1977). Some parents and teachers translate these expectations into parenting and teaching practices they subsequently use with younger siblings that influence the younger children's beliefs about their academic abilities, interests, and choice of friends; children often choose friends whom they perceive to be similar to themselves.

Rather than viewing behavioral influence as flowing in one direction, from parents to children, developmental psychologists now recognize that these influences are reciprocal. The behaviors that children use during everyday interactions with their parents partially determine the behaviors that the parents direct toward their children. Children with active or emotionally intense personalities receive different, usually more negative, parenting than do children with calm and easygoing personalities. Some studies suggest that older siblings' individual characteristics may contribute indirectly to the quality of parenting that younger siblings receive. For example, East (1998) discovered that negative experiences with an earlier-born child lead parents to question their ability to provide good care for their younger children and to lower their expectations for their younger children's behavior.

In our research, my colleagues and I explored the specific ways in which older siblings' characteristics contribute to the quality of parenting that younger siblings receive, which in turn contributes to younger siblings' development of conduct problems and depressive symptoms. The premise of the study was simple. Rearing older siblings who are doing well in school and are well liked by other children provides parents with opportunities for basking in their children's achievements. (Basking is a phenomenon in which one's psychological well-being increases because of the accomplishments of persons to whom one is close.) Using a longitudinal research design in which we collected data from families for 4 years, we found that academically and socially competent older siblings contributed to an increase in their mothers' self-esteem and a decrease in their mothers' depressive symptoms. Positive changes in mothers' psychological functioning forecast their use of adjustment-promoting parenting practices with younger siblings. Over time, these practices forecast high levels of self-control and low levels of behavior problems and depressive symptoms in the younger siblings (Brody, Kim, Murry, & Brown, 2003). We expect future research to clarify further the indirect pathways through which siblings influence one another's development, including the processes by which children's negative characteristics affect their parents' child-rearing practices. A difficult-to-rear older sibling, for example, may contribute over time to decreases in his or her parents' psychological well-being, resulting in increased tension in the family. Under these circumstances, the parents' negativity and distraction decrease the likelihood that a younger sibling will experience parenting that promotes self-worth, academic achievement, and social skills.

PARENTAL DIFFERENTIAL TREATMENT

Any discussion of siblings' contributions to development would be incomplete without acknowledging parental differential treatment. Having a sibling creates a context in which parental behavior assumes symbolic value, as children use it as a barometer indicating the extent to which they are loved, rejected, included, or excluded by their parents. Children's and adolescents' beliefs that they receive less warmth and more negative treatment from their parents than do their siblings is associated with poor emotional and behavioral functioning (Reiss, Neiderhiser, Hetherington, & Plomin, 2000).

Not all children who perceive differential treatment develop these problems, however. Differential parental treatment is associated with poor adjustment in a child only when the quality of the child's individual relationship with his or her parents is distant and negative. The association between differential treatment and adjustment is weak for children whose parents treat them well, even when their siblings receive even warmer and more positive treatment (Feinberg & Hetherington, 2001). Children's perceptions of the legitimacy of differential treatment also help determine its contribution to their adjustment. Children who perceive their parents' differential behavior to be justified report fewer behavior problems than do children who consider it to be unjust, even under conditions of relatively high levels of differential treatment. Children and adolescents who perceive differential treatment as unfair experience low levels of self-worth and have high levels of behavior problems (Kowal, Kramer, Krull, & Crick, 2002). Children justify differential treatment by citing ways in which they and their siblings differ in age, personality, and special needs. Sensitive parenting entails treating children as their individual temperaments and developmental needs require. Nevertheless, it is important that children understand why parents treat siblings differently from one another so that they will be protected from interpreting the differences as evidence that they are not valued or worthy of love.

FUTURE DIRECTIONS

Considerable work is needed to provide a comprehensive understanding of the processes through which siblings influence one another's cognitive development, language development, psychological adjustment, and social skills. Current studies can best be considered "first generation" research. They describe associations between older and younger siblings' behaviors and characteristics. Some studies have demonstrated that the prediction of younger siblings' outcomes is more accurate if it is based on older siblings' characteristics plus parenting, rather than parenting alone (Brody, Kim, et al., 2003). More research is needed to isolate influences other than parenting, such as shared genetics, shared environments, and social learning, before siblings' unique contributions to development can be specified. The next generation of research will address the ways in which sibling relationships contribute to children's self-images and personal identities, emotion regulation and coping skills, explanations of positive and negative events that occur in family and peer relationships, use of aggression, and involvement in high-risk behaviors.

Recommended Reading

Brody, G.H. (1998). Sibling relationship quality: Its causes and consequences. *Annual Review of Psychology, 49,* 1–24.
Feinberg, M., & Hetherington, E.M. (2001). (See References)
Kowal, A., Kramer, L., Krull, J.L., & Crick, N.R. (2002). (See References)
Maynard, A.E. (2002). (See References)
Whiteman, S.D., & Buchanan, C.M. (2002). (See References)

Acknowledgments—I would like to thank Eileen Neubaum-Carlan for helpful comments. Preparation of this article was partly supported by grants from the National Institute of Child Health and Human Development, the National Institute of Mental Health, and the National Institute on Alcohol Abuse and Alcoholism.

REFERENCES

Bank, L., Patterson, G.R., & Reid, J.B. (1996). Negative sibling interaction patterns as predictors of later adjustment problems in adolescent and young adult males. In G.H. Brody (Ed.), *Sibling relationships: Their causes and consequences* (pp. 197–229). Norwood, NJ: Ablex.
Brody, G.H., Ge, X., Kim, S.Y., Murry, V.M., Simons, R.L., Gibbons, F.X., Gerrard, M., & Conger, R. (2003). Neighborhood disadvantage moderates associations of parenting and older sibling problem attitudes and behavior with conduct disorders in African American children. *Journal of Consulting and Clinical Psychology, 71,* 211–222.
Brody, G.H., Kim, S., Murry, V.M., & Brown, A.C. (2003). Longitudinal direct and indirect pathways linking older sibling competence to the development of younger sibling competence. *Developmental Psychology, 39,* 618–628.
Bronfenbrenner, U. (1977). Toward an experimental ecology of human development. *American Psychologist, 32,* 513–531.
Dunn, J. (1988). Connections between relationships: Implications of research on mothers and siblings. In R.A. Hinde & J. Stevenson-Hinde (Eds.), *Relationships within families: Mutual influences* (pp. 168–180). New York: Oxford University Press.
East, P.L. (1998). Impact of adolescent childbearing on families and younger siblings: Effects that increase younger siblings' risk for early pregnancy. *Applied Developmental Science, 2,* 62–74.
Feinberg, M., & Hetherington, E.M. (2001). Differential parenting as a within-family variable. *Journal of Family Psychology, 15,* 22–37.
Hetherington, E.M. (1988). Parents, children, and siblings: Six years after divorce. In R.A. Hinde & J. Stevenson-Hinde (Eds.), *Relationships within families: Mutual influences* (pp. 311–331). New York: Oxford University Press.
Jenkins, J. (1992). Sibling relationships in disharmonious homes: Potential difficulties and protective effects. In F. Boer & J. Dunn (Eds.), *Children's sibling relationships: Developmental and clinical issues* (pp. 125–138). Hillsdale, NJ: Erlbaum.

Kowal, A., Kramer, L., Krull, J.L., & Crick, N.R. (2002). Children's perceptions of the fairness of parental preferential treatment and their socioemotional well-being. *Journal of Family Psychology, 16,* 297–306.

Marshall, N.L., Garcia-Coll, C., Marx, F., McCartney, K., Keefe, N., & Ruh, J. (1997). After-school time and children's behavioral adjustment. *Merrill-Palmer Quarterly, 43,* 497–514.

Maynard, A.E. (2002). Cultural teaching: The development of teaching skills in Maya sibling interactions. *Child Development, 73,* 969–982.

Reiss, D., Neiderhiser, J.M., Hetherington, E.M., & Plomin, R. (2000). *The relationship code: Deciphering genetic and social influences on adolescent development.* Cambridge, MA: Harvard University Press.

Whiteman, S.D., & Buchanan, C.M. (2002). Mothers' and children's expectations for adolescence: The impact of perceptions of an older sibling's experience. *Journal of Family Psychology, 16,* 157–171.

Zukow-Goldring, P.G. (1995). Sibling caregiving. In M.H. Bornstein (Ed.), *Handbook of parenting: Vol. 3. Status and social conditions of parenting* (pp. 177–208). Mahwah, NJ: Erlbaum.

Marital Conflict: Correlates, Structure, and Context

Frank D. Fincham[1]

Psychology Department, University of Buffalo, Buffalo, New York

Abstract

Marital conflict has deleterious effects on mental, physical, and family health, and three decades of research have yielded a detailed picture of the behaviors that differentiate distressed from nondistressed couples. Review of this work shows that the singular emphasis on conflict in generating marital outcomes has yielded an incomplete picture of its role in marriage. Recently, researchers have tried to paint a more textured picture of marital conflict by studying spouses' backgrounds and characteristics, investigating conflict in the contexts of support giving and affectional expression, and considering the ecological niche of couples in their broader environment.

Keywords

conflict patterns; marital distress; support

Systematic psychological research on marriage emerged largely among clinical psychologists who wanted to better assist couples experiencing marital distress. In the 30 years since this development, marital conflict has assumed a special status in the literature on marriage, as evidenced by three indices. First, many of the most influential theories of marriage tend to reflect the view that "distress results from couples' aversive and ineffectual response to conflict" (Koerner & Jacobson, 1994, p. 208). Second, research on marriage has focused on what spouses do when they disagree with each other, and reviews of marital interaction are dominated by studies of conflict and problem solving (see Weiss & Heyman, 1997). Third, psychological interventions for distressed couples often target conflict-resolution skills (see Baucom, Shoham, Mueser, Daiuto, & Stickle, 1998).

IS MARITAL CONFLICT IMPORTANT?

The attention given marital conflict is understandable when we consider its implications for mental, physical, and family health. Marital conflict has been linked to the onset of depressive symptoms, eating disorders, male alcoholism, episodic drinking, binge drinking, and out-of-home drinking. Although married individuals are healthier on average than the unmarried, marital conflict is associated with poorer health and with specific illnesses such as cancer, cardiac disease, and chronic pain, perhaps because hostile behaviors during conflict are related to alterations in immunological, endocrine, and cardiovascular functioning. Physical aggression occurs in about 30% of married couples in the United States, leading to significant physical injury in about 10% of couples. Marriage is also the most common interpersonal context for homicide, and more women are murdered by their partners than by anyone else. Finally, marital conflict is associated with important family outcomes, including poor parenting, poor adjustment of children, increased likelihood of parent-child conflict, and conflict between siblings. Marital conflicts that are frequent, intense, physical, unresolved, and child related have a particularly negative influence on children, as do marital conflicts that spouses attribute to their child's behavior (see Grych & Fincham, 2001).

WHAT ARE MARITAL CONFLICTS ABOUT?

Marital conflicts can be about virtually anything. Couples complain about sources of conflict ranging from verbal and physical abusiveness to personal characteristics and behaviors. Perceived inequity in a couple's division of labor is associated with marital conflict and with a tendency for the male to withdraw in response to conflict. Conflict over power is also strongly related to marital dissatisfaction. Spouses' reports of conflict over extramarital sex, problematic drinking, or drug use predict divorce, as do wives' reports of husbands being jealous and spending money foolishly. Greater problem severity increases the likelihood of divorce. Even though it is often not reported to be a problem by couples, violence among newlyweds is a predictor of divorce, as is psychological aggression (verbal aggression and nonverbal aggressive behaviors that are not directed at the partner's body).

HOW DO SPOUSES BEHAVE DURING CONFLICT?

Stimulated, in part, by the view that "studying what people say about themselves is no substitute for studying how they behave" (Raush, Barry, Hertel, & Swain, 1974, p. 5), psychologists have conducted observational studies, with the underlying hope of identifying dysfunctional behaviors that could be modified in couple therapy. This research has focused on problem-solving discussions in the laboratory and provides detailed information about how maritally distressed and nondistressed couples behave during conflict.

During conflict, distressed couples make more negative statements and fewer positive statements than nondistressed couples. They are also more likely to respond with negative behavior when their partner behaves negatively. Indeed, this negative reciprocity, as it is called, is more consistent across different types of situations than is the amount of negative behavior, making it the most reliable overt signature of marital distress. Negative behavior is both more frequent and more frequently reciprocated in couples that engage in physical aggression than in other couples. Nonverbal behavior, often used as an index of emotion, reflects marital satisfaction better than verbal behavior, and unlike verbal behavior does not change when spouses try to fake good and bad marriages.

Are There Typical Patterns of Conflict Behavior?

The sequences of behavior that occur during conflict are more predictable in distressed than in nondistressed marriages and are often dominated by chains of negative behavior that usually escalate and are difficult for the couple to stop. One of the greatest challenges for couples locked into negative exchanges is to find an adaptive way of exiting from such cycles. This is usually attempted through responses that are designed to repair the interaction (e.g., "You're not listening to me") but are delivered with negative affect (e.g., irritation, sadness). The partners tend to respond to the negative affect, thereby continuing the cycle. This makes their interactions structured and predictable. In contrast, nondistressed couples appear to be more responsive to attempts at repair and are thereby able to exit from negative exchanges early on. For example, a spouse may respond to "Wait, you're not letting me finish" with "Sorry . . . please finish what you were saying." Their interaction therefore appears more random and less predictable.

A second important behavior pattern exhibited by maritally distressed couples is the demand-withdraw pattern, in which one spouse pressures the other with demands, complaints, and criticisms, while the partner withdraws with defensiveness and passive inaction. Specifically, behavior sequences in which the husband withdraws and the wife responds with hostility are more common in distressed than in satisfied couples. This finding is consistent with several studies showing that wives display more negative affect and behavior than husbands, who tend to not respond or to make statements suggestive of withdrawal, such as irrelevant comments. Disengagement or withdrawal is, in turn, related to later decreases in marital satisfaction. However, inferring reliable gender differences in demand-withdraw patterns would be premature, as recent research shows that the partner who withdraws varies according to which partner desires change. So, for example, when a man desires change, the woman is the one who withdraws. Finally, conflict patterns seem to be relatively stable over time (see Karney & Bradbury, 1995).

Is There a Simple Way to Summarize Research Findings on Marital Conflict?

The findings of the extensive literature on marital conflict can be summarized in terms of a simple ratio: The ratio of agreements to disagreements is greater than 1 for happy couples and less than 1 for unhappy couples. Gottman (1993) utilized this ratio to identify couple types. He observed husbands and wives during conversation, recording each spouse's positive and negative behaviors while speaking, and then calculated the cumulative difference between positive and negative behaviors over time for each spouse. Using the patterns in these difference scores, he distinguished regulated couples (increase in positive speaker behaviors relative to negative behaviors for both spouses over the course of conversation) from nonregulated couples (all other patterns). The regulated couples were more satisfied in their marriage than the nonregulated couples, and also less likely to divorce. Regulated couples displayed positive problem-solving behaviors and positive affect approximately 5 times as often as negative problem-solving behaviors and negative affect, whereas the corresponding ratio was approximately 1:1 for nonregulated couples.

Interestingly, Gottman's perspective corresponds with the findings of two early, often overlooked studies on the reported frequency of sexual intercourse and of marital arguments (Howard & Dawes, 1976; Thornton, 1977). Both showed that the ratio of sexual intercourse to arguments, rather than their base rates, predicted marital satisfaction.

Don't Research Findings on Marital Conflict Just Reflect Common Sense?

The findings described in this article may seem like common sense. However, what we have learned about marital interaction contradicts the long-standing belief that satisfied couples are characterized by a *quid pro quo* principle according to which they exchange positive behavior and instead show that it is dissatisfied spouses who reciprocate one another's (negative) behavior. The astute reader may also be wondering whether couples' behavior in the artificial setting of the laboratory is a good reflection of their behavior in the real world outside the lab. It is therefore important to note that couples who participate in such studies themselves report that their interactions in the lab are reminiscent of their typical interactions. Research also shows that conflict behavior in the lab is similar to conflict behavior in the home; however, laboratory conflicts tend to be less severe, suggesting that research findings underestimate differences between distressed and nondistressed couples.

THE SEEDS OF DISCONTENT

By the early 1980s, researchers were attempting to address the limits of a purely behavioral account of marital conflict. Thus, they began to pay attention to subjective factors, such as thoughts and feelings, which might influence behavioral interactions or the relation between behavior and marital satisfaction. For example, it is now well documented that the tendency to explain a partner's negative behavior (e.g., coming home late from work) in a way that promotes conflict (e.g., "he thinks only about himself and his needs"), rather than in less conflictual ways (e.g., "he was probably caught in traffic"), is related to less effective problem solving, more negative communication in problem-solving discussions, more displays of specific negative affects (e.g., anger) during problem solving, and steeper declines in marital satisfaction over time (Fincham, 2001). Explanations that promote conflict are also related to the tendency to reciprocate a partner's negative behavior, regardless of a couple's marital satisfaction. Research on such subjective factors, like observational research on conflict, has continued to the present time. However, it represents an acceptance and expansion of the behavioral approach that accords conflict a central role in understanding marriage.

In contrast, very recently, some investigators have argued that the role of conflict in marriage should be reconsidered. Longitudinal research shows that conflict accounts for a relatively small portion of the variability in later marital outcomes, suggesting that other factors need to be considered in predicting these outcomes (see Karney & Bradbury, 1995). In addition, studies have demonstrated a troubling number of "reversal effects" (showing that greater conflict is a predictor of improved marriage; see Fincham & Beach, 1999). It is difficult to account for such findings in a field that, for much of its existence, has focused on providing descriptive data at the expense of building theory.

Rethinking the role of conflict also reflects recognition of the fact that most of what we know about conflict behavior comes from observation of problem-solving discussions and that couples experience verbal problem-solving situations infrequently; about 80% of couples report having overt disagreements once a month or less. As a result, cross-sectional studies of distressed versus nondistressed marriages and longitudinal studies of conflict are being increasingly complemented by research designs that focus on how happy marriages become unhappy.

Finally, there is evidence that marital conflict varies according to contextual factors. For example, diary studies illustrate that couples have more stressful marital interactions at home on days of high general life stress than on other days, and at times and places where they are experiencing multiple competing demands; arguments at work are related to marital arguments, and the occurrence of stressful life events is associated with more conflictual problem-solving discussions.

NEW BEGINNINGS: CONFLICT IN CONTEXT

Although domains of interaction other than conflict (e.g., support, companionship) have long been discussed in the marital literature, they are only now emerging from the secondary status accorded to them. This is somewhat ironic given the simple summary of research findings on marital conflict offered earlier, which points to the importance of the context in which conflict occurs.

Conflict in the Context of Support Giving and Affectional Expression

Observational laboratory methods have recently been developed to assess supportive behaviors in interactions in which one spouse talks about a personal issue he or she would like to change and the other is asked to respond as she or he normally would. Behaviors exhibited during such support tasks are only weakly related to the conflict behaviors observed during the problem-solving discussions used to study marital conflict. Supportive spouse behavior is associated with greater marital satisfaction and is more important than negative behavior in determining how supportive the partners perceive an interaction to be. In addition, the amount of supportive behavior partners exhibit is a predictor of later marital stress (i.e., more supportive behavior correlates with less future marital stress), independently of conflict behavior, and when support is poor, there is an increased risk that poor skills in dealing with conflict will lead to later marital deterioration. There is also evidence that support obtained by spouses outside the marriage can influence positively how the spouse behaves within the marriage.

In the context of high levels of affectional expression between spouses, the association between spouses' negative behavior and marital satisfaction decreases significantly. High levels of positive behavior in problem-solving discussions also mitigate the effect of withdrawal or disengagement on later marital satisfaction. Finally, when there are high levels of affectional expression between spouses, the demand-withdraw pattern is unrelated to marital satisfaction, but when affectional expression is average or low, the demand-withdraw pattern is associated with marital dissatisfaction.

Conflict in the Context of Spouses' Backgrounds and Characteristics

Focus on interpersonal behavior as the cause of marital outcomes led to the assumption that the characteristics of individual spouses play no role in those outcomes. However, increasing evidence that contradicts this assumption has generated recent interest in studying how spouses' backgrounds and characteristics might enrich our understanding of marital conflict.

The importance of spouses' characteristics is poignantly illustrated in the intergenerational transmission of divorce. Although there is a tendency for individuals whose parents divorced to get divorced themselves, this tendency varies depending on the offspring's behavior. Divorce rates are higher for offspring who behave in hostile, domineering, and critical ways, compared with offspring who do not behave in this manner.

An individual characteristic that is proving to be particularly informative for understanding marriage comes from recent research on attachment, which aims to address questions about how the experience of relationships early in life affects interpersonal functioning in adulthood. For example, spouses who tend to feel secure in relationships tend to compromise and to take into account both their own and their partner's interests during problem-solving interactions; those who tend to feel anxious or ambivalent in relationships show a greater tendency to oblige their partner, and focus on relationship maintenance, than do those who tend to avoid intimacy in relationships. And spouses who are preoccupied with being completely emotionally intimate in relationships show an elevated level of marital conflict after an involuntary, brief separation from the partner.

Of particular interest for understanding negative reciprocity are the findings that greater commitment is associated with more constructive, accommodative responses to a partner's negative behavior and that the dispositional tendency to forgive is a predictor of spouses' responses to their partners' transgressions; spouses having a greater tendency to forgive are less likely to avoid the partner or retaliate in kind following a transgression by the partner. Indeed, spouses themselves acknowledge that the capacity to seek and grant forgiveness is one of the most important factors contributing to marital longevity and satisfaction.

Conflict in the Context of the Broader Environment

The environments in which marriages are situated and the intersection between interior processes and external factors that impinge upon marriage are important to consider in painting a more textured picture of marital conflict. This is because problem-solving skills and conflict may have little impact on a marriage in the absence of external stressors. External stressors also may influence marriages directly. In particular, nonmarital stressors may lead to an increased number of negative interactions, as illustrated by the fact that economic stress is associated with marital conflict. There is a growing need to identify the stressors and life events that are and are not influential for different couples and for different stages of marriage, to investigate how these events influence conflict, and to clarify how individuals and marriages may inadvertently generate stressful events. In fact, Bradbury, Rogge, and Lawrence (2001), in considering the ecological niche of the couple (i.e., their life events, family constellation, socioeconomic standing, and stressful circumstances), have recently argued that it may be "at least as important to examine the struggle that exists between the couple . . . and the environment they inhabit as it is to examine the interpersonal struggles that are the focus of our work [observation of conflict]" (p. 76).

CONCLUSION

The assumption that conflict management is the key to successful marriage and that conflict skills can be modified in couple therapy has proved useful in propelling the study of marriage into the mainstream of psychology. However, it may have outlived its usefulness, and some researchers are now calling for greater attention to other mechanisms (e.g., spousal social support) that might be responsible for marital outcomes. Indeed, controversy over whether conflict has beneficial or detrimental effects on marriage over time is responsible, in part, for the recent upsurge in longitudinal research on marriage. Notwithstanding diverse opinions on just how central conflict is for understanding marriage, current efforts to study conflict in a broader marital context, which is itself seen as situated in a broader ecological niche, bode well for advancing understanding and leading to more powerful preventive and therapeutic interventions.

Recommended Reading

Bradbury, T.N., Fincham, F.D., & Beach, S.R.H. (2000). Research on the nature and determinants of marital satisfaction: A decade in review. *Journal of Marriage and the Family, 62*, 964–980.

Fincham, F.D., & Beach, S.R. (1999). (See References)

Grych, J.H., & Fincham, F.D. (Eds.). (2001). (See References)

Karney, B.R., & Bradbury, T.N. (1995). (See References)

Acknowledgments—This article was written while the author was supported by grants from the Templeton, Margaret L. Wendt, and J.M. McDonald Foundations.

Note

1. Address correspondence to Frank D. Fincham, Department of Psychology, University at Buffalo, Buffalo, NY 14260.

References

Baucom, D.H., Shoham, V., Mueser, K.T., Daiuto, A.D., & Stickle, T.R. (1998). Empirically supported couple and family interventions for marital distress and adult mental health problems. *Journal of Consulting and Clinical Psychology, 66*, 53–88.

Bradbury, T.N., Rogge, R., & Lawrence, E. (2001). Reconsidering the role of conflict in marriage. In A. Booth, A.C. Crouter, & M. Clements (Eds.), *Couples in conflict* (pp. 59–81). Mahwah, NJ: Erlbaum.

Fincham, F.D. (2001). Attributions and close relationships: From balkanization to integration. In G.J. Fletcher & M. Clark (Eds.), *Blackwell handbook of social psychology* (pp. 3–31). Oxford, England: Blackwell.

Fincham, F.D., & Beach, S.R. (1999). Marital conflict: Implications for working with couples. *Annual Review of Psychology, 50*, 47–77.

Gottman, J.M. (1993). The roles of conflict engagement, escalation, and avoidance in marital interaction: A longitudinal view of five types of couples. *Journal of Consulting and Clinical Psychology, 61*, 6–15.

Grych, J.H., & Fincham, F.D. (Eds.). (2001). *Interparental conflict and child development: Theory, research, and applications.* New York: Cambridge University Press.

Howard, J.W., & Dawes, R.M. (1976). Linear prediction of marital happiness. *Personality and Social Psychology Bulletin, 2*, 478–480.

Karney, B.R., & Bradbury, T.N. (1995). The longitudinal course of marital quality and stability: A review of theory, method, and research. *Psychological Bulletin, 118*, 3–34.

Koerner, K., & Jacobson, N.J. (1994). Emotion and behavior in couple therapy. In S.M. Johnson & L.S. Greenberg (Eds.), *The heart of the matter: Perspectives on emotion in marital therapy* (pp. 207–226). New York: Brunner/Mazel.

Raush, H.L., Barry, W.A., Hertel, R.K., & Swain, M.A. (1974). *Communication, conflict, and marriage*. San Francisco: Jossey-Bass.

Thornton, B. (1977). Toward a linear prediction of marital happiness. *Personality and Social Psychology Bulletin, 3*, 674–676.

Weiss, R.L., & Heyman, R.E. (1997). A clinical-research overview of couple interactions. In W.K. Halford & H. Markman (Eds.), *The clinical handbook of marriage and couples interventions* (pp. 13–41). Brisbane, Australia: Wiley.

Forgiveness: Who Does It and How Do They Do It?

Michael E. McCullough[1]
Department of Psychology, Southern Methodist University, Dallas, Texas

Abstract

Forgiveness is a suite of prosocial motivational changes that occurs after a person has incurred a transgression. People who are inclined to forgive their transgressors tend to be more agreeable, more emotionally stable, and, some research suggest, more spiritually or religiously inclined than people who do not tend to forgive their transgressors. Several psychological processes appear to foster or inhibit forgiveness. These processes include empathy for the transgressor, generous attributions and appraisals regarding the transgression and transgressor, and rumination about the transgression. Interpreting these findings in light of modern trait theory would help to create a more unified understanding of how personality might influence forgiveness.

Keywords

forgiveness; research; review; personality; theory

Relating to others—whether strangers, friends, or family—inevitably exposes people to the risk of being offended or harmed by those other people. Throughout history and across cultures, people have developed many strategies for responding to such transgressions. Two classic responses are avoidance and revenge—seeking distance from the transgressor or opportunities to harm the transgressor in kind. These responses are normal and common, but can have negative consequences for individuals, relationships, and perhaps society as a whole.

Psychologists have been investigating interpersonal transgressions and their aftermath for years. However, although many of the world's religions have advocated the concept of forgiveness as a productive response to such transgressions (McCullough & Worthington, 1999), scientists have begun only recently to devote sustained attention to forgiveness. Nevertheless, researchers have made substantial progress in illuminating forgiveness during this short amount of time.

WHAT IS FORGIVENESS?

Most psychologists concur with Enright, Gassin, and Wu (1992) that forgiveness is distinct from pardon (which is more apposite to the legal realm), condonation (which implies justifying the transgression), and excusing (which implies recognition that the transgressor had a good reason for committing the transgression). Most scholars also concur that forgiveness is distinct from reconciliation—a term implying restoration of a relationship. But what is forgiveness foundationally? The first definition for "forgive" in *Webster's New Universal Unabridged Dictionary* (1983) is "to give up resentment against or the desire to punish; to stop being angry with; to pardon" (p. 720). Although this definition conflates the concepts of forgiveness and pardon, it nearly suffices as an adequate psychological definition because it points to what is perhaps the essence of forgiveness: prosocial motivational change on the victim's part. By using the term "prosocial," I am suggesting that when people forgive, they become less motivated to harm their transgressor (or their relationship with the transgressor) and, simultaneously, become more motivated to act in ways that will benefit the transgressor (or their relationship with the transgressor).

My colleagues and I have assumed that most people are motivated (at least initially) to respond to transgressions with other forms of negative behavior—particularly, to avoid contact with the transgressor and to seek revenge. When people forgive, they counteract or modulate these motivations to avoid or seek revenge so that the probability of restoring benevolent and harmonious interpersonal relations with their transgressors is increased (McCullough, Bellah, Kilpatrick, & Johnson, 2001; McCullough et al., 1998; McCullough, Worthington, & Rachal, 1997). When people indicate that they have forgiven a transgressor, we believe they are indicating that their perceptions of the transgression and transgressor no longer stimulate motivations for avoidance and revenge. Instead, a forgiver experiences the return of benevolent, constructive motivations regarding the transgressor. In this conceptualization, forgiveness is not a motivation per se, but rather, a complex of prosocial changes in one's motivations.

Locating forgiveness at the motivational level, rather than at the level of overt behaviors, accommodates the fact that many people who would claim to have forgiven someone who has harmed them might not behave in any particularly new and benevolent way toward their transgressors. Forgiveness might not cause an employee who forgives her boss for an insult to behave any less negatively toward the boss: Avoidance and revenge in the workplace can put one's job at risk, so most people are probably careful to inhibit the expression of such negative motivations in the first place, regardless of how strong they might have been as a result of the transgression. The motivational definition does imply, however, that the employee would experience a reduced *potential* for avoidant and vengeful behavior (and an increased potential for benevolent behavior) toward the boss, which might or might not be expressed overtly. A motivational definition also accommodates the fact that someone can make public gestures of forgiveness toward his or her transgressor even in the absence of such prosocial motivational changes.

How would one describe the sorts of people who tend to engage in the motivational transformations collectively called forgiveness? What psychological processes appear to help people forgive? Several research teams have been investigating these questions in detail. In this article, I describe what psychological science has revealed about who tends to forgive and the psychological processes that may foster or hinder forgiveness for specific transgressions.

THE FORGIVING PERSONALITY

Researchers have found that the disposition to forgive is correlated (positively or negatively) with a broad array of variables, including several personality traits, psychological symptoms, moral emotions, hope, and self-esteem (e.g., see Berry,

Worthington, Parrott, O'Connor, & Wade, in press; Tangney, Fee, Reinsmith, Boone, & Lee, 1999). For simplicity, it is useful to reduce this potentially bewildering array of correlates to a smaller set of higher-order personality factors, such as those in the Five Factor (or Big Five) personality taxonomy (McCrae & Costa, 1999). Several recent research efforts suggest that the disposition to forgive may be related most strongly to two of these higher-order dimensions: agreeableness and emotional stability (Ashton, Paunonen, Helmes, & Jackson, 1998; Berry et al., in press; McCullough et al., 2001; McCullough & Hoyt, 1999). Some evidence also suggests that the disposition to forgive is related positively to religiousness and spirituality.

Agreeableness

Agreeableness is a personality dimension that incorporates traits such as altruism, empathy, care, and generosity. Highly agreeable people tend to thrive in the interpersonal realm and experience less conflict in relationships than less agreeable people do. Trait theorists and researchers have long been aware that agreeable people typically are rated highly on descriptors such as "forgiving" and low on descriptors such as "vengeful." Research specifically on the disposition to forgive has also confirmed the agreeableness-forgiveness association (Ashton et al., 1998; McCullough & Hoyt,1999).

People who appear dispositionally inclined to forgive also possess many of the lower-order traits that agreeableness subsumes. For instance, compared with people who are not inclined to forgive, they tend to be less exploitative of and more empathic toward others (Tangney et al., 1999). They also report higher levels of moral responsibility and demonstrate a greater tendency to share resources with people who have been rude and inconsiderate to them (Ashton et al., 1998).

Emotional Stability

Emotional stability is a personality dimension that involves low vulnerability to experiences of negative emotion. Emotionally stable people also tend not to be moody or overly sensitive. Several studies demonstrate that people who are high in emotional stability score higher on measures of the disposition to forgive than do their less emotionally stable counterparts (Ashton et al., 1998; Berry et al., in press; McCullough & Hoyt,1999).

Religiousness and Spirituality

A third personality trait that might be related to the disposition to forgive—and one that recent research suggests is empirically distinct from the Big Five personality factors—is religiousness or spirituality. A review of results from seven studies suggested that people who consider themselves to be highly religious or spiritual tend to value forgiveness more highly and see themselves as more forgiving than do people who consider themselves less religious or spiritual (McCullough & Worthington, 1999).

Despite the consistency of the existing evidence on this point, few studies have addressed whether religiousness and spirituality are associated with forgiving specific transgressors for specific, real-life transgressions. Indeed, studies addressing this issue hint that religiousness-spirituality and forgiveness of individual transgressions may be essentially unrelated (e.g., McCullough & Worthington, 1999). Therefore, it is possible that religious and spiritual people are no more forgiving than are less religious and spiritual people in real life, but only believe themselves (or aspire) to be highly forgiving. The connection of religiousness and spirituality to forgiveness of actual transgressions remains to be investigated more fully (McCullough & Worthington, 1999).

WHAT DO PEOPLE DO WHEN THEY FORGIVE?

Recent research has also helped to illuminate the psychological processes that people employ when they forgive. The processes that have been studied to date include empathy, attributions and appraisals, and rumination.

Empathy for the Transgressor

Empathy has been defined by some scholars as the vicarious experience of another person's emotional state, and by others as a specific emotion characterized by compassion, tenderness, and sympathy. Empathy (defined as a specific emotional state) for a particular transgressor correlates strongly with the extent to which a victim forgives the transgressor for a particular transgression. In several correlational studies (McCullough et al., 1997, 1998; Worthington et al., 2000), people's reports of the extent to which they had forgiven a specific transgressor were highly correlated with the extent to which they experienced empathy for the transgressor.

Empathy also helps explain why some social-psychological variables influence forgiveness. The well-known effect of transgressors' apologies on victims' likelihood of forgiving apparently is almost totally mediated by the effects of the apologies on victims' empathy for the transgressors (McCullough et al., 1997, 1998). When transgressors apologize, they implicitly express some degree of fallibility and vulnerability, which might cause victims to feel empathic, thereby motivating them to forgive the transgressors. Also, research on psychological interventions designed to help people forgive specific transgressors has revealed that empathy fosters forgiveness. Indeed, empathy for the transgressor is the only psychological variable that has, to date, been shown to facilitate forgiveness when induced experimentally (McCullough et al., 1997; Worthington et al., 2000), although experimental research on this issue is still in its infancy.

Generous Attributions and Appraisals

Another factor associated with the extent to which someone forgives a specific transgressor is the extent to which the victim makes generous attributions and appraisals about the transgression and transgressor. Compared with people who have not forgiven their transgressors, people who have forgiven their transgressors appraise the transgressors as more likable (Bradfield & Aquino, 1999), and the transgressors' explanations for the transgressions as more adequate and honest (Shapiro, 1991). In such situations, forgiveness is also related to the victim's appraisal of the severity of the transgression (Shapiro, 1991). People who tend to forgive their spouses also tend to attribute less responsibility to their spouses for their negative behavior than do people who do not tend to forgive their spouses (Fincham, 2000). Thus, forgivers apparently are inclined to give their transgressors "the benefit of the doubt." Whether the correlations between appraisals-attributions and forgiveness reflect the causal effects of attributional and appraisal processes, or simply reflect victims' accurate perceptions of the actual qualities of transgressors and transgressions that cause them to be more or less forgivable, remains to be explored more fully in the future.

Rumination About the Transgression

A third factor associated with the extent to which someone forgives a specific transgressor is the extent to which the victim ruminates about the transgression. Rumination, or the tendency to experience intrusive thoughts, affects, and images about past events, appears to hinder forgiveness. The more people brood about a transgression, the higher are their levels of revenge and avoidance motivation (McCullough et al., 1998, 2001). In a recent longitudinal study, my colleagues and I also found that victims who continued to ruminate about a particular transgression made considerably less progress in forgiving the transgressor during an 8-week follow-up period (McCullough et al., 2001). This longitudinal evidence indicates that the degree to which people reduce their ruminations about a particular transgression over time is a good predictor of how much progress they will make in forgiving their transgressor.

FUTURE RESEARCH AND THEORY

So far, research has shown that people who are more agreeable, more emotionally stable, and (possibly) more spiritual or religious have a stronger disposition to forgive than do their less agreeable, less emotionally stable, and less spiritually and religiously inclined counterparts. Moreover, research has shown that empathizing with the transgressor, making generous attributions and appraisals regarding the transgressor and transgression, and refraining from rumination about the transgression are associated with the extent to which a victim forgives a specific transgressor.

An interesting step for future research on the personality factors and psychological mechanisms associated with forgiveness would be to explore the specific cognitive and emotional habits of agreeable, emotionally stable, and (perhaps) religiously or spiritually inclined people that predispose them to forgive. For example, agreeableness reflects a tendency toward kindness and prosociality, so perhaps agreeable people are particularly inclined to experience empathy for their transgressors. They might also be inclined to perceive the transgressions they have incurred as less intentional and less severe, and their transgressors as more likable and contrite, than do less agreeable people.

Likewise, emotionally stable people might find forgiveness easier than people who are less emotionally stable because of perceptual processes: Emotionally stable people perceive many environmental factors—including physical pain and negative life events—less negatively than do less emotionally stable people. Emotionally stable people also ruminate less about negative life events. Research addressing such potential links between personality traits and psychological processes would enrich psychology's understanding of how personality might influence the extent to which people forgive particular transgressors.

Such empirical advances should be coupled with theoretical refinements. It might prove particularly useful to frame such investigations in the context of modern trait theory. Trait theorists such as McCrae and Costa (1999) have advocated for conceptualizing the empirical links between traits and real-life behavioral proclivities as causal connections that reflect how *basic tendencies* (i.e., traits) are "channelized" into *characteristic adaptations,* or approaches to negotiating life within one's own cultural and environmental context. Using McCrae and Costa's framework to theorize about forgiveness might explain how the basic, biologically based tendencies that are reflected in measures of higher-order personality dimensions lead people to use forgiveness to address certain problems encountered in daily life—namely, interpersonal transgressions.

Such a theoretical framework could lead to other interesting questions: Insofar as forgiveness can be viewed as a characteristic adaptation of agreeable and emotionally stable people, why might agreeable and emotionally stable people be predisposed to use forgiveness for navigating their social worlds? Is forgiveness a by-product of other characteristic adaptations resulting from agreeableness and emotional stability (such as a capacity for empathy, a tendency to make generous attributions regarding the negative behavior of other people, or an ability to refrain from rumination about negative events)? Or is it more accurate to view forgiveness as a goal to which agreeable and emotionally stable people actively strive, using the other characteristic psychological adaptations (e.g., capacity for empathy, tendency to form generous attributions, disinclination to ruminate) associated with agreeableness and emotional stability as footholds on the climb toward that goal? Answers to these questions would raise even more interesting questions. In any case, more sophisticated theorizing would transform this new area of research from simply a search for the correlates of forgiveness to a quest to truly understand forgiveness and its place in human personality and social functioning.

Recommended Reading

McCrae, R.R., & Costa, P.T., Jr. (1999). (See References)

McCullough, M.E., Bellah, C.G., Kilpatrick, S.D., & Johnson, J.L. (2001). (See References)

McCullough, M.E., Pargament, K.I., & Thoresen, C.T. (Eds.). (2000). *Forgiveness: Theory, research, and practice.* New York: Guilford.

McCullough, M.E., Rachal, K.C., Sandage, S.J., Worthington, E.L., Brown, S.W., & Hight, T.L. (1998). (See References)

McCullough, M.E., & Worthington, E.L. (1999). (See References)

Note

1. Address correspondence to Michael McCullough, Department of Psychology, Southern Methodist University, PO Box 750442, Dallas, TX 75275-0442; e-mail: mikem@mail.smu.edu.

References

Ashton, M.C., Paunonen, S.V., Helmes, E., & Jackson, D.N. (1998). Kin altruism, reciprocal altruism, and the Big Five personality factors. *Evolution and Human Behavior, 19,* 243-255.

Berry, J.W., Worthington, E.L., Parrott, L., O'Connor, L.E., & Wade, N.G. (in press). Dispositional forgivingness: Development and construct validity of the Transgression Narrative Test of Forgivingness (TNTF). *Personality and Social Psychology Bulletin.*

Bradfield, M., & Aquino, K. (1999). The effects of blame attributions and offender likeableness on forgiveness and revenge in the workplace. *Journal of Management, 25,* 607-631.

Enright, R.D., Gassin, E.A., & Wu, C. (1992). Forgiveness: A developmental view. *Journal of Moral Education, 21,* 99-114.

Fincham, F.D. (2000). The kiss of the porcupines: From attributing responsibility to forgiving. *Personal Relationships, 7,* 1-23.

McCrae, R.R., & Costa, P.T., Jr. (1999). A five-factor theory of personality. In L.A. Pervin & O.P. John (Eds.), *Handbook of personality: Theory and research* (pp. 139-153). New York: Guilford.

McCullough, M.E., Bellah, C.G., Kilpatrick, S.D., & Johnson, J.L. (2001). Vengefulness: Relationships with forgiveness, rumination, well-being, and the Big Five. *Personality and Social Psychology Bulletin, 27,* 601-610.

McCullough, M.E., & Hoyt, W.T. (1999, August). *Recovering the person from interpersonal forgiving.* Paper presented at the annual meeting of the American Psychological Association, Boston.

McCullough, M.E., Rachal, K.C., Sandage, S.J., Worthington, E.L., Brown, S.W., & Hight, T.L. (1998). Interpersonal forgiving in close relationships: II. Theoretical elaboration and measurement. *Journal of Personality and Social Psychology, 75,* 1586-1603.

McCullough, M.E., & Worthington, E.L. (1999). Religion and the forgiving personality. *Journal of Personality, 67,* 1141-1164.

McCullough, M.E., Worthington, E.L., & Rachal, K.C.(1997). Interpersonal forgiving in close relationships. *Journal of Personality and Social Psychology, 73,* 321-336.

Shapiro, D.L. (1991). The effects of explanations on negative reactions to deceit. *Administrative Science Quarterly, 36,* 614-630.

Tangney, J., Fee, R., Reinsmith, C., Boone, A.L., & Lee, N. (1999, August). *Assessing individual differences in the propensity to forgive.* Paper presented at the annual meeting of the American Psychological Association, Boston.

Webster's new universal unabridged dictionary. (1983). New York: Dorset and Baker.

Worthington, E.L., Kurusu, T.A., Collins, W., Berry, J.W., Ripley, J.S., & Baier, S.N. (2000). Forgiving usually takes time: A lesson learned by studying interventions to promote forgiveness. *Journal of Psychology and Theology, 28,* 3-20.

Critical Thinking Questions

1. Most of the papers in this section discuss processes that can be situated in the broader context of the nature vs. nurture debate. Discuss where these processes stand on this debate as well as your own view on how one can reconcile them.

2. The notion that individual differences in affect, cognition, and behavior may become visible most clearly in particular situations is illustrated by several papers in this section, most notably by Andersen & Berk, Brody, and Fincham. Discuss the similarities and differences in how each of these papers deals with the ways in which the characteristics of the person and of the situation influence each other and interact in their joint effects on behavior. At what level of specificity are situations being conceptualized?

3. The idea that the effect of broad personality traits is mediated by more specific social-cognitive and affective processes runs as a common theme through several papers in this section. Identify those articles and for each discuss the traits being examined and the process level variables associated with those traits. Discuss what if anything is gained from such a process-level analysis. (Does it add to our understanding and prediction of behavior?)

4. Based on the Fincham and the McCullough findings, describe the factors and processes that contribute to conflict vs. harmony in a marital relationship. Explain what are the contributions to these processes by personality factors. Based on both articles (and other things you have learned about personality processes thus far), what do you think are the most fruitful avenues for intervention? (I.e., what factors or processes would you try to change and why?) [Note: you might also want to consider the findings by Andersen and Berk in your answer.]

5. Drawing from all three of the preceding sections (biological, intrapersonal, and interpersonal mechanisms), think about how and to what degree people contribute to "constructing their own realities." Provide examples of the role of biological factors and intrapersonal mechanisms, as well as some interpersonal factors. How does this analysis contribute to the question of stability of personality (see Section One)?

Implications of Personality for Well-Being

The overarching goal of psychology is to predict human behavior. For personality psychology no goal is more important than the prediction of individuals' psychological and physical well-being. This goal requires that we understand the mechanisms that account for adaptive as well as maladaptive behavior, adjustment as well as maladjustment, risk as well as resiliency. It is only through examining human behavior both in its negative and positive manifestations that we can ultimately put ourselves in a position to intervene in the negative manifestations and to change suboptimal functioning towards more positive outcomes. This last section brings together a selection of seven articles discussing various programs of research that share this common goal. While the preceding sections of the reader included a number of articles that have discussed mechanisms relevant to negative outcomes (such as those related to impulsivity, stress reactivity, insecure attachment styles, and so on), the emphasis of the majority of the articles in this section is on the psychological mechanisms and personality traits that predict well-being and positive outcomes.

The section begins with Werner's (1995) discussion of the predictors of long-term resilience, psychological adjustment, and positive social outcomes in high-risk children growing up in chronic poverty. Resilient children tend to have easy-going temperaments and good communication skills. They are engaging and interesting to adults and their peers alike and they tend to have high self-confidence, striking a balance between autonomy and relatedness. These within-individual protective factors also coexist with protective factors that reside within the family interactions and the community, highlighting the social and relational nature of resiliency.

The second article by Asher and Paquette (2002) describes research on the types of developmental experiences that lead to chronic loneliness in children. Not surprisingly, peer rejection and overt victimization are the leading causes of loneliness in children. However, loneliness cannot be explained simply by whether or not children have friends. Rather it is the subjective perceptions of the quality of one's social connectedness (i.e., level of intimacy, support within the relationship) that predict loneliness. Purely objective assessments of children's peer relationships, therefore, are not sufficient in fully explaining its dynamics. To better understand why some children feel lonely even among friends whereas others do not experience loneliness despite their lack of close friendships, an examination of the relevant intra-individual mechanisms including children's expectations, appraisals, and beliefs about their social connections is necessary.

The following article focuses on just such intra-individual mechanisms, in that Folkman & Moskowitz (2000) examine cognitive mechanisms that underlie positive coping in the face of stress. They find that

165

coping by positive reappraisal, such as discovering opportunities for personal growth and finding new meaning in the stressor, and/or by engaging in instrumental behaviors that give the individual a sense of control and self-efficacy, are strategies that increase positive affect and effective coping even in the midst of dealing with an uncontrollable stressor such as caring for a loved one with terminal illness. While this research answers many important questions about positive coping, it also raises many new ones. Is it the frequency or the intensity with which positive emotions are experienced that is related to effective long-term coping? What are the dispositional variables that predict its use? Clearly these are questions worth exploring in future research.

Complementing the preceding article on positive coping, Keltner, Kring, and Bonanno (1999) investigate the impact of facial expressions of positive affect on the well-being of individuals grieving for the early death of their spouse. Expression of positive emotions, such as laughter and smiles, while talking about the deceased in early days of individuals' loss predict lower grief severity even a year after the loss. This argues against the Freudian notion that expression of negative emotions is necessary for effective "working through" of emotional experiences. While not conclusive, the mechanism for this effect may be that expressions of positive emotions enhance later well-being, at least in part, by eliciting more liking of the individual in others. Overall, then, the central thesis of this article is that facial expressions of emotion not only reflect intra-individual processes but also mediate social and interpersonal interactions, which in turn affect individuals' well-being.

Further evidence that subjective well-being has a lot to do with people's characteristic ways of processing emotional stimuli and events is provided in the next article. In a large meta-analysis of 137 personality traits, examining their link to subjective well-being (SWB), DeNeve (1999) found that happiness was related to personality traits in several domains. The most unhappy people tended to be those who avoided threatening information, denied negative emotions although they experienced them frequently, and who believed that they did not have control over the events in their lives. Happy people were those who had characteristically positive emotionality, explained events in optimistic, adaptive ways, and who had the desire and ability to form good relationships. Although this work is purely correlational, potential intra-individual and interpersonal mechanisms by which personality is linked to SWB that need to be followed up in future work are clearly implied in these findings.

In DeNeve's meta-analysis, although personality factors were strong predictors of SWB, they were second to one other factor, namely self-reported physical health. Given this, Gottfredson and Dreary's (2004) finding that intelligence (IQ) is a strong predictor of health and longevity is particularly interesting. In contrast to the usual assumption that IQ is simply a proxy for socioeconomic status (SES), these researchers find that the relationship holds, even after controlling for SES. A convincing argument is made that intelligence and problem-solving skills may facilitate individuals' self health-care behaviors by way of increasing people's understanding of the complexities of self-care, such as engaging in prevention, self-monitoring, self-medicating, and adhering to treatment. These findings show how even a largely biological trait such as IQ impacts well-being via specific mediating mechanisms and as such has important implications for prevention and intervention-related healthcare policy and practice.

This section concludes with an article on a prevalent and serious physical and mental health problem in today's Western societies—eating disorders. Thompson and Stice's (2001) systematic investigations on the topic have uncovered that a primary risk factor for these disorders is internalization of thin-ideal standards for attractiveness. It appears that society and significant others, perhaps inadvertently, communicate expectations concerning thinness; attitudes that are then internalized by some individuals, which in turn, predict eating pathology, increased dieting, and body dissatisfaction. As we have now seen many times, appraisals and social processes are once again key to understanding the link between intra-individual processes and outcomes. What still remains to be understood are what factors promote such internalizations of societal attitudes, as well as what may protect against them.

In summary, together the papers in this section address the relationship between personality and well-being by discussing some of its intrapersonal, interpersonal, and societal mediators. They emphasize the role of social-cognitive mechanisms and their interactions with the environment in promoting or hindering individuals' effective adaptation to their life circumstances.

Resilience in Development

Emmy E. Werner

During the past decade, a number of investigators from different disciplines—child development, psychology, psychiatry, and sociology—have focused on the study of children and youths who overcame great odds. These researchers have used the term resilience to describe three kinds of phenomena: good developmental outcomes despite high-risk status, sustained competence under stress, and recovery from trauma. Under each of these conditions, behavioral scientists have focused their attention on protective factors, or mechanisms that moderate (ameliorate) a person's reaction to a stressful situation or chronic adversity so that his or her adaptation is more successful than would be the case if the protective factors were not present.[1]

So far, only a relatively small number of studies have focused on children who were exposed to biological insults. More numerous in the current research literature are studies of resilient children who grew up in chronic poverty, were exposed to parental psychopathology, or experienced the breakup of their family or serious caregiving deficits. There has also been a growing body of literature on resilience in children who have endured the horrors of contemporary wars.

Despite the heterogeneity of all these studies, one can begin to discern a common core of individual dispositions and sources of support that contribute to resilience in development. These protective buffers appear to transcend ethnic, social-class, and geographic boundaries. They also appear to make a more profound impact on the life course of individuals who grow up in adversity than do specific risk factors or stressful life events.

Most studies of individual resilience and protective factors in children have been short-term, focusing on middle childhood and adolescence. An exception is the Kauai Longitudinal Study, with which I have been associated during the past three decades.[2] This study has involved a team of pediatricians, psychologists, and public-health and social workers who have monitored the impact of a variety of biological and psychosocial risk factors, stressful life events, and protective factors on the development of a multiethnic cohort of 698 children born in 1955 on the "Garden Island" in the Hawaiian chain. These individuals were followed, with relatively little attrition, from the prenatal period through birth to ages 1, 2, 10, 18, and 32.

Some 30% of the survivors in this study population were considered high-risk children because they were born in chronic poverty, had experienced perinatal stress, and lived in family environments troubled by chronic discord, divorce, or parental psychopathology. Two thirds of the children who had experienced four or more such risk factors by age 2 developed serious learning or behavior problems by age 10 or had delinquency records, mental health problems, or pregnancies by age 18. But one third of the children who had experi-

Emmy E. Werner is Professor of Human Development at the University of California, Davis. Address correspondence to Emmy E. Werner, Department of Applied Behavioral Sciences, University of California, Davis, 2321 Hart Hall, Davis, CA 95616.

enced four or more such risk factors developed instead into competent, confident, and caring adults.

PROTECTIVE FACTORS WITHIN THE INDIVIDUAL

Infancy and Early Childhood

Our findings with these resilient children are consistent with the results of several other longitudinal studies which have reported that young children with good coping abilities under adverse conditions have temperamental characteristics that elicit positive responses from a wide range of caregivers. The resilient boys and girls in the Kauai study were consistently characterized by their mothers as active, affectionate, cuddly, good-natured, and easy to deal with. Egeland and his associates observed similar dispositions among securely attached infants of abusing mothers in the Minnesota Mother-Child Interaction Project,[3] and Moriarty found the same qualities among infants with congenital defects at the Menninger Foundation.[4] Such infants were alert, easy to soothe, and able to elicit support from a nurturant family member. An "easy" temperament and the ability to actively recruit competent adult caregivers were also observed by Elder and his associates[5] in the resourceful children of the Great Depression.

By the time they reach preschool age, resilient children appear to have developed a coping pattern that combines autonomy with an ability to ask for help when needed. These characteristics are also predictive of resilience in later years.

Middle Childhood and Adolescence

When the resilient children in the Kauai Longitudinal Study were in elementary school, their teachers were favorably impressed by their communication and problem-solving skills. Although these children were not particularly gifted, they used whatever talents they had effectively. Usually they had a special interest or a hobby they could share with a friend, and that gave them a sense of pride. These interests and activities were not narrowly sex typed. Both the boys and the girls grew into adolescents who were outgoing and autonomous, but also nurturant and emotionally sensitive.

Similar findings have been reported by Anthony, who studied the resilient offspring of mentally ill parents in St. Louis;[6] by Felsman and Vaillant, who followed successful boys from a high-crime neighborhood in Boston into adulthood;[7] and by Rutter and Quinton, who studied the lives of British girls who had been institutionalized in childhood, but managed to become well-functioning adults and caring mothers.[8]

Most studies of resilient children and youths report that intelligence and scholastic competence are positively associated with the ability to overcome great odds. It stands to reason that youngsters who are better able to appraise stressful life events correctly are also better able to figure out strategies for coping with adversity, either through their own efforts or by actively reaching out to other people for help. This finding has been replicated in studies of Asian-American, Caucasian, and African-American children.[2,9,10]

Other salient protective factors that operated in the lives of the resilient youths on Kauai were a belief in their own effectiveness (an internal locus of control) and a positive self-concept. Such characteristics were also found by Farrington among successful and law-abiding British youngsters who grew up in high-crime neighborhoods in London,[11] and by Wallerstein and her associates among American children who coped effectively with the breakup of their parents' marriages.[12]

PROTECTIVE FACTORS WITHIN THE FAMILY

Despite the burden of chronic poverty, family discord, or parental psychopathology, a child identified as resilient usually has had the opportunity to establish a close bond with at least one competent and emotionally stable person who is attuned to his or her needs. The stress-resistant children in the Kauai Longitudinal Study, the well-functioning offspring of child abusers in the Minnesota Mother-Child Interaction Project, the resilient children of psychotic parents studied by Anthony in St. Louis, and the youngsters who coped effectively with the breakup of their parents' marriages in Wallerstein's studies of divorce all had received enough good nurturing to establish a basic sense of trust.[2,3,6,12]

Much of this nurturing came from substitute caregivers within the extended family, such as grandparents and older siblings. Resilient children seem to be especially adept at recruiting such surrogate parents. In turn, they themselves are often called upon to take care of younger siblings and to practice acts of "required helpfulness" for members of their family who are ill or incapacitated.[2]

Both the Kauai Longitudinal Study and Block and Gjerde's studies of ego-resilient children[9] found characteristic child-rearing orientations that appear to promote resiliency differentially in boys and girls. Resilient boys tend to come from households with structure and rules, where a male serves as a model of identification (father, grandfather, or older brother), and where there is some encouragement of emotional expressiveness. Resilient girls, in contrast, tend to come from households that combine an emphasis on risk taking and independence with reliable support from a female caregiver, whether mother, grandmother, or older sister. The example of a mother who is gainfully and steadily employed appears to be an especially powerful model of identification for resilient girls.[2] A number of studies of resilient children from a wide variety of socioeconomic and ethnic backgrounds have also noted that the families of these children held religious beliefs that provided stability and meaning in times of hardship and adversity.[2,6,10]

PROTECTIVE FACTORS IN THE COMMUNITY

The Kauai Longitudinal Study and a number of other prospective studies in the United States have shown that resilient youngsters tend to rely on peers and elders in the community as sources of emotional support and seek them out for counsel and comfort in times of crisis.[2,6]

Favorite teachers are often positive role models. All of the resilient high-risk children in the Kauai study could point to at least one teacher who was an important source of support. These teachers listened to the children, challenged them, and rooted for them—whether in grade school, high school, or community college. Similar findings have been reported by Wallerstein and her associates from their long-term observations of youngsters who coped effectively with their parents' divorces[12] and by Rutter and his associates from their studies of inner-city schools in London.[13]

Finally, in the Kauai study, we found that the opening of opportunities at major life transitions enabled the majority of the high-risk children who had a troubled adolescence to rebound in their 20s and early 30s. Among the most potent second chances for such youths were adult education programs in community colleges, voluntary military service, active participation in a church community, and a supportive friend or marital partner. These protective buffers were also observed by Elder in the adult lives of the children of the Great Depression,[14] by Furstenberg and his associates in the later lives of black teenage mothers,[15] and by Farrington[11] and Felsman and Vaillant[7] in the adult lives of young men who had grown up in high-crime neighborhoods in London and Boston.

PROTECTIVE FACTORS: A SUMMARY

Several clusters of protective factors have emerged as recurrent themes in the lives of children who overcome great odds. Some protective factors are characteristics of the individual: Resilient children are engaging to other people, adults and peers alike; they have good communication and problem-solving skills, including the ability to recruit substitute caregivers; they have a talent or hobby that is valued by their elders or peers; and they have faith that their own actions can make a positive difference in their lives.

Another factor that enhances resilience in development is having affectional ties that encourage trust, autonomy, and initiative. These ties are often provided by members of the extended family. There are also support systems in the community that reinforce and reward the competencies of resilient children and provide them with positive role models: caring neighbors, teachers, elder mentors, youth workers, and peers.

LINKS BETWEEN PROTECTIVE FACTORS AND SUCCESSFUL ADAPTATION IN HIGH-RISK CHILDREN AND YOUTHS

In the Kauai study, when we examined the links between protective factors within the individual and outside sources of support, we noted a certain continuity in the life course of the high-risk individuals who successfully overcame a variety of childhood adversities. Their individual dispositions led them to select or construct environments that, in turn, reinforced and sustained their active approach to life and rewarded their special competencies.

Although the sources of support available to the individuals in their childhood homes were modestly linked to the quality of the individuals' adaptation as adults, their competencies, temperament, and self-esteem had a greater impact. Many resilient high-risk youths on Kauai left the adverse conditions of

171

their childhood homes after high school and sought environments they found more compatible. In short, they picked their own niches.

Our findings lend some empirical support to Scarr and McCartney's theory[16] about how people make their own environment. Scarr and McCartney proposed three types of effects of people's genes on their environment: passive, evocative, and active. Because parents provide both children's genes and their rearing environments, children's genes are necessarily correlated with their own environments. This is the passive type of genotype-environment effect. The evocative type refers to the fact that a person's partially heritable characteristics, such as intelligence, personality, and physical attractiveness, evoke certain responses from other people. Finally, a person's interests, talents, and personality (genetically variable traits) may lead him or her to select or create particular environments; this is called an active genotype-environment effect. In line with this theory, there was a shift from passive to active effects as the youths and young adults in the Kauai study left stressful home environments and sought extrafamilial environments (at school, at work, in the military) that they found more compatible and stimulating. Genotype-environment effects of the evocative sort tended to persist throughout the different life stages we studied, as individuals' physical characteristics, temperament, and intelligence elicited differential responses from other people (parents, teachers, peers).

IMPLICATIONS

So far, most studies of resilience have focused on children and youths who have "pulled themselves up by their bootstraps," with informal support by kith and kin, not on recipients of intervention services. Yet there are some lessons such children can teach society about effective intervention: if we want to help vulnerable youngsters become more resilient, we need to decrease their exposure to potent risk factors and increase their competencies and self-esteem, as well as the sources of support they can draw upon.

In *Within Our Reach*, Schorr has isolated a set of common characteristics of social programs that have successfully prevented poor outcomes for children who grew up in high-risk families.[17] Such programs typically offer a broad spectrum of health, education, and family support services, cross professional boundaries, and view the child in the context of the family, and the family in the context of the community. They provide children with sustained access to competent and caring adults, both professionals and volunteers, who teach them problem-solving skills, enhance their communication skills and self-esteem, and provide positive role models for them.

There is an urgent need for more systematic evaluations of such programs to illuminate the process by which we can forge a chain of protective factors that enables vulnerable children to become competent, confident, and caring individuals, despite the odds of chronic poverty or a medical or social disability. Future research on risk and resiliency needs to acquire a cross-cultural perspective as well. We need to know more about individual dispositions and sources of support that transcend cultural boundaries and operate effectively in a variety of high-risk contexts.

Notes

1. A.S. Masten, K.M. Best, and N. Gannezy, Resilience and development: Contributions from the study of children who overcame adversity, *Development and Psychopathology*, 2, 425–444 (1991).

2. All results from this study that are discussed in this review were reported in E.E. Werner, Risk resilience, and recovery: Perspectives from the Kauai Longitudinal Study, *Development and Psychopathology*, 5, 503 515 (1993)

3. B. Egeland. D. Jacobvitz, and L.A. Sroufe, Breaking the cycle of child abuse, *Child Development*, 59, 1080–1088 (1988.)

4. A. Moriarty, John, a boy who acquired resilience, in *The Invulnerable Child*, E.I. Anthony and B.J. Cohler, Eds. (Guilford Press, New York, 1987).

5. G.H. Elder, K. Liker, and C.E. Cross, Parent-child behavior in the Great Depression, in *Life Span Development and Behavior*, Vol. 6. T.B. Baltes and O.G. Brim, Jr.. Eds. (Academic Press, New York, 1984).

6. E.J. Anthony, Children at risk for psychosis growing up successfully, in *The Invulnerable Child*, E.J. Anthony and B.J. Cohler, Eds. (Guilford Press, New York, 1987).

7. J.K. Felsman and G.E. Vaillant, Resilient children as adults: A 40 year study, in *The Invulnerable Child*, E.J. Anthony and B.J. Cohler, Eds. (Guilford Press, New York, 1987).

8. M. Rutter and D. Quinton, Long term follow-up of women institutionalized in childhood: Factors promoting good functioning in adult life, *British Journal of Developmental Psychology*, 18, 225–234 (1984).

9. J. Block and P.F. Gjerde, *Early antecedents of ego resiliency in late adolescence*, paper presented at the annual meeting of the American Psychological Association, Washington, DC (August 1986).

10. R. M. Clark, *Family Life and School Achievement: Why Poor Black Children Succeed or Fail* (University of Chicago Press, Chicago, 1983).

11. D.P. Farrington, *Protective Factors in the Development of Juvenile Delinquency and Adult Crime* {Institute of Criminology, Cambridge University, Cambridge, England, 1993).

12. J.S. Wallerstein and S. Blakeslee. *Second Chances: Men, Women and Children a Decade After Divorce* (Ticknor and Fields, New York, 1989).

13. M. Rutter, B. Maughan, P. Mortimore, and J. Ousten, *Fifteen Thousand Hours: Secondary Schools and Their Effects on Children* (Harvard University Press, Cambridge, MA, 1979).

14. G.H. Elder, Military times and turning points in men's lives, *Developmental Psychology*, 22, 233–245 (1986).

15. F.F. Furstenberg, J. Brooks-Gunn, and S.P. Morgan, *Adolescent Mothers in Later Life* (Cambridge University Press, New York, 1987).

16. S. Scarr and K. McCartney, How people make their own environments: A theory of genotype environment effects, *Child Development*, 54, 424–435 (1983).

17. L. Schorr, *Within Our Reach: Breaking the Cycle of Disadvantage* {Anchor Press, New York, 1988).

Recommended Reading

Haggerty, R., Garmezy, N., Rutter, M., and Sherrod, L., Eds. (1994). *Stress, Risk, and Resilience in Childhood and Adolescence* (Cambridge University Press, New York).

Luthar, S., and Zigler, E. (1991). Vulnerability and competence: A review of research on resilience in childhood. *American Journal of Orthopsychiatry, 61,* 6–22.

Werner, E.E., and Smith, R.S. (1992). *Overcoming the Odds: High Risk Children From Birth to Adulthood* (Cornell University Press, Ithaca, NY).

Loneliness and Peer Relations in Childhood

Steven R. Asher[1] and Julie A. Paquette
Department of Psychology, Duke University, Durham, North Carolina

Abstract

Although loneliness is a normative experience, there is reason to be concerned about children who are chronically lonely in school. Research indicates that children have a fundamental understanding of what it means to be lonely, and that loneliness can be reliably measured in children. Most of the research on loneliness in children has focused on the contributions of children's peer relations to their feelings of well-being at school. Loneliness in children is influenced by how well accepted they are by peers, whether they are overtly victimized, whether they have friends, and the durability and quality of their best friendships. Findings from this emerging area of research provide a differentiated picture of how children's peer experiences come to influence their emotional well-being.

Keywords

loneliness; peer acceptance; friendship

The study of children's peer-relationship difficulties has become a major focus of contemporary developmental and child-clinical psychology (see Rubin, Bukowski, & Parker, 1998). As part of this focus, increasing attention is being given to the internal, subjective, and emotional sides of children's social lives. Human beings have fundamental needs for inclusion in group life and for close relationships (e.g., Baumeister & Leary, 1995), so it is fitting to examine what happens when social needs go unmet. It is clear that a variety of strong affective consequences can result. In this article, we focus on one such emotional reaction, loneliness, and we describe what has been learned about the association between loneliness and various indicators of the quality of children's social lives with peers.

PERSPECTIVES ON LONELINESS

Loneliness is typically defined by researchers as involving the cognitive awareness of a deficiency in one's social and personal relationships, and the ensuing affective reactions of sadness, emptiness, or longing. For example, Parkhurst and Hopmeyer (1999) described loneliness as "a sad or aching sense of isolation, that is, of being alone, cut-off, or distanced from others . . . associated with a felt deprivation of, or longing for, association, contact, or closeness" (p. 58). Likewise, many other authors emphasize the perceived deficiencies in the qualitative or quantitative aspects of social relationships and the accompanying emotional discomfort or distress that results.

The subjective experience of loneliness should not be viewed as interchangeable with more objective features of children's peer experiences, such as how well accepted they are by peers, whether they have friends, and what their friendships are like. So, for example, it is possible to have many friends and still feel lonely. Likewise, it is possible to be poorly accepted by the peer group or to lack friends and yet to not feel lonely. Loneliness is an internal emotional state that can be strongly influenced by features of one's social life, but it is not to be confused with any particular external condition.

It is also important to note that loneliness in itself is not pathological. Loneliness is actually quite normative in that most people feel lonely at some point during their lives. As social animals who participate extensively in social relationships, humans open themselves up to the possibility of loneliness. This can occur not only when people lack ongoing relationships with others, but even when they have meaningful relationships that take negative turns. For example, loneliness can be a response to separations, such as when a friend is unavailable to play or moves away. These situational or short-term experiences of loneliness are typically not causes for concern. Chronic loneliness, however, is associated with various indices of maladjustment in adolescents and adults, such as dropping out of school, depression, alcoholism, and medical problems. At least 10% of elementary school-aged children report feeling lonely either always or most of the time (Asher, Hymel, & Renshaw, 1984), which suggests a level of loneliness that places children at risk for poor outcomes.

Systematic research on children's loneliness partially grew out of an earlier line of research on the effects of teaching social-relationship skills to children who were highly rejected by their peers. The question that emerged was whether the children who were the focus of these intensive intervention efforts were themselves unhappy with their situation in school. The research was also inspired by very interesting work on adults' loneliness. The study of loneliness in childhood offers unique opportunities that are typically not available to researchers who explore loneliness in adulthood. Much of children's social lives takes place in a "closed" full-time environment, the school, so it is much easier to capture children's peer world. The presence of a child's "colleagues" makes it possible to learn about a child not just by studying that child, but also by querying his or her interactive partners or directly observing the social interactions the child has with peers. By contrast, adults' relationships take place over more contexts, making it harder to get access to most of their social network. Furthermore, it is usually easier to gain research access to schools than the adult workplace.

CAN LONELINESS BE MEANINGFULLY STUDIED WITH CHILDREN?

Some people might think that the concept of loneliness does not have much meaning to children or that they cannot give reliable information about their subjective well-being in this regard. Indeed, Harry Stack Sullivan (the famous American psychiatrist who wrote eloquently about the role of "chumship" in middle childhood) argued that children cannot experience true loneliness until early adolescence, when they develop a need for intimacy within the context of close friendships. However, research indicates that children as young as 5 or 6 years of age have at least a rudimentary understanding of the concept of loneliness

(Cassidy & Asher, 1992). Their understanding that loneliness involves having no one to play with and feeling sad corresponds fairly well to typical definitions of loneliness in the literature in that children grasp that loneliness involves a combination of solitude and depressed affect. We call this a rudimentary understanding because young children do not yet appreciate that one can be "lonely in a crowd" or even when with a significant other.

Children's basic understanding of loneliness is accompanied by the ability to respond in meaningful ways to formal assessments of loneliness. The most widely used measures have children respond to some items that assess their feelings of loneliness and other items that involve appraisals of whether they have friends, whether they are good at making friends and getting along with others, and whether their basic relationship needs are being met. Because most of these self-report measures for children contain diverse item content that goes beyond loneliness per se (as does the widely used UCLA Loneliness Scale for adults), caution must be used when interpreting results. Some investigators (e.g., Asher, Gorman, Gabriel, & Guerra, 2003; Ladd, Kochenderfer, & Coleman, 1997; Parker & Asher, 1993) have therefore calculated "pure loneliness" scores by using only items that directly assess feelings of loneliness (e.g., "I am lonely at school"; "I feel left out of things at school"; "I feel alone at school").

Researchers in the field have examined whether, within a particular measure, children respond in an internally consistent manner from one loneliness item to another (e.g., Asher et al., 1984). They have also examined whether there is stability in children's reports of loneliness from one time of assessment to another (e.g., Renshaw & Brown, 1993). Several studies indicate that children's reports of loneliness are highly reliable by both of these criteria. Accordingly, researchers have used these methodologically sound measures to examine whether acceptance by peers and friendships influence children's feelings of loneliness.

PEER ACCEPTANCE AND LONELINESS

The preponderance of research on children's loneliness has focused on the influence of acceptance versus rejection by peers. Peer acceptance in school is typically assessed using sociometric measures in which children either nominate schoolmates they like most and like least or use a rating scale to indicate how much they like each of their peers. Regardless of method, there is a consistent association between acceptance by peers and loneliness. Children who are poorly accepted report experiencing greater loneliness. This finding holds whether loneliness is measured in classroom, lunchroom, playground, or physical education contexts (Asher et al., 2003), suggesting that there is no safe haven at school for poorly accepted children. The finding that rejected children experience more loneliness than other children holds for age groups ranging from kindergartners to elementary-school children to middle schoolers. Furthermore, these associations have been found in research in many different countries and for both genders (with mean differences in loneliness between boys and girls rarely significant).

Although rejected children report the most loneliness, there is considerable within-group variability. Researchers have found that there are distinct subgroups of rejected children. Withdrawn-rejected children consistently report greater loneliness than aggressive-rejected children, although in the elementary-school years both groups report more loneliness than children with an average degree of acceptance by their peers. One factor that may account for variability in rejected children's feelings of loneliness is overt victimization. Not all highly disliked children are overtly victimized, but those who are victimized are more likely than others to report elevated loneliness (for relevant research, see Boivin & Hymel, 1997; Ladd et al., 1997).

FRIENDSHIP AND LONELINESS

Variability in loneliness among children rejected by their peers also arises from the partial independence of acceptance and friendship. One way researchers assess whether children have friends is by giving them a roster of the names of their classmates and asking them to circle the names of their friends. Researchers typically consider that a friendship exists when two children identify one another as friends. With this mutual-nomination criterion, half of the children who are poorly accepted by their peers prove to have friends, making it possible to learn whether friendship has a buffering effect on the influence of low peer acceptance.

In studies of the connection between friendship and loneliness, children without friends report experiencing more loneliness than children with friends (Parker & Asher, 1993; Renshaw & Brown, 1993). This beneficial effect of friendship occurs for children at all levels of peer acceptance and for both boys and girls. Even children with deviant friends (i.e., friends who participate in delinquent behavior) report less loneliness than friendless children (Brendgen, Vitaro, & Bukowski, 2000).

There is no evidence to date that the number of friends children have (beyond one friend!) relates to loneliness; however, it is important for children to have friendships that endure. In a camp-based study, Parker and Seal (1996) found that children's ability to maintain, as well as form, friendships was related to loneliness. Children who frequently made new friends but who did not maintain their friendships experienced higher levels of loneliness than other children.

The quality of children's friendships also plays an important role in children's feelings of loneliness. Features such as the degree of companionship, help and guidance, intimacy, conflict, and ease of conflict resolution can all be reliably measured among elementary-school children. Children who participate in high-quality friendships experience less loneliness than other children (Parker & Asher, 1993); this result is found even in analyses that statistically control for level of peer acceptance. Furthermore, the effects of friendship quality on loneliness are comparable for boys and girls. One indicator of friendship quality is whether friends engage in relational aggression toward one another. Crick and Nelson (2002) recently found that among both boys and girls, having friends who ignored them when angry or tried to influence them by threatening termination of the friendship was associated with increased loneliness.

There is a need for research on how the influence of specific qualities of friendship might differ for children of different ages. As discussed by Parkhurst and Hopmeyer (1999), the experience of loneliness at different ages might be influenced by cognitive-developmental changes, changes in the kinds of close-ness or associations that are meaningful, and changes in the value that children place on certain kinds of relationships. Thus, what causes a 5- or 6-year-old child to feel lonely will likely be different from what causes an adolescent to feel lonely. For example, kindergartners might feel lonely if there is no one to play with, whereas older youth might feel lonely if they do not have someone with whom to discuss personal thoughts and feelings. These types of developmental predictions need direct tests.

FUTURE DIRECTIONS

Research to date consistently indicates that both acceptance by peers and friend-ship processes influence children's feelings of loneliness at school. However, acceptance and friendship variables, as typically measured, still leave much of the variance in loneliness unexplained. Partly this is because of the frequent reliance on single-shot assessments of key constructs. When repeated assess-ments of rejection or victimization are conducted, the associations with loneli-ness become stronger. Children who chronically experience negative peer relations are unquestionably at greater risk than children whose adverse cir-cumstances are more short term (e.g., Kochenderfer-Ladd & Wardrop, 2001). Repeated assessments help to account for more of the variance in children's loneliness.

At the same time, psychologists will never fully understand the dynamics of loneliness if they look only at objective indicators of children's adjustment and ignore children's subjective representations of their experiences. Little is known about the role of beliefs and expectations in children's loneliness. For example, children who have idealized views that friends will always "be there for them," will never fail to keep a commitment, or will never hurt their feelings are likely to experience disappointments in their friendships even when other people with different beliefs and expectations might think those friendships are going well. Likewise, children who believe that conflict is a sign of impending dissolution of a friendship are likely to experience higher levels of loneliness than other children because some level of conflict is virtually inevitable in all close rela-tionships. Examining children's beliefs and expectations may shed light on why some children who are highly accepted and have what seem to be high-quality friendships nevertheless are lonely.

Finally, there is a need for intervention research aimed at helping children who experience chronic loneliness. An earlier generation of intervention studies found that teaching children social-relationship skills had beneficial effects on children's peer acceptance (see Asher, Parker, & Walker, 1996, for a review). However, these studies generally predated the more recent research on loneliness in children and therefore did not assess whether the interventions had positive effects on loneli-ness. Intervention research not only would offer a potential aid to children, but also could be useful for testing specific hypotheses about the processes that lead particular kinds of children to become lonely. For example, intervention research is a way to learn whether increasing the social skills of poorly accepted children who lack friends leads to parallel increases in acceptance and friendship that in turn result in reductions in loneliness. Likewise, for children who are well accepted and have friends yet are lonely, interventions aimed at modifying their thoughts and beliefs about relationships can experimentally test hypothesized linkages between particular representations and loneliness.

Recommended Reading

Asher, S.R., Rose, A.J., & Gabriel, S.W. (2001). Peer rejection in everyday life. In M.R. Leary (Ed.), *Interpersonal rejection* (pp. 105–142). New York: Oxford University Press.

Ernst, J.M., & Cacioppo, J.T. (1999). Lonely hearts: Psychological perspectives on loneliness. *Applied & Preventive Psychology, 8*, 1–22.

Peplau, L.A., & Perlman, D. (Eds.). (1982). *Loneliness: A sourcebook of current theory, research, and therapy.* New York: Wiley.

Rotenberg, K.J., & Hymel, S. (Eds.). (1999). *Loneliness in childhood and adolescence.* New York: Cambridge University Press.

Note

1. Address correspondence to Steven R. Asher, Department of Psychology: Social and Health Sciences, Duke University, Box 90085, Durham, NC 27708-0085; e-mail: asher@duke.edu.

References

Asher, S.R., Gorman, A.H., Gabriel, S.W., & Guerra, V.S. (2003). *Children's loneliness in different school contexts.* Manuscript submitted for publication.

Asher, S.R., Hymel, S., & Renshaw, R.D. (1984). Loneliness in childhood. *Child Development, 55,* 1456–1464.

Asher, S.R., Parker, J.G., & Walker, D.L. (1996). Distinguishing friendship from acceptance: Implications for intervention and assessment. In W.M. Bukowski, A.F. Newcomb, & W.W. Hartup (Eds.), *The company they keep: Friendship during childhood and adolescence* (pp. 366–405). New York: Cambridge University Press.

Baumeister, R.F., & Leary, M.R. (1995). The need to belong: Desire for interpersonal attachments as a fundamental human motivation. *Psychological Bulletin, 117,* 497–529.

Boivin, M., & Hymel, S. (1997). Peer experiences and social self-perceptions: A sequential model. *Developmental Psychology, 33,* 135–145.

Brendgen, M., Vitaro, F., & Bukowski, W.M. (2000). Deviant friends and early adolescents' emotional and behavioral adjustment. *Journal of Research on Adolescence, 10,* 172–189.

Cassidy, J., & Asher, S.R. (1992). Loneliness and peer relations in young children. *Child Development, 63,* 350–365.

Crick N.R., & Nelson, D.A. (2002). Relational and physical victimization within friendships: Nobody told me there'd be friends like these. *Journal of Abnormal Child Psychology, 30,* 599–607.

Kochenderfer-Ladd, B.J., & Wardrop, J.L. (2001). Chronicity and instability of children's peer victimization experiences as predictors of loneliness and social satisfaction trajectories. *Child Development, 72,* 134–151.

Ladd, G.W., Kochenderfer, B.J., & Coleman, C.C. (1997). Classroom peer acceptance, friendship, and victimization: Distinct relational systems that contribute uniquely to children's school adjustment? *Child Development, 68,* 1181–1197.

Parker, J.G., & Asher, S.R. (1993). Friendship and friendship quality in middle childhood: Links with peer group acceptance and feelings of loneliness and social dissatisfaction. *Developmental Psychology, 29,* 611–621.

Parker, J.G., & Seal, J. (1996). Forming, losing, renewing, and replacing friendships: Applying temporal parameters to the assessment of children's friendship experiences. *Child Development, 67,* 2248–2268.

Parkhurst, J.T., & Hopmeyer, A. (1999). Developmental change in the source of loneliness in child-hood and adolescence: Constructing a theoretical model. In K.J. Rotenberg & S. Hymel (Eds.), *Loneliness in childhood and adolescence* (pp. 56–79). New York: Cambridge University Press.

Renshaw, P.D., & Brown, P.J. (1993). Loneliness in middle childhood: Concurrent and longitudinal predictors. *Child Development, 64,* 1271–1284.

Rubin, K.H., Bukowski, W., & Parker, J.G. (1998). Peer interactions, relationships, and groups. In W. Damon (Editor-in-Chief) & N. Eisenberg (Vol. Ed.), *Handbook of child psychology: Vol. 3. Social, emotional, and personality development* (pp. 619–700). New York: Wiley.

Stress, Positive Emotion, and Coping

Susan Folkman[1] and Judith Tedlie Moskowitz

Center for AIDS Prevention Studies, University of California-San Francisco, San Francisco, California

Abstract

There is growing interest in positive aspects of the stress process, including positive outcomes of stress and antecedents that dispose individuals to appraise stressful situations more as a challenge than as a threat. Less attention has been given to the adaptational significance of positive emotions during stress or to the coping processes that sustain positive emotions. We review evidence for the occurrence of positive emotions under conditions of stress, discuss the functional role that positive emotions play under such conditions, and present three types of coping that are associated with positive emotion during chronic stress. These findings point to new research questions about the role of positive emotions during stress and the nature of the coping processes that generate these positive emotions.

Keywords

coping; positive emotion; chronic stress

Decades of research have shown that stress is associated with a wide array of negative outcomes, such as depression, anxiety, physical symptoms, disease, and even death in extreme cases. In recent years, however, there has been a growing interest in positive aspects of the stress process, including positive outcomes such as personal transformation or growth (for review, see Tedeschi, Park, & Calhoun, 1998) and antecedents that dispose individuals to appraise situations more as a challenge than as a threat. With the exception of a few investigators such as Affleck and Tennen (1996), however, researchers have not given much attention to the actual coping mechanisms that link the positive dispositions, on the one hand, and the positive outcomes of stressful situations, on the other.

The growing interest in positive aspects of the stress process is paralleled by a growing interest in positive emotions and, of particular relevance here, the possibility that they may have important adaptational significance during the stress process. Fredrickson (1998), for example, cited evidence that positive emotions broaden the scope of attention, cognition, and action, and help build physical, intellectual, and social resources. Her "Broaden and Build Model of Positive Emotions," which is premised on this evidence, raises the possibility that positive emotions are important facilitators of adaptive coping and adjustment to acute and chronic stress and may underlie the beneficial effects of interventions such as relaxation therapies (Fredrickson, 2000). Twenty years ago, we (Lazarus, Kanner, & Folkman, 1980) suggested that positive emotions may have three important adaptive functions during stress: sustaining coping efforts, providing a "breather," and restoring depleted resources. However, until recently, there has been little effort to provide empirical support for these ideas.

The idea that people even experience positive emotions in the midst of

181

acute or chronic stress may at first seem counterintuitive. But people do experience these emotions, even under the most difficult of circumstances. For example, when we monitored gay men who were the primary informal caregivers of partners with AIDS for up to 5 years, the caregivers reported levels of depressed mood that were more than one standard deviation above levels in the general population, and increased to more than two standard deviations above the general population's levels during periods of crisis. Throughout the study, with the exception of the weeks immediately preceding and following their partners' deaths, however, the caregivers also reported experiencing positive mood at a frequency comparable to the frequency of their negative mood (Folkman, 1997).

COPING AND POSITIVE EMOTION

Given data demonstrating that positive emotions occur even under the most dire of circumstances, the compelling question becomes not whether people experience positive emotions during long periods of severe stress, but rather, how they do it. In our study of caregivers, we identified three classes of coping mechanisms that help answer this question: positive reappraisal, problem-focused coping, and the creation of positive events (Folkman, 1997; Folkman & Moskowitz, in press).

Positive Reappraisal

Positive reappraisal is a cognitive process through which people focus on the good in what is happening or what has happened. Forms of positive reappraisal include discovering opportunities for personal growth, perceiving actual personal growth, and seeing how one's own efforts can benefit other people. Through the process of positive reappraisal, the meaning of a situation is changed in a way that allows the person to experience positive emotion and psychological well-being. In our study of AIDS-related caregiving, we found that positive reappraisal was consistently associated with positive emotion both during caregiving and after the death of the partner. This association remained significant even when emotion at the previous interview and the other types of coping were statistically controlled (Moskowitz, Folkman, Collette, & Vittinghoff, 1996).

Not all forms of positive reappraisal necessarily generate positive emotion. For example, a cognitive reappraisal through which an individual devalues an important goal that has proven to be unrealistic, such as gaining admission to a prestigious Ivy League school, may be positive in that it lessens the personal significance of failing to achieve the goal, but it may do more to reduce distress than to enhance positive emotion.

Problem-Focused Coping

Problem-focused coping includes thoughts and instrumental behaviors that manage or solve the underlying cause of distress. It tends to be used more in situations in which there is personal control over an outcome and less in situations in which there is an absence of personal control. Problem-focused coping is usually considered maladaptive when there is no personal control (Lazarus & Folkman, 1984), but this general formula may be overly simplified; a situation that appears on its surface to be uncontrollable may still have controllable aspects.

In our research, for example, we found a significant increase in problem-focused coping by caregivers during the weeks leading up to the partner's death, a period of profound lack of control. A review of narrative data showed that during this period caregivers were often creating the proverbial "to-do" list, usually comprising seemingly mundane tasks such as getting a prescription filled, successfully administering a medication, or changing the partner's bed linens. Such lists served multiple purposes: In attending to even the most trivial task, the caregiver had an opportunity to feel effective and in control, thereby helping to combat the feelings of helplessness and lack of control that often characterized the overall situation; working on tasks helped the caregiver feel mobilized and focused, which was energizing; and the successful accomplishment of the various tasks was often helpful, in which case the caregiver often benefited from positive feedback from his partner or other people involved in the partner's care. An important finding was that this type of coping was responsible for increases in positive mood (as distinct from decreases in distress) during these weeks (Moskowitz et al., 1996).

Creation of Positive Events

This coping mechanism involves creating a positive psychological time-out by infusing ordinary events with positive meaning (Folkman, Moskowitz, Ozer, & Park, 1997), as when a person reflects on a compliment that was offered in passing, or pauses to take note of a beautiful sunset. Such time-outs provide momentary respite from the ongoing stress. In our study of caregivers, we were struck by the pervasiveness of this method of coping throughout caregiving and bereavement. Month after month, for example, more than 99% of the caregivers noted and remembered positive events in the midst of some of the most psychologically stressful circumstances people encounter. For the most part, these events were ordinary events of daily life that in less stressful moments might not even have been noted. We believe the occurrence of these positive events was not random. Rather, caregivers created them deliberately by planning positive events, noting positive events when they occurred serendipitously, or infusing neutral events with positive meaning, as a way of having a few moments of relief from the intense stress.

Sometimes the creation of these meaningful events depended on the caregiver's ability to find humor in the situation. Humor, which has long been recognized for its tension-reducing properties (e.g., Menninger, 1963), has the added benefit of generating positive emotion in the very darkest of moments, which may, in turn, help build social bonds that can be beneficial under conditions of stress. The term gallows humor attests to the widespread use of humor in situations that are particularly grim. Humor was common in the accounts provided by caregivers, even the accounts that described partners' deaths. The humor usually managed to capture positive qualities of the dying partner in a loving manner, which had the additional benefit of helping the caregiver create images of the partner that he wanted to remember.

183

COMPELLING UNANSWERED QUESTIONS

Research on coping and positive emotions is still in its earliest stages, and each new finding raises new questions. For example, researchers have only begun to understand the adaptive functions of positive emotions in the midst of stressful circumstances. Laboratory studies have provided provocative suggestions regarding the ways positive emotions may help people endure stress (e.g., Fredrickson & Levenson, 1998). But because constraints of the laboratory limit researchers' ability to simulate the meaning or duration of serious real-life stressors, we strongly encourage pursuing research under real-life circumstances, with all their complexity. In our newly launched study of maternal caregivers, for example, we are investigating positive emotions and relevant coping processes in the daily lives of women providing care for a child with HIV or other serious chronic illness.

There are several issues regarding measurement and conceptualization of emotion that need to be addressed in order to advance knowledge of the role of positive emotion in the stress process. At this point, there is little in the literature about the intensity and duration of positive emotions necessary to activate their adaptive functions during stress. In our study of AIDS-related caregiving, the quantitative measures assessed the frequency of emotions, not their duration or intensity. But qualitative data suggested that positive emotions were less intense and less enduring than negative emotions (Folkman et al., 1997). It may be that it is the frequency of positive emotion, and not its intensity or duration, that confers benefits on the individual.

A related issue has to do with whether different positive emotions are differentially effective with respect to motivating and sustaining coping, and if so, under what circumstances. For example, is excitement more adaptive than happiness at the outset of a stressful undertaking, but less so while the situation unfolds?

Answering these questions regarding intensity, duration, and differential effects of positive emotions will require close attention to the measurement and conceptualization of emotion. Recent debates regarding whether positive and negative emotion are independent or bipolar constructs (i.e., opposite extremes of the same construct) have reignited interest in these issues (see Russell & Carroll, 1999, for a review). As Russell and Carroll (1999) noted, when all the measurement issues are considered, a bipolar model fits the data best. By making the assertion that both positive and negative emotion occur in chronically stressful situations, we are not implying that they are independent and that at any given moment high levels of negative emotion co-occur with high levels of positive emotion. Rather, our point is that over a period of time, people in stressful situations experience not only negative emotion, but also positive emotion. Thus, in the case of our caregiver study, when participants reported their emotions over the previous week, as expected, they indicated that they experienced frequent negative affect, but they also experienced fairly frequent positive affect.

The coping processes that are associated with positive emotion involve another set of questions. Are the coping processes that generate positive emotion truly different from those that regulate distress? If so, how are they different? For example, many of the positive reappraisal processes that generate positive emotion depend on the individual's ability to access deeply held values that enhance the personal significance of ongoing coping activity. In contrast, coping processes that people are more likely to use to regulate distress (such as escape-avoidance or distancing), or even strategies that are intended to reduce tension (such as relaxation or meditation), do not seem to depend on accessing values in the same way. Further work that specifically addresses the distinction between coping processes that are associated with positive as opposed to negative emotions is clearly needed. If the ways of coping that decrease negative emotion differ from those that increase positive emotion, it may be necessary for researchers to expand the repertoire of coping measures in order to more fully tap into these positive ways of coping.

Another set of questions concerns the importance of the duration of stress, and whether the capacity or need for positive emotions differs in acute versus chronic stressful situations. Does the novelty, immediacy, or urgency of the demands of an acute stressful situation reduce the person's capacity for engaging in the coping strategies that generate positive emotions? Or perhaps it is not as important to generate positive emotions during an acute, time-limited situation as it is when a stressful situation persists over time, and the person needs to have respite from distress to become rededicated to the coping efforts in order to keep going. Studies directly comparing coping with acute, relatively short-lived stressors and coping with chronic stressors are necessary to answer this question.

Finally, to what extent can people be taught to generate positive emotions while they are also regulating distress? Is the ability to generate positive emotions attached to underlying personality dimensions, such as optimism, that may be relatively immutable? Or are there teachable skills that are independent of the underlying personality dimensions? Lewinsohn and his colleagues recognized the importance of pleasant events (and the associated positive emotions) in the treatment of depression years ago (e.g., Lewinsohn, Sullivan, & Grosscup, 1980). More recent work has pursued the idea that helping clients identify thoughts and beliefs that interfere with positive experiences is an important component of therapy (Fava, Rafanelli, Cazzaro, Conti, & Grandi, 1998).

We have highlighted some of the exciting new developments in the areas of stress, positive emotions, and coping. These developments point the way for systematic, programmatic research that may help explain the fascinating, fundamental question, namely, why it is that some people not only survive adversity mentally and physically, but manage somehow even to thrive.

Recommended Reading

Folkman, S. (1997). (See References)
Fredrickson, B.L. (1998). (See References)
Tedeschi, R.G., Park, C.L., & Calhoun, L.G. (Eds.). (1998). (See References)

Acknowledgments—This research was supported by Grants 49985 and 52517 from the National Institute of Mental Health, and by Grant 58069 from the National Institute of Mental Health and the National Institute of Nursing Research.

Note

1. Address correspondence to Susan Folkman, 74 New Montgomery, Suite 600, San Francisco, CA 94105; e-mail: sfolkman@psg.ucsf.edu.

References

Affleck, G., & Tennen, H. (1996). Construing benefits from adversity: Adaptational significance and dispositional underpinnings. *Journal of Personality, 64*, 899–922.

Fava, G.A., Rafanelli, C., Cazzaro, M., Conti, S., & Grandi, S. (1998). Well-being therapy: A novel psychotherapeutic approach for residual symptoms of affective disorders. *Psychological Medicine, 28*, 475–480.

Folkman, S. (1997). Positive psychological states and coping with severe stress. *Social Science and Medicine, 45*, 1207–1221.

Folkman, S., & Moskowitz, J.T. (in press). Positive affect and the other side of coping. *American Psychologist*.

Folkman, S., Moskowitz, J.T., Ozer, E.M., & Park, C.L. (1997). Positive meaningful events and coping in the context of HIV/AIDS. In B.H. Gottlieb (Ed.), *Coping with chronic stress* (pp. 293–314). New York: Plenum Press.

Fredrickson, B.L. (1998). What good are positive emotions? *Review of General Psychology, 2*, 300–319.

Fredrickson, B.L. (2000). Cultivating positive emotions to optimize health and well-being. *Prevention and Treatment* [On-line], 3. Available: http://journals.apa.org.prevention

Fredrickson, B.L., & Levenson, R.W. (1998). Positive emotions speed recovery from the cardiovascular sequelae of negative emotions. *Cognition and Emotion, 12*, 191–220.

Lazarus, R.S., & Folkman, S. (1984). *Stress, appraisal, and coping*. New York: Springer.

Lazarus, R.S., Kanner, A.D., & Folkman, S. (1980). Emotions: A cognitive-phenomenological analysis. In R. Plutchik & H. Kellerman (Eds.), *Theories of emotion* (pp. 189–217). New York: Academic Press.

Lewinsohn, P.M., Sullivan, J.M., & Grosscup, S.J. (1980). Changing reinforcing events: An approach to the treatment of depression. *Psychotherapy: Theory, Research, and Practice, 17*, 322–334.

Menninger, K. (1963). *The vital balance: The life process in mental health and illness*. New York: Viking.

Moskowitz, J.T., Folkman, S., Collette, L., & Vittinghoff, E. (1996). Coping and mood during AIDS-related caregiving and bereavement. *Annals of Behavioral Medicine, 18*, 49–57.

Russell, J.A., & Carroll, J.M. (1999). On the bipolarity of positive and negative affect. *Psychological Bulletin, 125*, 3–30.

Tedeschi, R.G., Park, C.L., & Calhoun, L.G. (Eds.). (1998). *Posttraumatic growth*. Mahwah, NJ: Erlbaum.

Fleeting Signs of the Course of Life:
Facial Expression and Personal Adjustment

Dacher Keltner,[1] Ann M. Kring, and George A. Bonanno
*Department of Psychology, University of California at Berkeley,
Berkeley, California (D.K., A.M.K.), and Department of Psychology,
Catholic University of America, Washington, D.C. (G.A.B.)*

Abstract

In this article, we consider whether facial expressions of emotion relate in theoretically interesting ways to personal adjustment. We first consider the conceptual benefits of this line of inquiry. Then, to anticipate why brief samples of emotional behavior should relate to personal adjustment, we review evidence indicating that facial expressions of emotion correspond to intrapersonal processes and social outcomes. We then review studies showing that facial expressions relate in theoretically significant ways to adjustment after the death of a spouse, in long-term relationships, and in the context of chronic psychological disorders.

Keywords

facial expression; personal adjustment; bereavement; psychopathology

In every asylum we find examples of absolutely unmotived fear, anger, melancholy, or conceit; and others of equally unmotived apathy which persists in spite of the best outward reasons why it should give way. (James, 1890, p. 459)

Writers, artists, lay observers, and many behavioral scientists, such as William James, have long believed that emotional expression reveals something fundamental about the life an individual leads. For several reasons, however, the scientific study of facial expression and personal adjustment has emerged only in the past 15 years. One reason is that reliable methods for measuring facial expression were developed only quite recently. Also, it is somewhat counterintuitive, if not methodologically ill conceived (and counter to principles of statistical aggregation), to expect brief observations of facial behavior to predict cumulative life outcomes. Moreover, some social scientists argued that facial expressions provide little coherent information about an individual's emotions, intentions, and dispositions.

The study of facial expression and personal adjustment, however, informs several lines of inquiry. It is widely assumed that emotions are associated with adaptive responses to significant events, suggesting that correlations between facial expression and adjustment are likely. Studies linking individual variation in facial expression to specific outcomes, therefore, lend credence to claims about the functions of particular emotions. Accounts of personal adjustment often specify how different patterns of emotional expression lead to positive or negative outcomes, pointing to the need for relevant research. Finally, studies of facial expression and psychopathology point to possible causes, consequences, and interventions related to emotional disturbances.

FACIAL EXPRESSIONS OF EMOTION: MARKERS OF THE INNER WORLD AND MEDIATORS OF THE SOCIAL WORLD

The well-known cross-cultural judgment studies of Paul Ekman and Carroll Izard in the late 1960s and early 1970s documented that members of dramatically different cultures make similar attributions when judging the emotions of individuals posting various facial expressions. These findings paved the way for research that has subsequently revealed that facial expressions are much more than markers of momentary emotion. One literature, encompassing various methods and theoretical traditions, indicates that facial expressions correspond to a constellation of intrapersonal processes (see Keltner & Ekman, in press). Facial expressions of negative emotions and different kinds of smiles correlate in distinct ways to different experiences. Movements of facial muscles into the configurations of various emotions generate specific activity in the autonomic nervous system (e.g., anger elevates heart rate and disgust reduces heart rate; Levenson, Ekman, & Friesen, 1990). Recent studies have begun to link facial expressions to the individual's appraisal of ongoing events. Thus, facial expression indexes the individual's interpretation and experiential and physiological responses to ongoing life events.

Facial expressions also play vital roles in interpersonal processes, coordinating social interactions in at least three ways (Keltner & Kring, 1998). First, facial expressions rapidly convey to receivers information about senders' emotions, intentions, and relational orientations, as well as information about objects in the environment (e.g., children rely on parents' facial expressions to assess whether ambiguous stimuli are safe or dangerous). Second, facial expressions evoke in other people emotions that are associated with behaviors that help meet the goals of the interacting individuals. For example, displays of distress evoke sympathy and soothing-related behaviors. Third, facial expressions serve as incentives or deterrents for other individuals' behavior. Thus, facial expressions shape early parent–child interactions, rewarding shifts in attention, goal-directed behavior, and learning. Facial expressions also influence a wide range of adult interactions, ranging from spontaneous conversations to ritualized appeasement and courtship practices.

The implications of these empirical advances are clear. Researchers can rely on brief observations of facial expressions to make inferences about the individual's experiential, cognitive, and physiological responses to life events. An individual's tendency to display certain facial expressions should also shape his or her social interactions in consistent ways, leading to cumulative life outcomes. Although fleeting and often beyond control, facial expressions appear to be measurable signs of the course of life; they are indeed windows into the human soul.

FACIAL EXPRESSION AND BEREAVEMENT

How might facial expressions relate to individual adjustment in response to one of life's most devastating losses—the early death of a spouse? Traditional bereavement theories offer clear predictions. These theories, based on Freudian notions of "working through" the emotional pain of loss, suggest that recovery depends on the expression of negative emotions, such as anger and sadness. The expression of positive emotion indicates denial and impedes grief resolution. Social-functional accounts of emotion, in contrast, suggest that negative emotional expression may bring about problematic outcomes, whereas positive emotional expression may facilitate the adaptive response to stress.

We pitted these contrasting hypotheses against one another in a longitudinal study of individuals whose spouses had died in midlife (Bonanno & Keltner, 1997). The facial expressions of bereaved adults were coded as they talked for 6 min in highly moving and emotional ways about their recently deceased spouses. We related measures of the participants' facial expressions of emotions to a well-validated measure of grief severity, administered in separate interviews 6, 14, and 25 months after the loss. Contrary to widespread assumptions, higher scores for facial expressions of negative emotion, and in particular anger, predicted increased grief severity both 14 and 25 months after the loss. More laughter and smiling, in contrast, predicted reduced grief over time. The initial level of grief and the tendency to report high levels of distress did not affect this relation between facial expressions and long-term adjustment.

These findings raised an intriguing question. Why would laughing while talking about the deceased partner relate to increased personal adjustment? Recent theorizing about the functions of positive emotion points to possible answers (Fredrickson, 1998). Specifically, positive emotions are believed to accompany the "undoing" of distress (what we call dissociation from the distress of stressful events) and to enhance social bonds. Clearly, dissociation from distress and enhanced social bonds would help the bereaved individual adjust to a profoundly changed life following the loss of a spouse.

To assess these putative functions of positive emotion, we divided our bereaved participants into two groups: those who showed Duchenne laughter and those who did not (Keltner & Bonanno, 1997). Duchenne smiles and laughter involve the action of the *orbicularis oculi* muscle that raises the upper cheeks, and are typically associated with the experience of pleasure; in contrast, non-Duchenne smiles and laughter do not involve this muscle and are not associated with pleasure. We compared the two groups on three measures: their scores on a well-validated index of emotional dissociation (the discrepancy between self-reports of distress and autonomic reactivity gathered during the bereavement interview); their ambivalence toward a current significant other; and the responses they evoked in strangers, who viewed silent videotapes of the participants. Consistent with theorizing about positive emotion, bereaved individuals who showed Duchenne laughter while talking about their deceased spouses showed a pattern of dissociation from distress, reported better relations with a current significant other, and evoked more positive responses in strangers (see Fig. 1). Duchenne laughers and nonlaughers did not differ in their self-rated personality, nor did certain circumstances of their spouses' deaths (e.g., unexpectedness or financial impact) differ between the groups.

FACIAL EXPRESSION AND INTERPERSONAL ADJUSTMENT

From studies relating facial expression to recovery from the loss of a loved one, we turn to studies of emotion and ongoing relationships. Facial expressions, we argued earlier, coordinate social interactions by providing information to others,

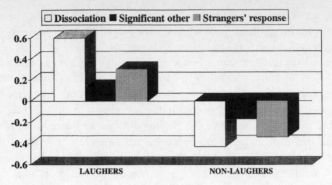

Fig. 1. Level of emotional dissociation and measures of social relationships of individuals who showed Duchenne laughter (laughers) and those who did not (nonlaughers) while talking about their deceased spouses. All measures are standardized z scores. Positive scores indicate increased emotional dissociation, less ambivalence toward a current significant other, and more positive than negative emotion evoked in strangers.

evoking responses, and serving as incentives for social behavior. Indeed, facial expressions are essential elements of interactions, such as attachment processes, flirtation, and appeasement and status rituals, that are crucial to human relationships. Individual differences in facial expressions of emotion, therefore, should relate to different levels of adjustment in interpersonal relationships.

Researchers have examined the contribution of emotional expression to problems in interpersonal adjustment. For example, Field and her colleagues have shown that mothers with depression express little positive emotion, and that this relative lack of positive emotional expression is linked with increased anxiety, distress, and disengagement in their children (Field, 1995). The emotional disturbance in depression is inexorably linked to the well-documented difficulties depressed individuals have in interpersonal relationships. In other work relating emotional expression to interpersonal adjustment, Gottman and Levenson (1992) have found that partners' expressions of contempt and wives' expressions of disgust during conversations about conflict predict dissatisfaction with the relationship and its eventual dissolution.

Given the emerging interest in positive emotions, we have begun to investigate whether positive emotional expression contributes to romantic adjustment. Theorists have proposed that the expression of positive emotion allows partners to increase intimacy, convey commitment, and dissociate from the distress that is likely to arise in any long-term relationship at times. As sensible as these claims are, the relevant empirical evidence is scarce. In a first study, therefore, we addressed whether nonverbal displays of love and desire contribute to romantic satisfaction (Gonzaga, Smith, & Keltner, 1998). Following ethological studies of humans and nonhumans, we coded the affiliative and sexual cues displayed by romantic partners as they talked together about a recent positive event. Romantic partners' affiliative cues, such as smiling and nodding the head, uniquely correlated with self-reports of love, and their sexual cues, such as licking the lips and glancing coyly, uniquely correlated with self-reports of desire. These facial signs of love and desire, in turn, related to romantic satisfaction.

In a follow-up study, we examined whether one marker of romantic love, the Duchenne smile,[2] predicts adjustment in romantic relations over the life course (Harker & Keltner, 1998). We measured positive emotional expression from the college yearbook photos taken of women at Mills College in 1957–1958 and related these measures to romantic outcomes when the women were 27, 43, and 52 years old. Would a measure of positive emotion gathered in one instant in time relate to romantic adjustment 30 years later? Indeed, women's smiling assessed at age 21 related to their reports of marital satisfaction 30 years later, even when we controlled for physical attractiveness and the tendency to report socially desirable answers on questionnaires, two variables that account for significant variance in interpersonal adjustment.

FACIAL EXPRESSION AND PSYCHOPATHOLOGY

Thus far, our review has revealed that brief observations of facial expression relate to how well the individual responds to the death of a spouse and to adjustment in ongoing interpersonal relationships. In this last section, we present evidence indicating that facial expressions relate in systematic ways to chronic, debilitating psychological disorders. This inquiry represents perhaps the most stringent test of the hypothesis that facial expressions relate to personal adjustment, and returns us to James's proposal cited at the outset of this essay.

How might facial expressions relate to psychological disorders? We have already noted that depression may be associated with certain patterns of emotional expression. Another widespread claim is that individuals who are less inclined toward self-conscious emotions, such as embarrassment, shame, or guilt, are more prone to antisocial behavior than are individuals who are more inclined toward self-conscious behavior. The rationale is rather simple: Self-conscious emotions motivate adherence to social norms and restorative interactions that follow norm violations. Individuals who experience and display little self-conscious emotion, by implication, should be more inclined to violate social norms and less likely to restore social relations following norm violations (e.g., in interpersonal conflict). Variants of this hypothesis were advanced long ago by Charles Darwin and Erving Goffman and are embedded in cultural conceptions of the "shameless" individual.

In a test of this hypothesis, the facial expressions of emotion that adolescent boys displayed while taking a brief interactive IQ test were coded and related to their teachers' ratings of the boys' levels of externalizing disorder, defined by aggression and delinquent behavior, and internalizing disorder, defined by anxiety, withdrawal, and complaints about physical problems (Keltner, Moffitt, & Stouthamer-Loeber, 1995). The IQ test produced frequent embarrassment, anger, and fear, as the boys made intellectual mistakes in front of an authority figure (one wonders what effects those emotions had on performance). As seen in Figure 2, the boys who were most prone to antisocial behavior, the externalizers, displayed the least embarrassment (and the most anger), lending credence to the claim that embarrassment motivates socially

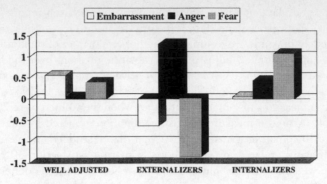

Fig. 2. Scores for facial expressions of embarrassment, anger, and fear shown by adolescent boys during an IQ test. Results are shown separately for boys rated as well adjusted, prone to externalizing behavior, and prone to internalizing behavior. All measures of facial expression are standardized z scores.

normative behavior. The data also suggest that externalizing and internalizing disorders have different emotional cores.

Whereas these early-childhood and adolescent disorders appear to be defined by tendencies to express certain emotions, it has long been believed that schizophrenia is marked by the relative absence of facial expression. Researchers have only recently sought to empirically test this observation, initially offered by Bleuler and Kraeplin. In a series of studies, we found that schizophrenic patients show fewer facial expressions of positive and negative emotions in response to emotionally evocative material than do nonpatients (Kring, Kerr, Smith, & Neale, 1993). These effects are not related to medication or a general deficit in social skills, and schizophrenic patients often report experiencing emotion similar to and in some instances greater than that of control participants. Schizophrenic patients with flat affect are likely to deprive other people of important information and fail to evoke emotions in others (e.g., sympathy) that may benefit themselves. As a consequence, flat affect is especially predictive of a poor prognosis. Interventions that help patients better match their feelings with their outward displays may therefore have positive effects on interpersonal adjustment.

CONCLUSIONS AND FUTURE PROSPECTS

Facial expressions of emotion are markers of intrapersonal processes and mediators of social interactions. This perspective allows researchers to test specific hypotheses concerning relations between facial expression and personal adjustment, thereby benefiting the study of emotion, personal adjustment, and psychopathology. We have shown that individual differences in facial expressions of emotion relate in theoretically coherent ways to personal adjustment in response to loss, in interpersonal relationships, and in the broad context of psychopathology. The findings we have presented, it should be noted, are primarily correlational in nature. It will be important to address how facial expressions contribute to personal adjustment.

Another kindred and promising line of research pertains to the relations between the perception of facial expressions and personal adjustment. Darwin and other researchers have claimed that humans evolved the capacity to reliably interpret facial expressions of emotion and respond accordingly. Consistent with this position, recent studies indicate that different facial expressions activate different regions in the brain in the perceiver and evoke different responses. We believe that these responses lead to behaviors that benefit social relations and, by implication, contribute to personal adjustment. A fairly coherent literature, based on many of the assumptions we have outlined in this review, indicates that individual differences in the perception of emotion relate to specific problems in personal adjustment. Emotion that is expressed and perceived in the face, as James noted long ago, shapes the course of life.

Recommended Reading

Bonanno, G.A. (in press). Grief and emotion: Experience, expression, and dissociation. In M. Stroebe, W. Stroebe, R.O. Hansson, & H. Schut (Eds.), *New handbook of bereavement: Consciousness, coping, and care.* Cambridge, England: Cambridge University Press.

Ekman, P. (1993). (See References)

Ekman, P., & Rosenberg, E. (Eds.). (1997). *What the face reveals.* New York: Oxford University Press.

Keltner, D., & Kring, A. (1998). (See References)

Kring, A., & Bachorowski, J.-A. (in press). Emotion and psychopathology. *Cognition and Emotion.*

Notes

1. Address correspondence to Dacher Keltner, Department of Psychology, 3210 Tolman Hall, University of California, Berkeley, CA 94720-1650.

2. We, like Ekman (1993), believe that the Duchenne smile is a marker of many positive emotional states.

References

Bonanno, G.A., & Keltner, D. (1997). Facial expressions of emotion and the course of conjugal bereavement. *Journal of Abnormal Psychology, 106,* 126–137.

Ekman, P. (1993). Facial expression and emotion. *American Psychologist, 48,* 384–392.

Field, T. (1995). Infants of depressed mothers. *Infant Behavior and Development, 18,* 1–13.

Fredrickson, B.L. (1998). What good are positive emotions? *Review of General Psychology, 2,* 300–319.

Gonzaga, G.C., Smith, M., & Keltner, D. (1998). *Displays of love and desire: Evidence for the commitment hypothesis.* Manuscript submitted for publication.

Gottman, J.M., & Levenson, R.W. (1992). Marital processes predictive of later dissolution: Behavior, physiology, and health. *Journal of Personality and Social Psychology, 63,* 221–233.

Harker, L.A., & Keltner, D. (1998). *Positive expressivity and personal adjustment over the life course.* Manuscript submitted for publication.

James, W. (1890). *Principles of psychology.* New York: Henry Holt.

Keltner, D., & Bonanno, G.A. (1997). A study of laughter and dissociation: The distinct correlates of laughter and smiling during bereavement. *Journal of Personality and Social Psychology, 73,* 687–702.

Keltner, D., & Ekman, P. (in press). Facial expression of emotion. In M. Lewis & J. Haviland (Eds.), *Handbook of emotions*. New York: Guilford Press.

Keltner, D., & Kring, A. (1998). Emotion, social function, and psychopathology. *Review of General Psychology, 2*, 320–342.

Keltner, D., Moffitt, T., & Stouthamer-Loeber, M. (1995). Facial expressions of emotion and psychopathology in adolescent boys. *Journal of Abnormal Psychology, 104*, 644–652.

Kring, A.M., Kerr, S.L., Smith, D.A., & Neale, J.M. (1993). Flat affect in schizophrenia does not reflect diminished subjective experience of emotion. *Journal of Abnormal Psychology, 102*, 507–517.

Levenson, R.W., Ekman, P., & Friesen, W.V. (1990). Voluntary facial action generates emotion-specific autonomic nervous system activity. *Psychophysiology, 27*, 363–384.

Happy as an Extraverted Clam? The Role of Personality for Subjective Well-Being

Kristina M. DeNeve[1]

Department of Psychology and Neuroscience, Baylor University, Waco, Texas

Abstract

Personality characteristics, especially the traits of extraversion and neuroticism, have been proposed as the primary determinant of subjective wellbeing (SWB). Meta-analytic evidence presented here suggests that personality is indeed strongly related with SWB, and that only health is more strongly correlated with SWB. In a study of 137 personality traits that have been correlated with SWB, neuroticism was one of the strongest negative correlates of SWB. However, extraversion was not the primary factor associated with increased SWB. Rather, several personality characteristics that focus on the characteristic experience of emotions, on enhancing relationships, and on one's characteristic style of explaining the causes of life events are most intimately tied to SWB.

Keywords

subjective well-being; personality; meta-analysis; extraversion; neuroticism

What makes people happy? Of course, this is an age-old question, yet it is one that psychologists did not really begin to address empirically until the 1970s. In the past three decades, psychologists have moved from examining demographic factors to focusing on personality as the primary determinant of individual reports of life quality, referred to as subjective well-being (SWB). Two personality constructs in particular, extraversion and neuroticism, have been proposed as the keys to the relation between personality and SWB (Diener, Suh, Lucas, & Smith, in press; McCrae & Costa, 1991). In this article, I summarize the utility of this view.

META-ANALYSES OF SUBJECTIVE WELL-BEING

By 1980, more than 550 research studies had examined various demographic variables in relation to SWB. A series of meta-analyses have analyzed the relation between SWB and variables ranging from age to socioeconomic status. A meta-analysis uses statistical methods to synthesize the empirical literature addressing a given topic and can often provide insight into contradictions that exist among the various studies.

For example, a meta-analysis might fruitfully be conducted on studies that examined whether drinking red wine might delay the development of cardiovascular disease. Let us assume that some studies reported that drinking red wine minimizes the risk for cardiovascular disease, some studies reported that drinking red wine actually increases the risk, and some studies found no connection whatsoever. All of the results from all of these studies could be statistically combined (taking into account factors ranging from the size of the sample to the quality of the study) in order to provide an overall conclusion as to whether drinking red wine can indeed minimize the risk for cardiovascular disease. A meta-analysis could then point out some reasons why the studies reported different results in the first place. For example, perhaps the studies that found drinking red wine was harmful asked participants to drink five glasses of wine a day, whereas the benefits arose in the studies in which participants drank one or two glasses a day.

Meta-analytic evidence indicates that self-reported health is one of the strongest correlates of SWB. In their meta-analysis, Okun, Stock, Haring, and Witter (1984) found an average correlation of $r = .32$ between health and SWB. Interestingly, the average correlation between SWB and health was significantly lower when health was rated by others (e.g., a physician) than when health was assessed via a self-report ($r = .16$ and .35, respectively). Additional research suggests that personality variables, such as neuroticism and characteristic perceptions, are largely responsible for the strong relation between individual reports of health and SWB (Diener et al., in press).

Other meta-analyses suggest that demographic variables do little to distinguish happy from unhappy people. (See DeNeve & Cooper, 1998, for a complete list of meta-analyses conducted to date, as well as their findings.) Men and women report equal amounts of SWB. SWB does not decline with age. Married individuals report being slightly happier than their nonmarried counterparts. Education is moderately related to SWB, but this effect is primarily due to an association between education, income level, and occupational status (Diener et al., in press). Income is also moderately correlated with SWB. However, contrary to popular belief, income appears to enhance SWB only to the point that it allows an individual to meet basic survival needs (Diener et al., in press). The socially active report more SWB than the less active. Finally, religious individuals tend to report more SWB than their nonreligious counterparts.

Demographic variables having the strongest associations with SWB, such as income and religion, do not provide an adequate picture of who is happy and who is not happy. No single demographic variable can explain more than 3% of the variation between individuals' SWB, and national studies find that combining all demographic variables explains less than 15% of the SWB differences between people (Andrews & Withey, 1976; Campbell, Converse, & Rodgers, 1976). Ultimately, psychologists have concluded that demographic variables are largely irrelevant for SWB. Instead, personality has been hypothesized as the major determinant of SWB.

THEORIES OF PERSONALITY AND SUBJECTIVE WELL-BEING

One recent perspective on SWB suggests that individuals who are happy have a genetic predisposition toward happiness. Research comparing identical and fraternal twins at the ages of 20 and 30 years revealed that approximately 50% of current well-being may be caused by genetic influences (Lykken & Tellegen, 1996). In addition, SWB has been tied to two neurologically based systems that were initially described by Gray (1991). The behavioral activation system (BAS) regulates behavior in the presence of rewards and is typically measured as extraversion or positive emotionality. The behavioral inhibition system (BIS) regulates behavior in the presence of punishment and is usually linked to neuroticism or negative emotionality. It has been hypothesized that extraversion predicts the presence of SWB, whereas neuroticism predicts its absence.

SWB researchers also emphasize personality when they adopt a top-down perspective (Diener, 1984). This perspective assumes all individuals have a global tendency to experience life consistently in a positive or negative manner and that this global tendency is determined by personality traits. This global tendency then influences the interpretation of momentary events. Although SWB changes when momentary events (either positive or negative) deviate from their typical pattern, personality characteristics (especially extraversion and neuroticism) will ultimately return the person to his or her previously stable level of SWB (Headey & Wearing, 1989). Personality theorists agree, proposing that extraversion and neuroticism represent enduring dispositions that lead directly to current positive and negative affective states (McCrae & Costa, 1991; Watson & Clark, 1992).

These theoretical formulations point to a single conclusion: Personality should be among the most influential factors for predicting SWB. More specifically, extraversion should be critical to the experience of SWB, and neuroticism should be critical for the lack of SWB.

A META-ANALYSIS OF PERSONALITY AND SUBJECTIVE WELL-BEING

By 1996, fully 137 personality traits had been correlated with SWB. My colleague, Harris Cooper, and I synthesized this literature using meta-analytic techniques (DeNeve & Cooper, 1998). We found 1,538 correlations between personality and SWB. These correlations were reported using 197 distinct samples of individuals, for a total of 42,171 adult respondents (average age of 53.2 years) from English-speaking countries. We found the overall correlation between personality and SWB to be $r = .19$. Thus, personality obtained a very strong relation with SWB, second only to subjective ratings of health in importance. This result is especially noteworthy given that the personality-SWB correlation ignored distinctions among the 137 distinct personality traits.

Of the 137 personality traits, extraversion and neuroticism were expected to be the strongest correlates of SWB, followed by personality traits that focus on control variables, such as desire for control (the extent to which a person wants control over the events in his or her life) and perceived control (the extent to which a person feels he or she has control over the events in his or her life). Contrary to this prediction, the most important personality trait was repressive-defensiveness (the tendency to avoid threatening information), with an average correlation of $r = -.40$. Seven additional personality correlates of SWB that were examined in three or more different samples obtained an average absolute correlation above $r = .30$. Of these seven variables, five were positive correlates: trust, emotional stability, desire for control, hardiness (the tendency to cope positively with stressful life events), and positive affectivity. The remaining two were negative correlates: locus of control-chance (the tendency to think that events happen based on chance alone) and tension (the tendency to experience negative emotions).

Although extraversion and neuroticism have received extensive empirical and theoretical attention, they were not the strongest correlates of SWB. One might argue that because extraversion and neuroticism have been researched with a larger number of diverse individuals, the results for these variables are more accurate than the results for other personality variables that have not been so widely examined. To test this possibility, we examined the average correlation for all personality traits that had been used in 10 or more distinct samples. (A total of 13 personality traits met this criterion.) Of these personality traits, affiliation (the tendency to want to relate with other people; $r = .29$) and perceived control ($r = .29$) were the strongest correlates, followed by neuroticism ($r = -.27$), internal locus of control (the tendency to credit or blame the self for events that happen; $r = .25$), social desirability (the tendency to respond in a manner that one believes will lead to approval from others; $r = .23$), and then sociability (the tendency to relate well with others; $r = .20$) and extraversion ($r = .20$). In sum, extraversion was still not one of the most important correlates, ranking 6th of the 13 most commonly researched traits.

HOW PERSONALITY MIGHT INFLUENCE SUBJECTIVE WELL-BEING

This pattern of results suggests that SWB cannot be explained solely in terms of extraversion and neuroticism. Rather, three general trends can be described. First, SWB is intimately tied to personality traits that focus on emotional tendencies, namely, emotional stability, positive affectivity, and tension. This finding makes intuitive sense; measures of characteristic emotions should be related to measures of current emotions.

Second, relationship-enhancing traits are also important for SWB. Affiliation refers to the desire and ability to form good relationships. Trust focuses on how a person views the behavior of another person. Social desirability and sociability refer to adaptive ways to relate to others. In addition to fostering better relationships, these personality traits appear to provide the bonus of facilitating SWB. This general trend extends Myers and Diener's (1995) suggestion that happy individuals tend to have strong relationships. Not only do happy people have strong relationships, but happy people are also characteristically good at fostering strong relationships.

Finally, several of the strongest SWB correlates suggest that the way people think about and explain what happens in their lives is intimately tied to SWB. Results on repressive-defensiveness, control variables, hardiness, and trust point to this conclusion. On the one hand, individuals who tend to be repressive-defensive and who tend to believe that they do not control the events in their own lives are among the least happy individuals. On the other hand, making positive attributions can enhance SWB. Unlike repressive-defensives who deny the very existence of threatening events, hardy individuals diminish the impact of stressful life events by appraising these events in an optimistic fashion and then engaging in active coping efforts. In contrast with individuals who believe that powerful others or chance events control their lives, individuals with a desire for control are more likely to make attributions that give them a sense of control over their lives

(Burger & Hemans, 1988). Likewise, SWB is related to the belief that one has a great deal of control over the events in one's life and that one is largely responsible for these events (as measured by internal locus of control and perceived control). Finally, Costa and McCrae (1992) indicated that people low on the trust scale "tend to be cynical and skeptical and to assume that others may be dishonest or dangerous" (p. 17). Thus, trust essentially measures the tendency to make attributions of people's actions in an optimistic or pessimistic fashion. In short, the pattern of correlations suggests that making positive, optimistic attributions and avoiding negative, pessimistic attributions is one key to experiencing SWB.

CONCLUSION

The research I have reviewed here suggests that personality is indeed of considerable importance for the experience of SWB. As previous theoretical frameworks indicated, unhappy individuals tend to be neurotic, with the most unhappy individuals being especially prone to denying threatening life events. In addition, unhappy individuals tend to deny the existence of negative emotions although they actually experience negative emotions more frequently than their happy counterparts. However, to "be as happy as a clam," a person does not need to be extraverted. Rather, the happiest people seem to be those who characteristically explain their life events in optimistic, adaptive ways. Happy people are also those who are characteristically able to foster their relationships. Taken together, these results challenge past theoretical models that suggested extraversion is the key for promoting SWB. New models that incorporate the personality characteristics found to have the highest correlations with SWB need to be developed. Given that most of these important traits have been examined in fewer than 10 SWB studies, additional research examining the processes by which these personality traits might influence SWB is also sorely needed.

In addition to relationship-enhancing and optimistic traits, characteristic positive emotionality relates strongly to SWB. This result, together with the findings that SWB has a large genetic basis and is stable across the life span (Diener et al., in press), suggests that SWB itself has some of the qualities of a personality trait.

Finally, SWB researchers should begin to utilize experimental methodologies more and survey methodologies less to begin to examine causal links. One promising experimental paradigm was described by Lyubomirsky and Ross (1997). In this work, participants were characterized as happy or unhappy some time prior to being invited to the lab, at which point they then participated in one of several experimental conditions. Using this type of methodology, SWB researchers can begin to move from identifying which personality traits are most closely associated with SWB to examining how characteristically happy people differ from characteristically unhappy people as they live their lives.

Recommended Reading

DeNeve, K.M., & Cooper, H. (1998). (See References)
Diener, E. (1996). Traits can be powerful, but are not enough: Lessons from subjective well-being. *Journal of Research in Personality, 30*, 389–399.

Diener, E., Suh, E.M., Lucas, R.E., & Smith, H.L. (in press). (See References)

Kahneman, D., Diener, E., & Schwarz, N. (Eds.). (1999). *Hedonic psychology: Scientific perspectives on enjoyment, suffering, and well-being*. New York: Russell Sage Foundation.

Note

1. Address correspondence to Kristina M. DeNeve, Department of Psychology and Neuroscience, Baylor University, P.O. Box 97334, Waco, TX 76798-7334; e-mail: kristina_deneve@baylor.edu.

References

Andrews, F.M., & Withey, S.B. (1976). *Social indicators of well-being: America's perception of life quality*. New York: Plenum Press.

Burger, J.M., & Hemans, L.T. (1988). Desire for control and the use of attribution processes. *Journal of Personality, 56*, 531–546.

Campbell, A., Converse, P.E., & Rodgers, W.L. (1976). *The quality of American life*. New York: Russell Sage Foundation.

Costa, P.T., & McCrae, R.R. (1992). *Revised NEO Personality Inventory (NEO PI-R) and NEO Five-Factor Inventory professional manual*. Odessa, FL: Psychological Assessment Resources.

DeNeve, K.M., & Cooper, H. (1998). The happy personality: A meta-analysis of 137 personality traits and subjective well-being. *Psychological Bulletin, 124*, 197–229.

Diener, E. (1984). *Subjective well-being. Psychological Bulletin, 95*, 542–575.

Diener, E., Suh, E.M., Lucas, R.E., & Smith, H.L. (in press). Subjective well-being: Three decades of progress. *Psychological Bulletin*.

Gray, J.A. (1991). Neural systems, emotion, and personality. In J. Madden, IV (Ed.), *Neurobiology of learning, emotion, and affect* (pp. 273–306). New York: Raven Press.

Headey, B., & Wearing, A. (1989). Personality, life events, and subjective well-being: Toward a dynamic equilibrium model. *Journal of Personality and Social Psychology, 57*, 731–739.

Lykken, D., & Tellegen, A. (1996). Happiness is a stochastic phenomenon. *Psychological Science, 7*, 186–189.

Lyubomirsky, S., & Ross, L. (1997). Hedonic consequences of social comparison: A contrast of happy and unhappy people. *Journal of Personality and Social Psychology, 73*, 1141–1157.

McCrae, R.R., & Costa, P.T. (1991). Adding Liebe und Arbeit: The full five-factor model and well-being. *Personality and Social Psychology Bulletin, 17*, 227–232.

Myers, D.G., & Diener, E. (1995). Who is happy? *Psychological Science, 6*, 10–19.

Okun, M.A., Stock, W.A., Haring, M.J., & Witter, R.A. (1984). Health and subjective well-being: A meta-analysis. *International Journal of Aging and Human Development, 19*, 111–132.

Watson, D., & Clark, L.M. (1992). On traits and temperament: General and specific factors of emotional experience and their relation to the five-factor model. *Journal of Personality, 60*, 441–476.

Intelligence Predicts Health and Longevity, but Why?

Linda S. Gottfredson[1] and Ian J. Deary[2]

[1]*School of Education, University of Delaware, and* [2]*Department of Psychology, University of Edinburgh, Edinburgh, Scotland, United Kingdom*

Abstract

Large epidemiological studies of almost an entire population in Scotland have found that intelligence (as measured by an IQ-type test) in childhood predicts substantial differences in adult morbidity and mortality, including deaths from cancers and cardiovascular diseases. These relations remain significant after controlling for socioeconomic variables. One possible, partial explanation of these results is that intelligence enhances individuals' care of their own health because it represents learning, reasoning, and problem-solving skills useful in preventing chronic disease and accidental injury and in adhering to complex treatment regimens.

Keywords

intelligence; health; longevity

Health psychologists examine the impact of volition on health, but might not competence matter too? Managing one's physical health is, after all, one of life's jobs, and personnel psychology has established that psychometric intelligence, that is, intelligence as measured by IQ tests, is the best single predictor of job performance. Indeed, intelligence is the best single predictor of major socioeconomic outcomes, both favorable (good education, occupation, income) and unfavorable (adult poverty, incarceration, chronic welfare use; Gottfredson, 2002).

HOW WELL DOES EARLY INTELLIGENCE PREDICT LATER HEALTH AND LONGEVITY?

Intelligence has been linked with various health behaviors and outcomes. On the positive side, physical fitness, a preference for low-sugar and low-fat diets, and longevity increase with higher intelligence; on the negative side, alcoholism, infant mortality, smoking, and obesity increase with lower intelligence (Gottfredson, in press). Especially informative are two epidemiological studies correlating IQ in childhood to adult morbidity and mortality.

Australian Veterans Health Studies

O'Toole and Stankov (1992) used IQ at induction into the military, along with 56 other psychological, behavioral, health, and demographic variables, to predict

---

Address correspondence to Linda S. Gottfredson, School of Education, University of Delaware, Newark, DE 19716.

201

noncombat deaths by age 40 among 2,309 Australian veterans. When all other variables were statistically controlled, each additional IQ point predicted a 1% decrease in risk of death. Also, IQ was the best predictor of the major cause of death, motor vehicle accidents. Vehicular death rates doubled and then tripled at successively lower IQ ranges (100–115, 85–100, 80–85; O'Toole, 1990).

Scottish Mental Survey 1932 (SMS1932)

To date, Scotland is the only country to have conducted IQ testing on almost a whole year-of-birth cohort. This took place in the remarkable Scottish Mental Survey of 1932 (SMS1932). On June 1, 1932, a version of the Moray House Test (MHT) was administered to almost all children born in 1921 and attending schools in Scotland on that day ($N = 87,498$). The MHT is a well-validated intelligence test that has a high correlation (about .8) with the Stanford Binet. Recent follow-up studies of the SMS1932 (Deary, Whiteman, Starr, Whalley, & Fox, in press) provide novel findings on what intelligence differences during childhood portend for health in the rest of life.

Health data for subsets of the SMS1932 participants were collected in later decades. In one such follow-up study, Whalley and Deary (2001) identified the 2,792 children from the city of Aberdeen who participated in the SMS1932, and searched the Register of Deaths from 1932 to 1997 for whether they were alive or dead on January 1, 1997. Subjects not found were then sought in the Scottish Community Health Index, which records people who are registered with a general medical practitioner (more than 99% of the population). Many women were still untraced, mostly because they had married and changed their surname. Therefore, the Register of Marriages in Scotland was searched from 1937 onward. When a woman was traced to a marriage, the prior searches were repeated. Subjects still untraced were sought using computer and hand searches of the United Kingdom National Health Service Central Register.

Using these procedures, the researchers traced 2,230 (79.9%) of those children who took the MHT in Aberdeen: 1,084 were dead, 1,101 were alive, and 45 had moved away from Scotland. In addition, 562 were untraced. IQ at age 11 had a significant association with survival to about age 76. On average, individuals who were at a 1-standard-deviation (15-point) disadvantage in IQ relative to other participants were only 79% as likely to live to age 76. The effect of IQ was stronger for women (71%) than for men (83%), partly because men who died in active service during World War II had relatively high mean IQ scores. Further analyses of the Aberdeen subjects found that a drop of 1 standard deviation in IQ was associated with a 27% increase in cancer deaths among men and a 40% increase in cancer deaths among women (Deary, Whalley, & Starr, 2003). The effect was especially pronounced for stomach and lung cancers, which are specifically associated with low socioeconomic status (SES) in childhood.

Additional data for many SMS1932 participants are available in the Midspan studies, which began in the 1970s in the western and central areas of Scotland and are still ongoing. These studies investigated cardiovascular and respiratory diseases and their risk factors in the community. The participants were adults who completed a questionnaire and underwent physical examinations. Their social class—based on occupation at midlife—was recorded, as was the degree of deprivation or affluence of the area where they resided. The Midspan studies continue to follow participants, tracking their hospital admissions and the dates and causes of their deaths. Of the 1,251 Midspan participants born in 1921, 1,032 (82.5%) were matched to people in the SMS1932 ledgers, and 938 had an MHT score (Hart, Deary, et al., 2003). Higher IQ in 1932 had strong correlations with both higher social class and greater affluence of the area of residence at the time of Midspan participation. The risk of dying in the 25 years since participation in the Midspan studies increased 17% for each drop of 1 standard deviation in IQ at age 11 (Hart, Taylor, et al., 2003). Controlling for social class and deprivation recorded in the 1970s, when people were about 50 years old, reduced this figure to 12%.

IQ and deprivation interacted, such that the increase in mortality associated with deprivation was greatest in the lowest IQ quartile; put another way, IQ had a larger effect on mortality among people living in deprived areas than among people living in affluent areas at about age 50. Age-11 IQ had a small indirect effect on mortality from all causes combined, through its effects on adult social class and deprivation; however, the direct effects of age-11 IQ on mortality were stronger. Investigating specific causes of death among the Midspan participants, Hart, Taylor, et al. (2003) found that lower age-11 IQ predicted a significantly higher likelihood of dying from cardiovascular disease in general, coronary heart disease, and lung cancer.

Higher intelligence might lower mortality from all causes and from specific causes partly by affecting known risk factors for disease, such as smoking. In the combined SMS1932-Midspan database, there was no significant childhood IQ difference between participants who had ever smoked and those who had never smoked (Taylor, Hart, et al., 2003). However, at the time of the Midspan studies, participants who were current smokers had significantly lower childhood IQs than ex-smokers. For each standard deviation increase in IQ, there was a 33% increased rate of quitting smoking. Adjusting for social class reduced this rate only mildly, to 25%. Thus, childhood IQ was not associated with starting smoking (mostly in the 1930s, when the public were not aware of health risks), but was associated with giving up smoking as health risks became evident.

WHY DOES EARLY INTELLIGENCE PREDICT LATER HEALTH?

Health epidemiologists tend to ascribe inequalities in health to inequalities in socioeconomic resources, and then presume that intelligence is a product of such resources, and thus related to health because it is a proxy for privilege. Do differences in socioeconomic advantage explain the influence of intelligence on health?

Is Intelligence a Proxy for Material Resources?

A robust relation between childhood IQ and late-life morbidity and mortality remains after analyses control statistically for deprived living conditions. Residual confounding is possible, which means that social factors measured to date might not reliably assess all relevant aspects of social disadvantage. However, health inequalities tend to *increase* when health resources become more available to everyone (Gottfredson, in press). That is, increased availability of health resources improves health overall, but the improvements are smaller for people who are poorly educated and have low incomes than for people with more education and better incomes. Compared with people in high-SES groups, people with low SES seek more but not necessarily appropriate care when cost is no barrier; adhere less often to treatment regimens; learn and understand less about how to protect their health; seek less preventive care, even when it is free; and less often practice the healthy behaviors so important for preventing or slowing the progression of chronic diseases, the major killers and disablers in developed nations today.

Yet social class correlates with virtually every indicator of health, health behavior, and health knowledge. The link between SES and health transcends the particulars of material advantage, decade, nation, health system, social change, or disease, regardless of its treatability. Health scientists view the pervasiveness and finely graded nature of this relationship between SES and health as a paradox, leading them to speculate that SES creates health inequality via some yet-to-be-identified, highly generalizable "fundamental cause" (Gottfredson, in press). The socioeconomic measures that best predict health inequality also correlate most with intelligence (education best, then occupation, then income). This means that instead of IQ being a proxy for SES in health matters, SES measures might be operating primarily as rough proxies for social-class differences in mental rather than material resources.

Does Intelligence Provide Health-Enhancing Mental Resources?

Psychometric intelligence is manifested in generic thinking skills such as efficient learning, reasoning, problem solving, and abstract thinking. High intelligence is a useful tool in any life domain, but especially when tasks are novel, untutored, or complex and situations are ambiguous, changing, or unpredictable (Gottfredson, 1997).

Dealing with the novel, ever-changing, and complex is what health self-care demands. Preventive information proliferates, and new treatments often require regular self-monitoring and complicated self-medication. Good health depends as much on preventing as on ameliorating illness, injury, and disability. Preventing some aspects of chronic disease is arguably no less cognitive a process than preventing accidents, the fourth leading cause of death in the United States, behind cancer, heart disease, and stroke (Gottfredson, in press). Preventing both illness and accidents requires anticipating the unexpected and "driving defensively," in a well-informed way, through life. The cognitive demands of preventing illness and accidents are comparable—remain vigilant for hazards and recognize them when present, remove or evade them in a timely manner, contain incidents to prevent or limit damage, and modify behavior and environments to prevent reoccurrence. Health workers can diagnose and treat incubating problems, such as high blood pressure or diabetes, but only when people seek preventive screening and follow treatment regimens. Many do not. In fact, perhaps a third of all prescription medications are taken in a manner that jeopardizes the patient's health. Nonadherence to prescribed treatment regimens doubles the risk of death among heart patients (Gallagher, Viscoli, & Horwitz, 1993). For better or worse, people are substantially their own primary health care providers.

Researchers have concluded that high rates of noncompliance reflect many patients' inability, not unwillingness, to understand and implement the treatments their physicians recommend, especially as regimens become more complex. Many people are unable to perform some fundamental tasks in the "job" of patient, and some researchers have studied this issue using health literacy tests. Although these tests focus specifically on health content, they mimic IQ tests in assessing the same general ability to learn, reason, and solve problems. For instance, one study (Williams et al., 1995) found that, overall, 26% of the outpatients at two urban hospitals were unable to determine from an appointment slip when their next appointment was scheduled, and 42% did not understand directions for taking medicine on an empty stomach. The percentages specifically among outpatients with "inadequate" literacy were worse: 40% and 65%, respectively. In comparison, the percentages were 5% and 24% among outpatients with "adequate" literacy.

In another study (Williams, Baker, Parker, & Nurss, 1998), many insulin-dependent diabetics did not understand fundamental facts for maintaining daily control of their disease: Among those classified as having inadequate literacy, about half did not know the signs of very low or very high blood sugar, and 60% did not know the corrective actions they needed to take if their blood sugar was too low or too high. Among diabetics, intelligence at time of diagnosis correlates significantly (.36) with diabetes knowledge measured 1 year later (Taylor, Frier, et al., 2003). Like hypertension and many other chronic illnesses, diabetes requires self-monitoring and frequent judgments to keep physiological processes within safe limits. In general, low functional health literacy is linked to more illnesses, greater severity of illnesses, worse self-rated health, far higher medical costs, and (prospectively) more frequent hospitalization (Gottfredson, in press).

Most new information about health diffuses through the public media. Like improved access to health care, greater access to health information does not necessarily lead to greater equality. Rather, knowledge gaps tend to grow. When more knowledge about health risks (e.g., smoking) and new diagnostic options (e.g., Pap smears) infuse into the public sphere, already-informed persons learn the most and act on the new information more often than people who started out relatively uninformed (Gottfredson, in press). This might explain why IQ was related to smoking cessation in the SMS1932.

CONCLUSION

The SMS1932 studies have established that psychometric intelligence is an important factor in public health. Major challenges for future research are to identify the causal mechanisms for the relation between IQ and health and to capitalize on the findings to develop programs that will provide more effective health education and health care.

Correlations Have Causes

Four possible mechanisms relating childhood IQ to longevity (Whalley & Deary, 2001) provide a partial research agenda for the field. IQ at age 11 might be (a) an "archaeological record" of prior (e.g., perinatal and childhood) insults, (b) a record of the integrity of the body as a whole, (c) a predictor of healthy behaviors (e.g., avoid injuries, do not smoke), and (d) a predictor of entry into healthy environments (e.g., nonhazardous occupations). In the present article, we have focused on examining the third possibility, conceptualizing health self-care as a job, and cognitive competence as a correlate of performance in that job. However, none of these possibilities is exclusive of the others, and all four need to be considered.

A possible example of IQ as a record of prior insults is that cognitive differences, and risk of illnesses such as diabetes and cardiovascular disease later in life, are correlated with fetal development and birth weight. Investigating the second possibility requires clearly conceptualizing the construct of integrity. For example, oxidative stress (involving the generation of damaging free radicals in the body) is a factor in bodily aging and health. Perhaps people who have low levels of oxidative stress and good antioxidant defenses have better health and cognitive functions in later life than do people with more oxidative stress and poorer antioxidant defenses. Earlier in the article, we noted a confirmatory example of the third possibility: In the SMS1932-Midspan studies, people who gave up smoking between the 1930s and the 1970s tended to have had higher mental test scores at age 11 than people who continued to smoke. However, men with higher IQs were more likely to die in active service in World War II than were men with lower IQs: The association between higher IQ and longer life is not immutable.

With regard to exposure to safe versus healthy environments, the fourth possibility, many social scientists think that inequities in social structures, and perhaps education, are the fundamental causal influences that explain why IQ is related to health. The SMS1932-Midspan studies found that adjusting for occupational social class attenuated the effects of IQ on morbidity and mortality somewhat, but the effects remained significant and substantial. In the same studies, the finding of an interaction between childhood IQ and deprivation on later health attests to the importance of both intellectual and social factors. However, the fact that SES-health correlations have sometimes disfavored higher-SES groups but then reversed direction in a matter of decades (Gottfredson, in press), as groups differentially sought, understood, and acted upon new health discoveries, speaks against purely socioeconomic (or, indeed, body-integrity) explanations for some of the IQ-health relations found in the Scottish epidemiological studies. It implicates psychometric intelligence as a significant influence on effective health self-care. A key test of the influence of social background will be to examine whether siblings who have dissimilar IQs but are reared in the same family have discordant health and longevity.

Health Education and Health Care

The epidemiological studies we have discussed suggest that health care policy and practice will be more effective if they take into account how cognitive competence influences health and survival. One possibility we have raised is that the cognitive complexities of health self-care exceed the learning and reasoning capabilities of many individuals. Health educators already advocate that health materials be written at no higher than the fifth-grade reading level. However, many aspects of health self-care—for example, self-monitoring and self-medicating among individuals with chronic disease—are inherently complex and perhaps cannot be simplified without rendering care less effective. Health care workers can use this knowledge to help all patients attain optimal levels of skill and knowledge.

Recommended Reading

Deary, I.J. (2001). *Intelligence: A very short introduction.* Oxford, England: Oxford University Press.

Gottfredson, L.S. (1998). The general intelligence factor. *Scientific American Presents, 9,* 24–29.

Acknowledgments—Ian Deary is the recipient of a Royal Society-Wolfson Research Merit Award.

References

Deary, I.J., Whalley, L.J., & Starr, J.M. (2003). IQ at age 11 and longevity: Results from a follow up of the Scottish Mental Survey 1932. In C.E. Finch, J.-M. Robine, & Y. Christen (Eds.), *Brain and longevity: Perspectives in longevity* (pp. 153–164). Berlin, Germany: Springer.

Deary, I.J., Whiteman, M.C., Starr, J.M., Whalley, L.J., & Fox, H.C. (in press). The impact of childhood intelligence on later life: Following up the Scottish Mental Surveys of 1932 and 1947. *Journal of Personality and Social Psychology.*

Gallagher, E.J., Viscoli, C.M., & Horwitz, R.I. (1993). The relationship of treatment adherence to the risk of death after myocardial infarction in women. *Journal of the American Medical Association, 270,* 742–744.

Gottfredson, L.S. (1997). Why g matters: The complexity of everyday life. *Intelligence, 24,* 79–132.

Gottfredson, L.S. (2002). g: Highly general and highly practical. In R.J. Sternberg & E.L. Grigorenko (Eds.), *The general factor of intelligence: How general is it?* (pp. 331–380). Mahwah, NJ: Erlbaum.

Gottfredson, L.S. (in press). Intelligence: Is it the epidemiologists' elusive "fundamental cause" of social class inequalities in health? *Journal of Personality and Social Psychology.*

Hart, C.L., Deary, I.J., Taylor, M.D., MacKinnon, P.L., Davey Smith, G., Whalley, L.J., Wilson, V., Hole, D.J., & Starr, J.M. (2003). The Scottish Mental Survey 1932 linked to the Midspan studies: A prospective investigation of childhood intelligence and future health. *Public Health, 117,* 187–195.

Hart, C.L., Taylor, M.D., Davey Smith, G., Whalley, L.J., Starr, J.M., Hole, D.J., Wilson, V., & Deary, I.J. (2003). Childhood IQ, social class, deprivation and their relationships with mortality and morbidity risk in later life. *Psychosomatic Medicine, 65,* 877–883.

O'Toole, B.J. (1990). Intelligence and behavior and motor vehicle accident mortality. *Accident Analysis and Prevention, 22,* 211–221.

O'Toole, B.J., & Stankov, L. (1992). Ultimate validity of psychological tests. *Personality and Individual Differences, 13,* 699–716.

Taylor, M.D., Frier, B.M., Gold, A.E., & Deary, I.J. (2003). Psychosocial factors and diabetes-related outcomes following diagnosis of Type 1 diabetes. *Diabetic Medicine, 20,* 135–146.

Taylor, M.D., Hart, C.L., Davey Smith, G., Starr, J.M., Hole, D.J., Whalley, L.J., Wilson, V., & Deary, I.J. (2003). Childhood mental ability and smoking cessation in adulthood. *Journal of Epidemiology and Community Health, 57,* 464–465.

Whalley, L.J., & Deary, I.J. (2001). Longitudinal cohort study of childhood IQ and survival up to age 76. *British Medical Journal, 322,* 1–5.

Williams, M.V., Baker, D.W., Parker, R.M., & Nurss, J.R. (1998). Relationship of functional health literacy to patients' knowledge of their chronic disease. *Archives of Internal Medicine, 158,* 166–172.

Williams, M.V., Parker, R.M., Baker, D.W., Pirikh, N.S., Pitkin, K., Coates, W.C., & Nurss, J.R. (1995). Inadequate functional health literacy among patients at two public hospitals. *Journal of the American Medical Association, 274,* 1677–1682.

Thin-Ideal Internalization: Mounting Evidence for a New Risk Factor for Body-Image Disturbance and Eating Pathology

J. Kevin Thompson[1] and Eric Stice

Department of Psychology, University of South Florida, Tampa, Florida (J.K.T.), and Department of Psychology, University of Texas at Austin, Austin, Texas (E.S.)

Abstract

Body-image disturbance and eating disorders are a Significant physical and mental health problem in Western countries. We describe emerging work on one newly identified variable that appears to be a potent risk factor for the development of these problems—internalization of societal standards of attractiveness. Work conducted independently in our labs over the past decade has included scale development, correlational studies, prospective risk-factor studies, randomized experiments, and randomized prevention trials. Findings collectively suggest that internalization is a causal risk factor for body-image and eating disturbances, and that it appears to operate in conjunction with other established risk factors for these outcomes, including dieting and negative affect. Future research is needed to examine the specific familial, peer, and media influences that promote internalization and to replicate and extend our prospective and experimental studies.

Keywords

internalization; body image; eating disturbance; risk factors; prevention

Eating disorders are one of the most common psychiatric problems faced by women, and are characterized by a persistent course, co-occurrence with other psychopathology, medical complications, and elevated mortality. Body-image disturbance, generally consisting of a subjective unhappiness with some aspect of one's appearance, is also extremely prevalent and may be associated with psychological distress (e.g., depression) and functional impairment (Thompson, Heinberg, Altabe, & Tantleff-Dunn, 1999). Exciting advances have recently occurred in social scientists' understanding of the risk factors that promote body-image and eating disturbances. One promising avenue of new research concerns the role of internalization of societal ideals of attractiveness (thin-ideal internalization[2]) in the development of these problems. Thin-ideal internalization refers to the extent to which an individual cognitively "buys into" socially defined ideals of attractiveness and engages in behaviors designed to produce an approximation of these ideals (Thompson et al., 1999).

Theoretically, thin-ideal internalization results because individuals internalize attitudes that are approved of by significant or respected others (Kandel, 1980). This process is referred to as social reinforcement. Specifically, family, peers, and media (i.e., the socialization agents) are thought to reinforce the thin-ideal body image for women through comments or actions that serve to support and perpetuate this ideal (e.g., criticism or teasing regarding weight, encouragement to diet, and glorification of ultra-slender models). These sources communicate expectations concerning the benefits of thinness, such as increased social acceptance, and these expectations likely play a key role in the propagation of this ideal (Hohlstein, Smith, & Atlas, 1998).

Thin-ideal internalization is thought to directly foster body dissatisfaction because this ideal is virtually unattainable for most females (Thompson et al., 1999). Additionally, thin-ideal internalization is thought to work in conjunction with other established risk factors for eating pathology, including body dissatisfaction, dieting, and negative affect (e.g., Killen et al., 1996), in promoting eating-disordered symptoms. Specifically, the body dissatisfaction that is thought to result from thin-ideal internalization theoretically promotes dieting and negative affect, which in turn increase the risk for onset of bulimic symptoms (Stice, 2001). Body dissatisfaction putatively leads to dieting because of the common belief that this is an effective weight-control technique. Body dissatisfaction may also foster negative affect because appearance is a central evaluative dimension for women in our culture. Dieting is theorized to result in a greater risk for bulimic symptoms because individuals might binge-eat in an effort to counteract the effects of caloric deprivation. Finally, negative affect may increase the likelihood of bulimic symptoms because of the belief that eating provides comfort and distraction from negative emotions.

RESEARCH BACKGROUND

Our initial work on thin-ideal internalization focused on the operationalization of the internalization construct and an evaluation of the reliability and validity of the resulting measures. We asked young women and men to describe the current ideal for attractiveness for females in Western culture and used these qualitative responses to create our initial scales (Heinberg, Thompson, & Stormer, 1995; Stice, Schupak-Neuberg, Shaw, & Stein, 1994). These two paper-and-pencil questionnaires and their revisions have received extensive examination, with adult and child-adolescent samples, and have demonstrated strong internal consistencies, test-retest reliabilities, predictive validity, and convergent validity (i.e., they correlate significantly with other measures that are similar or that they should theoretically correlate with, such as measures of body image; Cusumano & Thompson, 2001; Heinberg et al., 1995; Stice, 2001; Stice & Agras, 1998; Stice, Mazotti, Weibel, & Agras, 2000). The convergent validity of our two internalization scales was supported by research indicating that they were highly correlated ($r = .69$) in a sample of young adult females (Stice et al., 2000). (See Table 1 for sample items from our two internalization scales.)

The second phase of our research consisted of preliminary studies that tested whether thin-ideal internalization is positively correlated with body-image and eating disturbances. Research with female college students confirmed these correlations (e.g., Stice et al., 1994). In addition, in studies that separated out the role of awareness of societal standards from internalization of such messages and images, internalization was a more potent correlate of eating and body-image problems (Cusumano & Thompson, 2001; Heinberg et al., 1995; Thompson et al., 1999).

Table 1. Sample internalization items

I would like my body to look like the women that appear in TV shows and movies.
I wish I looked like the women pictured in magazines that model underwear.
Music videos that show women who are in good physical shape make me wish that I
were in better physical shape.
I do not wish to look like the female models that appear in magazines. (reverse-keyed)
From Thompson, Heinberg, Altabe, and Tantleff-Dunn (1999)

Slender women are more attractive.
Women with toned bodies are more attractive.
Women with long legs are more attractive.
From Stice and Agras (1998)

Our third line of research tested whether thin-ideal internalization prospectively predicts body-image and eating disturbances. It is important to demonstrate temporal precedence between a putative risk factor and the pathologic outcomes to rule out the possibility that the factor is simply a concomitant or consequence of the disorder (Kraemer et al., 1997). An initial prospective study found that thin-ideal internalization predicted the onset of bulimic symptoms among initially asymptomatic adolescent girls (Stice & Agras, 1998), thereby establishing that thin-ideal internalization is a risk factor for eating pathology. Two additional findings support the theorized mediational processes that link thin-ideal internalization to eating disturbances. First, analyses also revealed that internalization predicted increased dieting (Stice, Mazotti, Krebs, & Martin, 1998). Second, an independent study found that thin-ideal internalization predicted subsequent increases in body dissatisfaction, dieting, and negative affect, which in turn predicted subsequent increase in bulimic symptoms (Stice, 2001).

The fourth phase of our research used randomized experiments to reduce the impact of one major promoter of thin-ideal internalization: thin-ideal images portrayed in the media. Specifically, Stormer and Thompson (1998) developed a program to teach women how to be more critical consumers of the media so as to reduce thin-ideal internalization. For example, one component of this intervention provides information on the degree to which photographic images in magazines are altered through computer modification. Two controlled trials showed that this intervention reduced thin-ideal internalization (Stormer & Thompson, 1998), and the effect has been replicated in other independent trials (e.g., Irving, DuPen, & Berel, 1998).

The fifth phase in this line of research entailed the experimental manipulation of thin-ideal internalization in an effort to rule out potential third variables that might explain the prospective findings and to establish that internalization is a causal risk factor for body-image and eating disturbances (Kraemer et al., 1997). In a dissonance-based intervention, women with higher than average thin-ideal internalization were persuaded to voluntarily argue against this ideal through a series of verbal, written, and behavioral exercises. Assessments conducted both at the time the intervention ended and at a later follow-up indicated that this intervention resulted in reductions in level of internalization, as well as decreased body dissatisfaction, dieting, negative affect, and bulimic pathology (Stice et al., 2000). These findings were replicated in an independent randomized experiment (Stice, Chase, Stormer, & Appel, 2001). Because there is experimental evidence that a reduction in thin-ideal internalization resulted in decreased body dissatisfaction and bulimic symptoms, thin-ideal internalization can be considered a causal risk factor for these outcomes according to the criteria of Kraemer et al. (1997).

FUTURE DIRECTIONS

These preliminary findings suggest that thin-ideal internalization is an important risk factor for body-image and eating disturbances, but several avenues of future research are indicated. First, our findings appear to suggest that internalization is a causal risk factor, and not a proxy for some other variable. Manipulation of thin-ideal internalization would not have affected body image if a proxy effect were operating. Nonetheless, our confidence in this conclusion would be strengthened by replication from other laboratories. Second, further work is needed in the prevention area to verify that interventions targeting internalization do not inadvertently manipulate other variables, such as body dissatisfaction. A temporal analysis indicating that internalization decreased prior to any changes in eating or body-image measures would be a key demonstration. Third, it would be desirable to elucidate possible physiological and cognitive correlates of internalization, such as reaction time or processing biases in response to weight and shape stimuli.

Finally, additional theoretical work is needed to investigate the factors that promote thin-ideal internalization, as well as the factors that buffer and heighten the effects of this risk variable. Variables that have been hypothesized or found to moderate the pernicious effects of internalization include self-esteem, exposure to the media, and tendency to compare one's appearance with other people's appearance (Thompson et al., 1999). More theory-driven work based on social-comparison and cognitive-processing models may also yield important information about the dispositional and contextual factors related to internalization. Furthermore, as we noted at the outset of this article, social-reinforcement theory may help explain the development of internalization. However, prospective studies are needed to document that social reinforcement from family, peers, and the media predicts subsequent development of thin-ideal internalization. Research should also attempt to manipulate parental and peer social reinforcement of the thin-ideal, to generate experimental evidence that these processes foster thin-ideal internalization.

Recommended Reading

Piran, N., Levine, M.P., & Steiner-Adair, C. (Eds.). (1999). *Preventing eating disorders: A handbook of interventions and special challenges.* Philadelphia: Brunner/Mazel.

Stice, E. (2001). Risk factors for eating pathology: Recent advances and future directions. In R.H. Striegel-Moore & L. Smolak (Eds.), *Eating disorders: Innovative directions for research and practice* (pp. 51–73). Washington, DC: American Psychological Association.

Thompson, J.K., & Heinberg, L.J. (1999). The media's influence on body image disturbance and eating disorders: We've reviled them, now can we rehabilitate them? *Journal of Social Issues, 55,* 339–353.

Thompson, J.K., & Smolak, L. (Eds.). (2001). *Body image, eating disorders, and obesity in youth: Assessment, prevention and treatment.* Washington, DC: American Psychological Association.

Notes

1. Address correspondence to J. Kevin Thompson, Department of Psychology, University of South Florida, Tampa, FL 33620-8200; e-mail: jthompso@chuma1.cas.usf.edu.

2. The societal ideal of attractiveness encompasses more than just thinness. However, we use the term thin-ideal internalization because this is the convention in the literature. Furthermore, it is the weight component of the ideal that is thought to give rise to eating pathology.

References

Cusumano, D.L., & Thompson, J.K. (2001). Media influence and body image in 8–11 year old boys and girls: A preliminary report on the Multidimensional Media Influence Scale. *International Journal of Eating Disorders, 29,* 37–44.

Heinberg, L.J., Thompson, J.K., & Stormer, S. (1995). Development and validation of the Sociocultural Attitudes Towards Appearance Questionnaire (SATAQ). *International Journal of Eating Disorders, 17,* 81–89.

Hohlstein, L.A., Smith, G.T., & Atlas, J.G. (1998). An application of expectancy theory to eating disorders: Development and validation of measures of eating and dieting expectancies. *Psychological Assessment, 10,* 49–58.

Irving, L.M., DuPen, J., & Berel, S. (1998). A media literacy program for high school females. *Eating Disorders: The Journal of Treatment and Prevention, 6,* 119–131.

Kandel, D.B. (1980). Drug and drinking behavior among youth. *Annual Review of Sociology, 6,* 235–285.

Killen, J.D., Taylor, C.B., Hayward, C., Haydel, K.F., Wilson, D.M., Hammer, L., Kraemer, H., Blair-Greiner, A., & Strachowski, D. (1996). Weight concerns influence the development of eating disorders: A 4 year prospective study. *Journal of Consulting and Clinical Psychology, 64,* 936–940.

Kraemer, H.C., Kazdin, A.E., Offord, D.R., Kessler, R.C., Jensen, P.S., & Kupfer, D.J. (1997). Coming to terms with the terms of risk. *Archives of General Psychiatry, 54,* 337–343.

Stice, E. (2001). A prospective test of the dual pathway model of bulimic pathology: Mediating effects of dieting and negative affect. *Journal of Abnormal Psychology, 110,* 124–135.

Stice, E., & Agras, W.S. (1998). Predicting the onset and remission of bulimic behaviors in adolescence: A longitudinal grouping analysis. *Behavior Therapy, 29,* 257–276.

Stice, E., Chase, A., Stormer, S., & Appel, A. (2001). A randomized trial of a dissonance-based eating disorder prevention program. *International Journal of Eating Disorders, 29,* 247–262.

Stice, E., Mazotti, L., Krebs, M., & Martin, S. (1998). Predictors of adolescent dieting behaviors: A longitudinal study. *Psychology of Addictive Behaviors, 12,* 195–205.

Stice, E., Mazotti, L., Weibel, D., & Agras, W.S. (2000). Dissonance prevention program decreases thin-ideal internalization, body dissatisfaction, dieting, negative affect, and bulimic symptoms: A preliminary experiment. *International Journal of Eating Disorders, 27,* 206–217.

Stice, E., Schupak-Neuberg, E., Shaw, H.E., & Stein, R.I. (1994). Relation of media exposure to eating disorder symptomatology: An examination of mediating mechanisms. *Journal of Abnormal Psychology, 103,* 836–840.

Stormer, S.M., & Thompson, J.K. (1998, November). *Challenging media messages regarding appearance: A psychoeducational program for males and females.* Paper presented at the annual meeting of the Association for the Advancement of Behavior Therapy, Washington, DC.

Thompson, J.K., Heinberg, L.J., Altabe, M.N., & Tantleff-Dunn, S. (1999). *Exacting beauty: Theory, assessment and treatment of body image disturbance.* Washington, DC: American Psychological Association.

Critical Thinking Questions

1. Discuss how within-individual, within-family, and within-community protective factors operate. In what ways might these factors reciprocally interact with each other in facilitating resiliency? Discuss the ways in which resiliency arises from interactions between the person and (the affordances of) situations.

2. Asher and Paquette call for more research examining the intra-individual processes that account for chronic loneliness. Discuss whether and how attachment theory and the intra-individual processes reviewed in Section Three might inform such an investigation.

3. Through several articles in this section runs the notion that our conceptualizations of personality should also incorporate individual differences in the situations people encounter. Identify which articles promote this idea and discuss the mechanisms through which personality impacts the kinds of situations that characterize an individual's life space. How do these mechanisms relate back to Saudino's discussion of heritability of situations?

4. Discuss the potential links between positive coping strategies identified by Folkman & Moskowitz and the traits and mechanisms summarized by DeNeve as characteristics of happy people.

5. Keltner, Kring, and Bonanno indicate that they advocate a functionalist approach to emotions. What do they mean by a functionalist approach? According to this view, what are the functions of facial expressions? Discuss and give examples for a few specific emotions. Extrapolate and discuss what Keltner and colleagues' findings might imply about the potential effectiveness of the usual emergency PTSD interventions, where counselors rush to the scene and help people try to work through the traumatic event and the associated emotions.

6. Think about how you would develop a study that would represent the next logical step in the Thompson & Stice work on eating disorders. What would be the research question, what the independent and dependent variables, and how would you conduct the study (i.e., what is the method)? Remember to also consider what population you would use, who would be the participants, as well as the ethics of what you propose.

7. Running through several of these papers is the idea that some people are resilient to negative experiences and can experience positive emotions even in the face of stressful life circumstances. Drawing from a variety of papers in this section, discuss the various mechanisms through which they achieve this. Evaluate how successful you think these people are in their coping efforts. That is, are they just pretending and/or "covering up", or does it really work— do they feel better? Explain your answer.